# Learning Concurrency in Python

Speed up your Python code with clean, readable, and advanced concurrency techniques

**Elliot Forbes**

BIRMINGHAM - MUMBAI

# Learning Concurrency in Python

First published: August 2017

Production reference: 1140817

Published by Packt Publishing Ltd.
Livery Place
35 Livery Street
Birmingham
B3 2PB, UK.

ISBN 978-1-78728-537-8

www.packtpub.com

# Credits

**Author**
Elliot Forbes

**Reviewer**
Nikolaus Gradwohl

**Commissioning Editor**
Merint Mathew

**Acquisition Editor**
Chaitanya Nair

**Content Development Editor**
Rohit Kumar Singh

**Technical Editors**
Ketan Kamble

**Copy Editor**
Sonia Mathur

**Project Coordinator**
Vaidehi Sawant

**Proofreader**
Safis Editing

**Indexer**
Francy Puthiry

**Graphics**
Abhinash Sahu

**Production Coordinator**
Nilesh Mohite

# About the Author

**Elliot Forbes** he worked as a full-time software engineer at JPMorgan Chase for the last two years. He graduated from the University of Strathclyde in Scotland in the spring of 2015 and worked as a freelancer developing web solutions while studying there.

He has worked on numerous different technologies such as GoLang and NodeJS and plain old Java, and he has spent years working on concurrent enterprise systems. It is with this experience that he was able to write this book.

Elliot has even worked at Barclays Investment Bank for a summer internship in London and has maintained a couple of software development websites for the last three years.

# About the Reviewer

**Nikolaus Gradwohl** was born 1976 in Vienna, Austria and always wanted to become an inventor like Gyro Gearloose. When he got his first Atari, he figured out that being a computer programmer is the closest he could get to that dream. For a living, he wrote programs for nearly anything that can be programmed, ranging from an 8-bit microcontroller to mainframes. In his free time, he likes to master on programming languages and operating systems.

Nikolaus authored the *Processing 2: Creative Coding Hotshot* book, and you can see some of his work on his blog at `http://www.local-guru.net/`.

# www.PacktPub.com

For support files and downloads related to your book, please visit www.PacktPub.com.

Did you know that Packt offers eBook versions of every book published, with PDF and ePub files available? You can upgrade to the eBook version at www.PacktPub.com and as a print book customer, you are entitled to a discount on the eBook copy. Get in touch with us at service@packtpub.com for more details.

At www.PacktPub.com, you can also read a collection of free technical articles, sign up for a range of free newsletters and receive exclusive discounts and offers on Packt books and eBooks.

https://www.packtpub.com/mapt

Get the most in-demand software skills with Mapt. Mapt gives you full access to all Packt books and video courses, as well as industry-leading tools to help you plan your personal development and advance your career.

## Why subscribe?

- Fully searchable across every book published by Packt
- Copy and paste, print, and bookmark content
- On demand and accessible via a web browser

# Customer Feedback

Thanks for purchasing this Packt book. At Packt, quality is at the heart of our editorial process. To help us improve, please leave us an honest review on this book's Amazon page at `https://www.amazon.com/dp/1787285375`.

If you'd like to join our team of regular reviewers, you can e-mail us at `customerreviews@packtpub.com`. We award our regular reviewers with free eBooks and videos in exchange for their valuable feedback. Help us be relentless in improving our products!

# Table of Contents

# Preface

Python is a very high-level, general-purpose language that features a large number of powerful high-level and low-level libraries and frameworks that complement its delightful syntax. This easy-to-follow guide teaches you new practices and techniques to optimize your code and then moves on to more advanced ways to effectively write efficient Python code. Small and simple practical examples will help you test the concepts introduced, and you will be able to easily adapt them to any application.

Throughout this book, you will learn to build highly efficient, robust, and concurrent applications. You will work through practical examples that will help you address the challenges of writing concurrent code, and also you will learn to improve the overall speed of execution in multiprocessor and multicore systems and keep them highly available.

## What this book covers

Chapter 1, *Speed It Up!*, helps you get to grips with threads and processes, and you'll also learn about some of the limitations and challenges of Python when it comes to implementing your own concurrent applications.

Chapter 2, *Parallelize It*, covers a multitude of topics including the differences between concurrency and parallelism. We will look at how they both leverage the CPU in different ways, and we also branch off into the topic of computer system design and how it relates to concurrent and parallel programming.

Chapter 3, *Life of a Thread*, delves deeply into the workings of Python's native threading library. We'll look at the numerous different thread types. We'll also look in detail at various concepts such as the multithreading model and the numerous ways in which we can make user threads to their lower-level siblings, the kernel threads.

Chapter 4, *Synchronization between Threads*, covers the various key issues that can impact our concurrent Python applications. We will delve into the topic of deadlocks and the famous "dining philosophers" problem and see how this can impact our own software.

Chapter 5, *Communication between Threads*, discusses quite a number of different mechanisms that we can employ to implement communication in our multithreaded systems. We delve into the thread-safe queue primitives that Python features natively.

Chapter 6, *Debug and Benchmark*, takes a comprehensive look at some of the techniques that you can utilize in order to ensure your concurrent Python systems are as free as practically possible from bugs before they plague your production environment. We will also cover testing strategies that help to ensure the soundness of your code's logic.

Chapter 7, *Executors and Pools*, covers everything that you need to get started with thread pools, process pools, and future objects. We will look at the various ways in which you can instantiate your own thread and process pools as well the advantages of using thread and process pool executors over traditional methods.

Chapter 8, *Multiprocessing*, discusses multiprocessing and how it can be utilized within our systems. We will follow the life of a process from its creation all the way through to its timely termination.

Chapter 9, *Event-Driven Programming*, covers the paradigm of event-driven programming before covering how asyncio works and how we can use it for our own event-driven Python systems.

Chapter 10, *Reactive Programming*, covers some of the key principles of reactive programming. We will look at the key differences between both reactive programming and typical event-driven programming and delve more deeply into the specifics of the very popular RxPY Python library.

Chapter 11, *Using the GPU*, covers some of the more realistic scenarios that data scientists typically encounter and why these are ideal scenarios for us to leverage the GPU wrapper libraries.

Chapter 12, *Choosing a Solution*, briefly discusses some libraries that are not covered in this book. We'll also take a look at the process that you should follow in order to effectively choose which libraries and programming paradigms you leverage for your Python software projects.

# What you need for this book

For this book, you will need the following software installed on your systems:

- Beautiful Soup
- RxPy
- Anaconda
- Theano
- PyOpenCL

# Who this book is for

This book is for Python developers who would like to get started with concurrent programming. You are expected to have a working knowledge of the Python language, as this book will build on its fundamental concepts.

# Conventions

In this book, you will find a number of text styles that distinguish between different kinds of information. Here are some examples of these styles and an explanation of their meaning.

Code words in text, database table names, folder names, filenames, file extensions, pathnames, dummy URLs, user input, and Twitter handles are shown as follows: "We can include other contexts through the use of the `include` directive."

A block of code is set as follows:

```
import urllib.request
import time
t0 = time.time()
req = urllib.request.urlopen('http://www.example.com')
pageHtml = req.read()
t1 = time.time()
print("Total Time To Fetch Page: {} Seconds".format(t1-t0))
```

When we wish to draw your attention to a particular part of a code block, the relevant lines or items are set in bold:

```
import urllib.request
import time
t0 = time.time()
req = urllib.request.urlopen('http://www.example.com')
pageHtml = req.read()
t1 = time.time()
print("Total Time To Fetch Page: {} Seconds".format(t1-t0))
```

Any command-line input or output is written as follows:

```
pip install rx
```

**New terms** and **important words** are shown in bold. Words that you see on the screen, for example, in menus or dialog boxes, appear in the text.

Warnings or important notes appear like this.

Tips and tricks appear like this.

# Reader feedback

Feedback from our readers is always welcome. Let us know what you think about this book-what you liked or disliked. Reader feedback is important for us as it helps us develop titles that you will really get the most out of. To send us general feedback, simply e-mail feedback@packtpub.com, and mention the book's title in the subject of your message. If there is a topic that you have expertise in and you are interested in either writing or contributing to a book, see our author guide at www.packtpub.com/authors.

# Downloading the example code

You can download the example code files for this book from your account at http://www.packtpub.com. If you purchased this book elsewhere, you can visit http://www.packtpub.com/support and register to have the files e-mailed directly to you. You can download the code files by following these steps:

1. Log in or register to our website using your e-mail address and password.
2. Hover the mouse pointer on the **SUPPORT** tab at the top.
3. Click on **Code Downloads & Errata**.
4. Enter the name of the book in the **Search** box.
5. Select the book for which you're looking to download the code files.
6. Choose from the drop-down menu where you purchased this book from.
7. Click on **Code Download**.

Once the file is downloaded, please make sure that you unzip or extract the folder using the latest version of:

- WinRAR / 7-Zip for Windows
- Zipeg / iZip / UnRarX for Mac
- 7-Zip / PeaZip for Linux

The code bundle for the book is also hosted on GitHub at `https://github.com/PacktPubl ishing/Learning-Concurrency-in-Python`. We also have other code bundles from our rich catalog of books and videos available at `https://github.com/PacktPublishing/`. Check them out!

# Errata

Although we have taken every care to ensure the accuracy of our content, mistakes do happen. If you find a mistake in one of our books-maybe a mistake in the text or the code-we would be grateful if you could report this to us. By doing so, you can save other readers from frustration and help us improve subsequent versions of this book. If you find any errata, please report them by visiting `http://www.packtpub.com/submit-errata`, selecting your book, clicking on the **Errata Submission Form** link, and entering the details of your errata. Once your errata are verified, your submission will be accepted and the errata will be uploaded to our website or added to any list of existing errata under the Errata section of that title. To view the previously submitted errata, go to `https://www.packtpub.com/book s/content/support` and enter the name of the book in the search field. The required information will appear under the **Errata** section.

# Piracy

Piracy of copyrighted material on the Internet is an ongoing problem across all media. At Packt, we take the protection of our copyright and licenses very seriously. If you come across any illegal copies of our works in any form on the Internet, please provide us with the location address or website name immediately so that we can pursue a remedy. Please contact us at `copyright@packtpub.com` with a link to the suspected pirated material. We appreciate your help in protecting our authors and our ability to bring you valuable content.

# Questions

If you have a problem with any aspect of this book, you can contact us at `questions@packtpub.com`, and we will do our best to address the problem.

# 1
# Speed It Up!

*"For over a decade prophets have voiced the contention that the organization of a single computer has reached its limits and that truly significant advances can be made only by interconnection of a multiplicity of computers."*

*-Gene Amdahl.*

Getting the most out of your software is something all developers strive for, and concurrency, and the art of concurrent programming, happens to be one of the best ways in order for you to improve the performance of your applications. Through the careful application of concurrent concepts into our previously single-threaded applications, we can start to realize the full power of our underlying hardware, and strive to solve problems that were unsolvable in days gone past.

With concurrency, we are able to improve the perceived performance of our applications by concurrently dealing with requests, and updating the frontend instead of just hanging until the backend task is complete. Gone are the days of unresponsive programs that give you no indication as to whether they've crashed or are still silently working.

This improvement in the performance of our applications comes at a heavy price though. By choosing to implement systems in a concurrent fashion, we typically see an increase in the overall complexity of our code, and a heightened risk for bugs to appear within this new code. In order to successfully implement concurrent systems, we must first understand some of the key concurrency primitives and concepts at a deeper level in order to ensure that our applications are safe from these new inherent threats.

In this chapter, I'll be covering some of the fundamental topics that every programmer needs to know before going on to develop concurrent software systems. This includes the following:

- A brief history of concurrency
- Threads and how multithreading works
- Processes and multiprocessing
- The basics of event-driven, reactive, and GPU-based programming
- A few examples to demonstrate the power of concurrency in simple programs
- The limitations of Python when it comes to programming concurrent systems

# History of concurrency

Concurrency was actually derived from early work on railroads and telegraphy, which is why names such as *semaphore* are currently employed. Essentially, there was a need to handle multiple trains on the same railroad system in such a way that every train would safely get to their destinations without incurring casualties.

It was only in the 1960s that academia picked up interest in concurrent computing, and it was Edsger W. Dijkstra who is credited with having published the first paper in this field, where he identified and solved the mutual exclusion problem. Dijkstra then went on to define fundamental concurrency concepts, such as semaphores, mutual exclusions, and deadlocks as well as the famous Dijkstra's Shortest Path Algorithm.

Concurrency, as with most areas in computer science, is still an incredibly young field when compared to other fields of study such as math, and it's worthwhile keeping this in mind. There is still a huge potential for change within the field, and it remains an exciting field for all--academics, language designers, and developers--alike.

The introduction of high-level concurrency primitives and better native language support have really improved the way in which we, as software architects, implement concurrent solutions. For years, this was incredibly difficult to do, but with this advent of new concurrent APIs, and maturing frameworks and languages, it's starting to become a lot easier for us as developers.

Language designers face quite a substantial challenge when trying to implement concurrency that is not only safe, but efficient and easy to write for the users of that language. Programming languages such as Google's Golang, Rust, and even Python itself have made great strides in this area, and this is making it far easier to extract the full potential from the machines your programs run on.

# Threads and multithreading

In this section of the book, we'll take a brief look at what a thread is, as well as at how we can use multiple threads in order to speed up the execution of some of our programs.

# What is a thread?

A thread can be defined as an ordered stream of instructions that can be scheduled to run as such by operating systems. These threads, typically, live within processes, and consist of a program counter, a stack, and a set of registers as well as an identifier. These threads are the smallest unit of execution to which a processor can allocate time.

Threads are able to interact with shared resources, and communication is possible between multiple threads. They are also able to share memory, and read and write different memory addresses, but therein lies an issue. When two threads start sharing memory, and you have no way to guarantee the order of a thread's execution, you could start seeing issues or minor bugs that give you the wrong values or crash your system altogether. These issues are, primarily, caused by race conditions which we'll be going, in more depth in Chapter 4, *Synchronization Between Threads*.

The following figure shows how multiple threads can exist on multiple different CPUs:

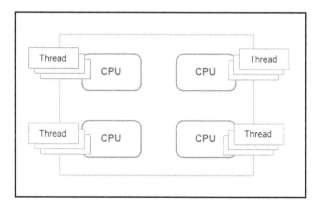

# Types of threads

Within a typical operating system, we, typically, have two distinct types of threads:

- User-level threads: Threads that we can actively create, run, and kill for all of our various tasks
- Kernel-level threads: Very low-level threads acting on behalf of the operating system

Python works at the user-level, and thus, everything we cover in this book will be, primarily, focused on these user-level threads.

# What is multithreading?

When people talk about multithreaded processors, they are typically referring to a processor that can run multiple threads simultaneously, which they are able to do by utilizing a single core that is able to very quickly switch context between multiple threads. This switching context takes place in such a small amount of time that we could be forgiven for thinking that multiple threads are running in parallel when, in fact, they are not.

When trying to understand multithreading, it's best if you think of a multithreaded program as an office. In a single-threaded program, there would only be one person working in this office at all times, handling all of the work in a sequential manner. This would become an issue if we consider what happens when this solitary worker becomes bogged down with administrative paperwork, and is unable to move on to different work. They would be unable to cope, and wouldn't be able to deal with new incoming sales, thus costing our metaphorical business money.

With multithreading, our single solitary worker becomes an excellent multitasker, and is able to work on multiple things at different times. They can make progress on some paperwork, and then switch context to a new task when something starts preventing them from doing further work on said paperwork. By being able to switch context when something is blocking them, they are able to do far more work in a shorter period of time, and thus make our business more money.

In this example, it's important to note that we are still limited to only one worker or processing core. If we wanted to try and improve the amount of work that the business could do and complete work in parallel, then we would have to employ other workers or processes as we would call them in Python.

Let's see a few advantages of threading:

- Multiple threads are excellent for speeding up blocking I/O bound programs
- They are lightweight in terms of memory footprint when compared to processes
- Threads share resources, and thus communication between them is easier

There are some disadvantages too, which are as follows:

- CPython threads are hamstrung by the limitations of the **global interpreter lock (GIL)**, about which we'll go into more depth in the next chapter.
- While communication between threads may be easier, you must be very careful not to implement code that is subject to race conditions
- It's computationally expensive to switch context between multiple threads. By adding multiple threads, you could see a degradation in your program's overall performance.

# Processes

Processes are very similar in nature to threads--they allow us to do pretty much everything a thread can do--but the one key advantage is that they are not bound to a singular CPU core. If we extend our office analogy further, this, essentially, means that if we had a four core CPU, then we can hire two dedicated sales team members and two workers, and all four of them would be able to execute work in parallel. Processes also happen to be capable of working on multiple things at one time much as our multithreaded single office worker.

These processes contain one main primary thread, but can spawn multiple sub-threads that each contain their own set of registers and a stack. They can become multithreaded should you wish. All processes provide every resource that the computer needs in order to execute a program.

In the following image, you'll see two side-by-side diagrams; both are examples of a process. You'll notice that the process on the left contains only one thread, otherwise known as the primary thread. The process on the right contains multiple threads, each with their own set of registers and stacks:

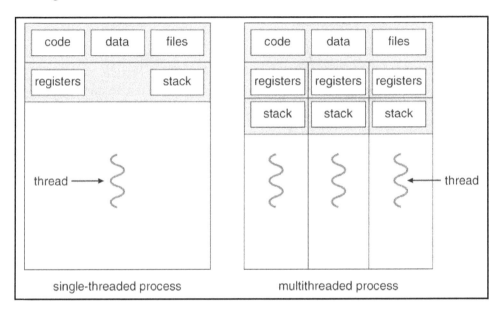

With processes, we can improve the speed of our programs in specific scenarios where our programs are CPU bound, and require more CPU horsepower. However, by spawning multiple processes, we face new challenges with regard to cross-process communication, and ensuring that we don't hamper performance by spending too much time on this **inter-process communication** (IPC).

# Properties of processes

UNIX processes are created by the operating system, and typically contain the following:

- Process ID, process group ID, user ID, and group ID
- Environment
- Working directory
- Program instructions
- Registers
- Stack
- Heap

- File descriptors
- Signal actions
- Shared libraries
- Inter-process communication tools (such as message queues, pipes, semaphores, or shared memory)

The advantages of processes are listed as follows:

- Processes can make better use of multi-core processors
- They are better than multiple threads at handling CPU-intensive tasks
- We can sidestep the limitations of the GIL by spawning multiple processes
- Crashing processes will not kill our entire program

Here are the disadvantages of processes:

- No shared resources between processes--we have to implement some form of IPC
- These require more memory

# Multiprocessing

In Python, we can choose to run our code using either multiple threads or multiple processes should we wish to try and improve the performance over a standard single-threaded approach. We can go with a multithreaded approach and be limited to the processing power of one CPU core, or conversely we can go with a multiprocessing approach and utilize the full number of CPU cores available on our machine. In today's modern computers, we tend to have numerous CPUs and cores, so limiting ourselves to just the one, effectively renders the rest of our machine idle. Our goal is to try and extract the full potential from our hardware, and ensure that we get the best value for money and solve our problems faster than anyone else:

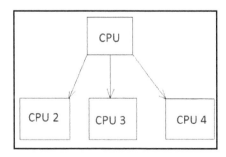

With Python's multiprocessing module, we can effectively utilize the full number of cores and CPUs, which can help us to achieve greater performance when it comes to CPU-bounded problems. The preceding figure shows an example of how one CPU core starts delegating tasks to other cores.

In all Python versions less than or equal to 2.6, we can attain the number of CPU cores available to us by using the following code snippet:

```
# First we import the multiprocessing module
import multiprocessing
# then we call multiprocessing.cpu_count() which
# returns an integer value of how many available CPUs we have
multiprocessing.cpu_count()
```

Not only does multiprocessing enable us to utilize more of our machine, but we also avoid the limitations that the Global Interpreter Lock imposes on us in CPython.

One potential disadvantage of multiple processes is that we inherently have no shared state, and lack communication. We, therefore, have to pass it through some form of IPC, and performance can take a hit. However, this lack of shared state can make them easier to work with, as you do not have to fight against potential race conditions in your code.

# Event-driven programming

Event-driven programming is a huge part of our lives--we see examples of it every day when we open up our phone, or work on our computer. These devices run purely in an event-driven way; for example, when you click on an icon on your desktop, the operating system registers this as an event, and then performs the necessary action tied to that specific style of event.

Every interaction we do can be characterized as an event or a series of events, and these typically trigger callbacks. If you have any prior experience with JavaScript, then you should be somewhat familiar with this concept of callbacks and the callback design pattern. In JavaScript, the predominant use case for callbacks is when you perform RESTful HTTP requests, and want to be able to perform an action when you know that this action has successfully completed and we've received our HTTP response:

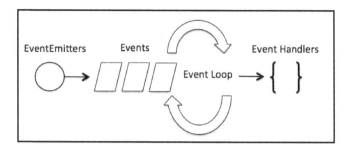

If we look at the previous image, it shows us an example of how event-driven programs process events. We have our **EventEmitters** on the left-hand side; these fire off multiple **Events**, which are picked up by our program's **Event Loop**, and, should they match a predefined **Event Handler**, that handler is then fired to deal with the said event.

Callbacks are often used in scenarios where an action is asynchronous. Say, for instance, you applied for a job at Google, you would give them an email address, and they would then get in touch with you when they make their mind up. This is, essentially, the same as registering a callback except that, instead of having them email you, you would execute an arbitrary bit of code whenever the callback is invoked.

# Turtle

Turtle is a graphics module that has been written in Python, and is an incredible starting point for getting kids interested in programming. It handles all the complexities that come with graphics programming, and lets them focus purely on learning the very basics whilst keeping them interested.

It is also a very good tool to use in order to demonstrate event-driven programs. It features event handlers and listeners, which is all that we need:

```
import turtle
turtle.setup(500,500)
window = turtle.Screen()
window.title("Event Handling 101")
window.bgcolor("lightblue")
nathan = turtle.Turtle()
def moveForward():
    nathan.forward(50)
def moveLeft():
    nathan.left(30)
def moveRight():
    nathan.right(30)
def start():
```

```
        window.onkey(moveForward, "Up")
        window.onkey(moveLeft, "Left")
        window.onkey(moveRight, "Right")
        window.listen()
        window.mainloop()
    if __name__ == '__main__':
        start()
```

# Breaking it down

In the first line of this preceding code sample, we import the turtle graphics module. We then go up to set up a basic turtle window with the title *Event Handling 101* and a background color of light blue.

After we've got the initial setup out of the way, we then go on to define three distinct event handlers:

- moveForward: This is for when we want to move our character forward by 50 units
- moveLeft/moveRight: This is for when we want to rotate our character in either direction by 30 degrees

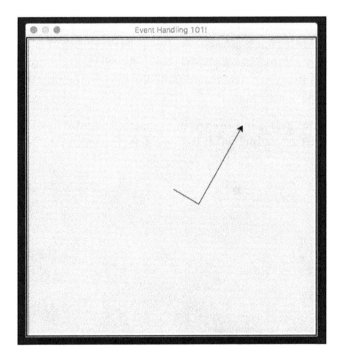

Once we've defined our three distinct handlers, we then go on to map these event handlers to the up, left, and right key presses using the `onkey` method.

Now that we've set up our handlers, we then tell them to start listening. If any of the keys are pressed after our program has started listening, then we will fire its event handler function. Finally, when you run the preceding code, you should see a window appear with an arrow in the center, which you can move about with your arrow keys.

# Reactive programming

Reactive programming is very similar to that of event-driven, but instead of revolving around events, it focuses on data. More specifically, it deals with streams of data, and reacts to specific data changes.

# ReactiveX - RxPy

RxPy is the Python equivalent of the very popular ReactiveX framework. If you've ever done any programming in Angular 2 and proceeding versions, then you will have used this when interacting with HTTP services. This framework is a conglomeration of the observer pattern, the iterator pattern, and functional programming. We essentially subscribe to different streams of incoming data, and then create observers that listen for specific events being triggered. When these observers are triggered, they run the code that corresponds to what has just happened.

We'll take a data center as a good example of how reactive programming can be utilized. Imagine this data center has thousands of server racks, all constantly computing millions upon millions of calculations. One of the biggest challenges in these data centers is keeping all these tightly packed server racks cool enough so that they don't damage themselves. We could set up multiple thermometers throughout our data center to ensure that we aren't getting too hot anywhere, and send the readings from these thermometers to a central computer as a continuous stream:

Within our central control station, we could set up a RxPy program that observes this continuous stream of temperature information. Within these observers, we could then define a series of conditional events to listen out for, and then react whenever one of these conditionals is hit.

One such example would be an event that only triggers if the temperature for a specific part of the data center gets too warm. When this event is triggered, we could then automatically react and increase the flow of any cooling system to that particular area, and thus bring the temperature back down again:

```
import rx
from rx import Observable, Observer
# Here we define our custom observer which
# contains an on_next method, an on_error method
# and an on_completed method
class temperatureObserver(Observer):
  # Every time we receive a temperature reading
  # this method is called
  def on_next(self, x):
    print("Temperature is: %s degrees centigrade" % x)
    if (x > 6):
      print("Warning: Temperate Is Exceeding Recommended Limit")
```

```
    if (x == 9):
      print("DataCenter is shutting down. Temperature is too high")
  # if we were to receive an error message
  # we would handle it here
  def on_error(self, e):
    print("Error: %s" % e)
  # This is called when the stream is finished
  def on_completed(self):
    print("All Temps Read")
# Publish some fake temperature readings
xs = Observable.from_iterable(range(10))
# subscribe to these temperature readings
d = xs.subscribe(temperatureObserver())
```

# Breaking it down

The first two lines of our code import the necessary rx module, and then from there import both observable and observer.

We then go on to create a temperatureObserver class that extends the observer. This class contains three functions:

- on_next: This is called every time our observer observes something new
- on_error: This acts as our error-handler function; every time we observe an error, this function will be called
- on_completed: This is called when our observer meets the end of the stream of information it has been observing

In the on_next function, we want it to print out the current temperature, and also to check whether the temperature that it receives is under a set of limits. If the temperature matches one of our conditionals, then we handle it slightly differently, and print out descriptive errors as to what has happened.

After our class declaration, we go on to create a fake observable which contains 10 separate values using Observable.from_iterable(), and finally, the last line of our preceding code then subscribes an instance of our new temperatureObserver class to this observable.

# GPU programming

GPUs are renowned for their ability to render high resolution, fast action video games. They are able to crunch together the millions of necessary calculations per second in order to ensure that every vertex of your game's 3D models are in the right place, and that they are updated every few milliseconds in order to ensure a smooth 60 FPS.

Generally speaking, GPUs are incredibly good at performing the same task in parallel, millions upon millions of times per minute. But if GPUs are so performant, then why do we not employ them instead of our CPUs? While GPUs may be incredibly performant at graphics processing, they aren't however designed for handling the intricacies of running an operating system and general purpose computing. CPUs have fewer cores, which are specifically designed for speed when it comes to switching context between operating tasks. If GPUs were given the same tasks, you would see a considerable degradation in your computer's overall performance.

But how can we utilize these high-powered graphics cards for something other than graphical programming? This is where libraries such as PyCUDA, OpenCL, and Theano come into play. These libraries try to abstract away the complicated low-level code that graphics APIs have to interact with in order to utilize the GPU. They make it far simpler for us to repurpose the thousands of smaller processing cores available on the GPU, and utilize them for our computationally expensive programs:

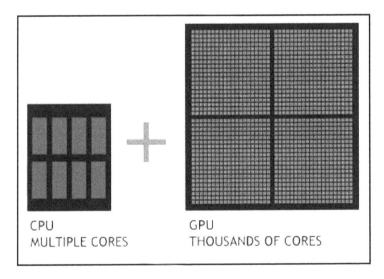

CPU
MULTIPLE CORES

GPU
THOUSANDS OF CORES

These **Graphics Processing Units** (**GPU**) encapsulate everything that scripting languages are not. They are highly parallelizable, and built for maximum throughput. By utilizing these in Python, we are able to get the best of both worlds. We can utilize a language that is favored by millions due to its ease of use, and also make our programs incredibly performant.

In the following sections, we will have a look at the various libraries that are available to us, which expose the power of the GPU.

# PyCUDA

PyCUDA allows us to interact with Nvidia's CUDA parallel computation API in Python. It offers us a lot of different advantages over other frameworks that expose the same underlying CUDA API. These advantages include things such as an impressive underlying speed, complete control of the CUDA's driver API, and most importantly, a lot of useful documentation to help those just getting started with it.

Unfortunately however, the main limitation for PyCUDA is the fact that it utilizes Nvidia-specific APIs, and as such, if you do not have a Nvidia-based graphics card, then you will not be able to take advantage of it. However, there are other alternatives which do an equally good job on other non-Nvidia graphics cards.

# OpenCL

OpenCL is one such example of an alternative to PyCUDA, and, in fact, I would recommend this over PyCUDA due to its impressive range of conformant implementations, which does also include Nvidia. OpenCL was originally conceived by Apple, and allows us to take advantage of a number of heterogeneous platforms such as CPUs, GPUs, digital signal processors, field-programmable gate arrays, and other different types of processors and hardware accelerators.

There currently exist third-party APIs for not only Python, but also Java and .NET, and it is therefore ideal for researchers and those of us who wish to utilize the full power of our desktop machines.

# Theano

Theano is another example of a library that allows you to utilize the GPU as well as to achieve speeds that rival C implementations when trying to solve problems that involve huge quantities of data.

It's a different style of programming, though, in the sense that Python is the medium in which you craft expressions that can be passed into Theano.

 The official website for Theano can be found here: `http://deeplearning.net/software/theano/`

# The limitations of Python

Earlier in the chapter, I talked about the limitations of the **GIL** or the **Global Interpreter Lock** that is present within Python, but what does this actually mean?

First, I think it's important to know exactly what the GIL does for us. The GIL is essentially a mutual exclusion lock which prevents multiple threads from executing Python code in parallel. It is a lock that can only be held by one thread at any one time, and if you wanted a thread to execute its own code, then it would first have to acquire the lock before it could proceed to execute its own code. The advantage that this gives us is that while it is locked, nothing else can run at the same time:

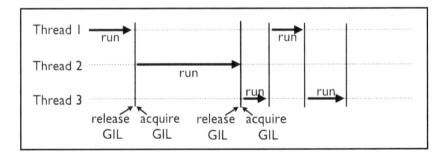

In the preceding diagram, we see an example of how multiple threads are hampered by this GIL. Each thread has to wait and acquire the GIL before it can progress further, and then release the GIL, typically before it has had a chance to complete its work. It follows a random round-robin approach, and you have no guarantees as to which thread will acquire the lock first.

Why is this necessary, you might ask? Well, the GIL has been a long-disputed part of Python, and over the years has triggered many a debate over its usefulness. But it was implemented with good intentions and to combat the non-thread safe Python memory management. It prevents us from taking advantage of multiprocessor systems in certain scenarios.

Guido Van Rossum, the creator of Python, posted an update on the removal of the GIL and its benefits in a post here: `http://www.artima.com/weblogs/viewpost.jsp?thread =214235`. He states that he wouldn't be against someone creating a branch of Python that is GIL-less, and he would accept a merge of this code if, and only if, it didn't negatively impact the performance of a single-threaded application.

There have been prior attempts at getting rid of the GIL, but it was found that the addition of all the extra locks to ensure thread-safety actually slowed down an application by a factor of more then two. In other words, you would have been able to get more work done with a single CPU than you would have with just over two CPUs. There are, however, libraries such as NumPy that can do everything they need to without having to interact with the GIL, and working purely outside of the GIL is something I'm going to be exploring in greater depth in the future chapters of this book.

It must also be noted that there are other implementations of Python, such as Jython and IronPython, that don't feature any form of Global Interpreter Lock, and as such can fully exploit multiprocessor systems. Jython and IronPython both run on different virtual machines, so, they can take advantage of their respective runtime environments.

# Jython

Jython is an implementation of Python that works directly with the Java platform. It can be used in a complementary fashion with Java as a scripting language, and has been shown to outperform CPython, which is the standard implementation of Python, when working with some large datasets. For the majority of stuff though, CPython's single-core execution typically outperforms Jython and its multicore approach.

The advantage to using Jython is that you can do some pretty cool things with it when working in Java, such as import existing Java libraries and frameworks, and use them as though they were part of your Python code.

# IronPython

IronPython is the .NET equivalent of Jython and works on top of Microsoft's .NET framework. Again, you'll be able to use it in a complementary fashion with .NET applications. This is somewhat beneficial for .NET developers, as they are able to use Python as a fast and expressive scripting language within their .NET applications.

# Why should we use Python?

If Python has such obvious, known limitations when it comes to writing performant, concurrent applications, then why do we continue to use it? The short answer is that it's a fantastic language to get work done in, and by work, I'm not necessarily talking about crunching through a computationally expensive task. It's an intuitive language, which is easy to pick up and understand for those who don't necessarily have a lot of programming experience.

The language has seen a huge adoption rate amongst data scientists and mathematicians working in incredibly interesting fields such as machine learning and quantitative analysis, who find it to be an incredibly useful tool in their arsenal.

In both the Python 2 and 3 ecosystems, you'll find a huge number of libraries that are designed specifically for these use cases, and by knowing about Python's limitations, we can effectively mitigate them, and produce software that is efficient and capable of doing exactly what is required of it.

So now that we understand what threads and processes are, as well as some of the limitations of Python, it's time to have a look at just how we can utilize multi-threading within our application in order to improve the speed of our programs.

# Concurrent image download

One excellent example of the benefits of multithreading is, without a doubt, the use of multiple threads to download multiple images or files. This is, actually, one of the best use cases for multithreading due to the blocking nature of I/O.

To highlight the performance gains, we are going to retrieve 10 different images from `http ://lorempixel.com/400/200/sports`, which is a free API that delivers a different image every time you hit that link. We'll then store these 10 different images within a temp folder so that we can view/use them later on.

All the code used in these examples can be found in my GitHub repository here:
`https://github.com/elliotforbes/Concurrency-With-Python`.

# Sequential download

First, we should have some form of a baseline against which we can measure the performance gains. To do this, we'll write a quick program that will download these 10 images sequentially, as follows:

```
import urllib.request
def downloadImage(imagePath, fileName):
  print("Downloading Image from ", imagePath)
  urllib.request.urlretrieve(imagePath, fileName)
def main():
  for i in range(10):
    imageName = "temp/image-" + str(i) + ".jpg"
    downloadImage("http://lorempixel.com/400/200/sports", imageName)
if __name__ == '__main__':
  main()
```

# Breaking it down

In the preceding code, we begin by importing `urllib.request`. This will act as our medium for performing HTTP requests for the images that we want. We then define a new function called `downloadImage`, which takes in two parameters, `imagePath` and `fileName`. `imagePath` represents the URL image path that we wish to download. `fileName` represents the name of the file that we wish to use to save this image locally.

In the `main` function, we then start up a `for` loop. Within this `for` loop, we generate an `imageName` which includes the `temp/` directory, a string representation of what iteration we are currently at--**str**(*i*)--and the file extension `.jpg`. We then call the `downloadImage` function, passing in the `lorempixel` location, which provides us with a random image as well as our newly generated `imageName`.

Upon running this script, you should see your `temp` directory sequentially fill up with 10 distinct images.

# Concurrent download

Now that we have our baseline, it's time to write a quick program that will concurrently download all the images that we require. We'll be going over creating and starting threads in future chapters, so don't worry if you struggle to understand the code. The key point of this is to realize the potential performance gains to be had by writing programs concurrently:

```python
import threading
import urllib.request
import time
def downloadImage(imagePath, fileName):
  print("Downloading Image from ", imagePath)
  urllib.request.urlretrieve(imagePath, fileName)
  print("Completed Download")
def executeThread(i):
  imageName = "temp/image-" + str(i) + ".jpg"
  downloadImage("http://lorempixel.com/400/200/sports", imageName)
def main():
  t0 = time.time()
  # create an array which will store a reference to
  # all of our threads
  threads = []
  # create 10 threads, append them to our array of threads
  # and start them off
  for i in range(10):
    thread = threading.Thread(target=executeThread, args=(i,))
    threads.append(thread)
    thread.start()
  # ensure that all the threads in our array have completed
  # their execution before we log the total time to complete
  for i in threads:
    i.join()
  # calculate the total execution time
  t1 = time.time()
  totalTime = t1 - t0
  print("Total Execution Time {}".format(totalTime))
if __name__ == '__main__':
  main()
```

# Breaking it down

In the first line of our newly modified program, you should see that we are now importing the threading module; this will enable us to create our first multithreaded application. We then abstract our filename generation, and call the downloadImage function into our own executeThread function.

Within the main function, we first create an empty array of threads, and then iterate 10 times, creating a new thread object, appending this to our array of threads, and then starting that thread.

Finally, we iterate through our array of threads by calling for *i* in threads, and call the join method on each of these threads. This ensures that we do not proceed with the execution of our remaining code until all of our threads have finished downloading the image.

If you execute this on your machine, you should see that it almost instantaneously starts the download of the 10 different images. When the downloads finish, it again prints out that it has successfully completed, and you should see the temp folder being populated with these images.

Both the preceding scripts do exactly the same tasks using the exact same urllib.request library, but if you take a look at the total execution time, then you should see an order of magnitude improvement on the time taken for the concurrent script to fetch all 10 images.

# Improving number crunching with multiprocessing

So, we've seen exactly how we can improve things such as downloading images, but how do we improve the performance of our number crunching? Well, this is where multiprocessing shines if used in the correct manner.

In this example, we'll try to find the prime factors of 10,000 random numbers that fall between 20,000 and 100,000,000. We are not necessarily fussed about the order of execution so long as the work gets done, and we aren't sharing memory between any of our processes.

# Sequential prime factorization

Again, we'll write a script that does this in a sequential manner, which we can easily verify is working correctly:

```
import time
import random
def calculatePrimeFactors(n):
  primfac = []
  d = 2
  while d*d <= n:
    while (n % d) == 0:
      primfac.append(d)   # supposing you want multiple factors repeated
      n //= d
    d += 1
  if n > 1:
    primfac.append(n)
  return primfac
def main():
  print("Starting number crunching")
  t0 = time.time()
  for i in range(10000):
    rand = random.randint(20000, 100000000)
    print(calculatePrimeFactors(rand))
  t1 = time.time()
  totalTime = t1 - t0
  print("Execution Time: {}".format(totalTime))
if __name__ == '__main__':
  main()
```

# Breaking it down

The first two lines make up our required imports--we'll be needing both the time and the random modules. After our imports, we then go on to define the calculatePrimeFactors function, which takes an input of *n*. This efficiently calculates all of the prime factors of a given number, and appends them to an array, which is then returned once that function completes execution.

After this, we define the main function, which calculates the starting time and then cycles through 10,000 numbers, which are randomly generated by using random's randint. We then pass these generated numbers to the calculatePrimeFactors function, and we print out the result. Finally, we calculate the end time of this for loop and print it out.

If you execute this on your computer, you should see the array of prime factors being printed out for 10,000 different random numbers, as well as the total execution time for this code. For me, it took roughly 3.6 seconds to execute on my Macbook.

# Concurrent prime factorization

So now let us have a look at how we can improve the performance of this program by utilizing multiple processes.

In order for us to split this workload up, we'll define an executeProc function, which, instead of generating 10,000 random numbers to be factorized, will generate 1,000 random numbers. We'll create 10 processes, and execute the function 10 times, though, so the total number of calculations should be the exact same as when we performed the sequential test:

```
import time
import random
from multiprocessing import Process
# This does all of our prime factorization on a given number 'n'
def calculatePrimeFactors(n):
  primfac = []
  d = 2
  while d*d <= n:
    while (n % d) == 0:
      primfac.append(d)   # supposing you want multiple factors repeated
      n //= d
    d += 1
  if n > 1:
    primfac.append(n)
  return primfac
# We split our workload from one batch of 10,000 calculations
# into 10 batches of 1,000 calculations
def executeProc():
  for i in range(1000):
    rand = random.randint(20000, 100000000)
    print(calculatePrimeFactors(rand))
def main():
  print("Starting number crunching")
  t0 = time.time()
  procs = []
  # Here we create our processes and kick them off
  for i in range(10):
    proc = Process(target=executeProc, args=())
    procs.append(proc)
    proc.start()
  # Again we use the .join() method in order to wait for
```

```
    # execution to finish for all of our processes
    for proc in procs:
      proc.join()
    t1 = time.time()
    totalTime = t1 - t0
    # we print out the total execution time for our 10
    # procs.
    print("Execution Time: {}".format(totalTime))
  if __name__ == '__main__':
    main()
```

# Breaking it down

This last code performs the exact same function as our originally posted code. The first change, however, is on line three. Here, we import the process from the multiprocessing module. Our following, the `calculatePrimeFactors` method has not been touched.

You should then see that we pulled out the `for` loop that initially ran for 10,000 iterations. We now placed this in a function called `executeProc`, and we also reduced our `for` loops range to 1,000.

Within the `main` function, we then create an empty array called `procs`. We then create 10 different processes, and set the target to be the `executeProc` function, and pass in no args. We append this newly created process to our `procs` arrays, and then we start the process by calling `proc.start()`.

After we've created 10 individual processes, we then cycle through these processes which are now in our `procs` array, and join them. This ensures that every process has finished its calculations before we proceed to calculate the total execution time.

If you execute this now, you should see the 10,000 outputs now print out in your console, and you should also see a far lower execution time when compared to your sequential execution. For reference, the sequential program executed in 3.9 seconds on my computer compared to 1.9 seconds when running the multiprocessing version.

This is just a very basic demonstration as to how we can implement multiprocessing into our applications. In future chapters, we'll explore how we can create pools and utilize executors. The key point to take away from this is that we can improve the performance of some CPU-bound tasks by utilizing multiple cores.

# Summary

By now, you should have an appreciation of some of the fundamental concepts that underlie concurrent programming. You should have a grasp of threads, processes, and you'll also know some of the limitations and challenges of Python when it comes to implementing your own concurrent applications. Finally, you have also seen firsthand some of the performance improvements that you can achieve if you were to add different types of concurrency to your applications.

I should make it clear now that there is no silver bullet that you can apply to every application and see consistent performance improvements. One style of concurrent programming might work better than another depending on the requirements of your application, so in the next few chapters, we'll look at all the different mechanisms you can employ and when to employ them.

In the next chapter, we'll have a more in-depth look at the concept of concurrency and parallelism, as well as the differences between the two concepts. We'll also look at some of the main bottlenecks that constrain our concurrent systems, and you'll learn the different styles of computer system architecture, and how it can help us achieve greater performance.

# 2
# Parallelize It

Concurrency and parallelism are two concepts that are commonly confused. The reality, though, is that they are quite different, and if you designed software to be concurrent when instead you needed parallel execution, then you could be seriously impacting your software's true performance potential.

Due to this, it's vital to know exactly what the two concepts mean so that you can understand the differences. Through knowing these differences, you'll be putting yourself at a distinct advantage when it comes to designing your own high performance software in Python.

In this chapter, we'll be covering the following topics:

- What is concurrency and what are the major bottlenecks that impact our applications
- What is parallelism and how does this differ from concurrency
- The different styles of computer system architecture and how we can utilize these effectively, using either concurrency or parallelism
- A brief overview of computer memory architecture

# Understanding concurrency

Concurrency is, essentially, the practice of doing multiple things at the same time, but not, specifically, in parallel. It can help us to improve the perceived performance of our applications, and it can also improve the speed at which our applications run.

The best way to think of how concurrency works is to imagine one person working on multiple tasks and quickly switching between these tasks. Imagine this one person working concurrently on a program, and, at the same time, dealing with support requests. This person would focus primarily on the writing of their program, and quickly context switch to fixing a bug or dealing with a support issue should there be one. Once they complete the support task, they could switch context again, back to writing their program really quickly.

However, in computing, there are typically two performance bottlenecks that we have to watch out for and guard against when writing our programs. It's important to know the differences between the two bottlenecks, as if you try to apply concurrency to a CPU-based bottleneck, then you would find that the program actually starts to see a decrease in performance as opposed to an increase. And if you tried to apply parallelism to a task that really requires a concurrent solution, then you could again see the same performance hits.

# Properties of concurrent systems

All concurrent systems share a similar set of properties; these can be defined as follows:

- Multiple actors: This represents the different processes and threads all trying to actively make progress on their own tasks. We could have multiple processes that contain multiple threads all trying to run at the same time.
- Shared resources: This feature represents the memory, disk, and other resources that the actors in the preceding group must utilize in order to perform what they need to do.
- Rules: These are a strict set of rules that all concurrent systems must follow, and which define when actors can and can't acquire locks, access memory, modify state, and so on. These rules are vital in order for these concurrent systems to work, otherwise, our programs would tear themselves apart.

# I/O bottlenecks

I/O bottlenecks, or I/O bottlenecks for short, are bottlenecks where your computer spends more time waiting on various inputs and outputs than it does on processing the information.

You'll typically find this type of bottleneck when you are working with an I/O heavy application. We could take your standard web browser as an example of a heavy I/O application. In a browser, we typically spend a significantly longer amount of time waiting for network requests to finish for things such as style sheets, scripts, or HTML pages to load as opposed to rendering this on the screen.

If the rate at which data is requested is slower than the rate at which it is consumed, then you have an I/O bottleneck.

One of the main ways to improve the speed of these applications is to either improve the speed of the underlying I/O by buying more expensive and faster hardware, or to improve the way in which we handle these I/O requests.

A great example of a program bound by I/O bottlenecks would be a web crawler. Now the main purpose of a web crawler is to traverse the web, and essentially index web pages so that they can be taken into consideration when Google runs its search ranking algorithm to decide the top 10 results for a given keyword.

We'll start by creating a very simple script that just requests a page and times how long it takes to request said web page, as follows:

```
import urllib.request
import time
t0 = time.time()
req = urllib.request.urlopen('http://www.example.com')
pageHtml = req.read()
t1 = time.time()
print("Total Time To Fetch Page: {} Seconds".format(t1-t0))
```

If we break down this code, first we import the two necessary modules, `urllib.request` and the `time` module. We then record the starting time and request the web page, `example.com`, and then record the ending time and print out the time difference.

Now, say we wanted to add a bit of complexity and follow any links to other pages so that we could index them in the future. We could use a library such as BeautifulSoup in order to make our lives a little easier, as follows:

```python
import urllib.request
import time
from bs4 import BeautifulSoup

t0 = time.time()
req = urllib.request.urlopen('http://www.example.com')
t1 = time.time()
print("Total Time To Fetch Page: {} Seconds".format(t1-t0))
soup = BeautifulSoup(req.read(), "html.parser")

for link in soup.find_all('a'):
  print(link.get('href'))

t2 = time.time()
print("Total Execeution Time: {} Seconds".format)
```

When I execute the preceding program, I see the results like so on my terminal:

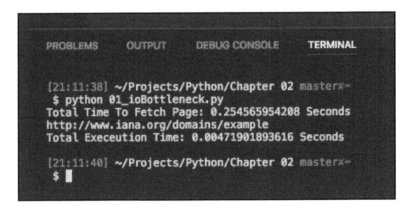

You'll notice from this output that the time to fetch the page is over a quarter of a second. Now imagine if we wanted to run our web crawler for a million different web pages, our total execution time would be roughly a million times longer.

The real main cause for this enormous execution time would purely boil down to the I/O bottleneck we face in our program. We spend a massive amount of time waiting on our network requests, and a fraction of that time parsing our retrieved page for further links to crawl.

# Understanding parallelism

In the first chapter, we covered a bit about Python's multiprocessing capabilities, and how we could use this to take advantage of more of the processing cores in our hardware. But what do we mean when we say that our programs are running in parallel?

Parallelism is the art of executing two or more actions simultaneously as opposed to concurrency in which you make progress on two or more things at the same time. This is an important distinction, and in order to achieve true parallelism, we'll need multiple processors on which to run our code at the same time.

A good analogy for parallel processing is to think of a queue for **Coke**. If you have, say, two queues of 20 people, all waiting to use a coke machine so that they can get through the rest of the day with a bit of a sugar rush, well, this would be an example of concurrency. Now say you were to introduce a second coke machine into the mix--this would then be an example of something happening in parallel. This is exactly how parallel processing works-- each of the coke machines in that room represents one processing core, and is able to make progress on tasks simultaneously:

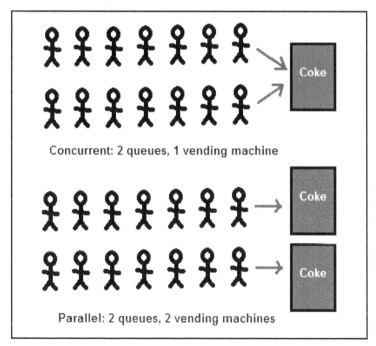

Source: https://github.com/montanaflynn/programming-articles/blob/master/articles/parallelism-and-concurrency-need-different-tools.md

A real-life example that highlights the true power of parallel processing is your computer's graphics card. These graphics cards tend to have hundreds, if not thousands, of individual processing cores that live independently, and can compute things at the same time. The reason we are able to run high-end PC games at such smooth frame rates is due to the fact we've been able to put so many parallel cores onto these cards.

# CPU-bound bottlenecks

A CPU-bound bottleneck is, typically, the inverse of an I/O-bound bottleneck. This bottleneck is found in applications that do a lot of heavy number crunching, or any other task that is computationally expensive. These are programs for which the rate at which they execute is bound by the speed of the CPU--if you throw a faster CPU in your machine you should see a direct increase in the speed of these programs.

 If the rate at which you are processing data far outweighs the rate at which you are requesting data, then you have a CPU-bound bottleneck.

In Chapter 1, *Speed It Up!*, we had a quick look at how to combat a CPU-bound program when we tried to compute the prime factors of 10,000 large random numbers, a problem that relies heavily on the CPU. We then implemented this same prime factorization program in a way that enabled us to utilize more of our CPU, and thus, directly improve the speed at which the program executed.

# How do they work on a CPU?

Understanding the differences outlined in the previous section between both concurrency and parallelism is essential, but it's also very important to understand more about the systems that your software will be running on. Having an appreciation of the different architecture styles as well as the low-level mechanics helps you make the most informed decisions in your software design.

# Single-core CPUs

Single-core processors will only ever execute one thread at any given time as that is all they are capable of. However, in order to ensure that we don't see our applications hanging and being unresponsive, these processors rapidly switch between multiple threads of execution many thousands of times per second. This switching between threads is what is called a "context switch," and involves storing all the necessary information for a thread at a specific point in time, and then restoring it at a different point further down the line.

Using this mechanism of constantly saving and restoring threads allows us to make progress on quite a number of threads within a given second, and it appears like the computer is doing multiple things at once. It is, in fact, doing only one thing at any given time, but doing it at such speed that it's imperceptible to the users of that machine.

When writing multithreaded applications in Python, it is important to note that these context switches are, computationally, quite expensive. There is no way to get around this, unfortunately, and much of the design of operating systems these days is about optimizing for these context switches so that we don't feel the pain quite as much.

The following are the advantages of single-core CPUs:

- They do not require any complex communication protocols between multiple cores
- Single-core CPUs require less power, which makes them better suited for IoT devices

Single-core CPUs, however, have these disadvantages:

- They are limited in speed, and larger applications cause them to struggle and potentially freeze
- Heat dissipation issues place a hard limit on how fast a single-core CPU can go

# Clock rate

One of the key limitations to a single-core application running on a machine is the clock speed of the CPU. When we talk about clock rate, we are essentially talking about how many clock cycles a CPU can execute every second.

For the past 10 years, we have watched as manufacturers managed to surpass Moore's law, which was essentially an observation that the number of transistors one was able to place on a piece of silicon doubled roughly every two years.

This doubling of transistors every two years paved the way for exponential gains in single-CPU clock rates, and CPUs went from the low MHz to the 4-5 GHz clock speeds that we now see on Intel's i7 6700k processor.

But with transistors getting as small as a few nanometers across, this is inevitably coming to an end. We've started to hit the boundaries of physics, and, unfortunately, if we go any smaller, we'll start being hit by the effects of quantum tunneling. Due to these physical limitations, we need to start looking at other methods in order to improve the speeds at which we are able to compute things.

This is where Materlli's Model of Scalability comes into play.

# Martelli model of scalability

The author of *Python Cookbook*, Alex Martelli, came up with a model on scalability, which Raymond Hettinger discussed in his brilliant hour-long talk on "Thinking about Concurrency" that he gave at PyCon Russia 2016. This model represents three different types of problems and programs:

- 1 core: This refers to single-threaded and single process programs
- 2-8 cores: This refers to multithreaded and multiprocessing programs
- 9+ cores: This refers to distributed computing

The first category, the single core, single-threaded category, is able to handle a growing number of problems due to the constant improvements in the speed of single-core CPUs, and as a result, the second category is being rendered more and more obsolete. We will eventually hit a limit with the speed at which a 2-8 core system can run at, and then we'll have to start looking at other methods, such as multiple CPU systems or even distributed computing.

If your problem is worth solving quickly, and it requires a lot of power, then the sensible approach is to go with the distributed computing category and spin up multiple machines and multiple instances of your program in order to tackle your problems in a truly parallel manner. Large enterprise systems that handle hundreds of millions of requests are the main inhabitants of this category. You'll typically find that these enterprise systems are deployed on tens, if not hundreds, of high performance, incredibly powerful servers in various locations across the world.

# Time-sharing - the task scheduler

One of the most important parts of the operating system is the task scheduler. This acts as the maestro of the orchestra, and directs everything with impeccable precision and incredible timing and discipline. This maestro has only one real goal, and that is to ensure that every task has a chance to run through till completion; the when and where of a task's execution, however, is non-deterministic. That is to say, if we gave a task scheduler two identical competing processes one after the other, there is no guarantee that the first process will complete first. This non-deterministic nature is what makes concurrent programming so challenging.

An excellent example that highlights this non-deterministic behavior is the following code:

```python
import threading
import time
import random
counter = 1
def workerA():
  global counter
  while counter < 1000:
    counter += 1
    print("Worker A is incrementing counter to {}".format(counter))
    sleepTime = random.randint(0,1)
    time.sleep(sleepTime)
def workerB():
  global counter
  while counter > -1000:
    counter -= 1
    print("Worker B is decrementing counter to {}".format(counter))
    sleepTime = random.randint(0,1)
    time.sleep(sleepTime)
def main():
  t0 = time.time()
  thread1 = threading.Thread(target=workerA)
  thread2 = threading.Thread(target=workerB)
  thread1.start()
  thread2.start()
  thread1.join()
  thread2.join()
  t1 = time.time()
  print("Execution Time {}".format(t1-t0))
if __name__ == '__main__':
  main()
```

Here in the preceding code, we have two competing threads in Python that are each trying to accomplish their own goal of either decrementing the counter to 1,000, or conversely incrementing it to 1,000. In a single-core processor, there is the possibility that worker *A* manages to complete its task before worker *B* has a chance to execute, and the same can be said for worker *B*. However, there is a third potential possibility, and that is that the task scheduler continues to switch between worker *A* and worker *B* an infinite number of times and never completes.

The preceding code, incidentally, also shows one of the dangers of multiple threads accessing shared resources without any form of synchronization. There is no accurate way to determine what will happen to our counter, and as such, our program could be considered unreliable.

# Multi-core processors

We've now got some idea as to how single-core processors work, but now it's time to take a look at multi-core processors. Multi-core processors contain multiple independent processing units or "cores". Each core contains everything it needs in order to execute a sequence of stored instructions. These cores each follow their own cycle, which consists of the following processes:

- Fetch: This step involves fetching instructions from the program memory. This is dictated by a **program counter** (**PC**), which identifies the location of the next step to execute.
- Decode: The core converts the instruction that it has just fetched, and converts it into a series of signals that will trigger various other parts of the CPU.
- Execute: Finally, we perform the execute step. This is where we run the instruction that we have just fetched and decoded, and the results of this execution are then stored in a CPU register.

Having multiple cores offers us the advantage of being able to work independently on multiple Fetch -> Decode -> Execute cycles. This style of architecture enables us to create higher performance programs that leverage this parallel execution.

The following are the advantages of multi-core processors:

- We are no longer bound by the same performance limitations that a single-core processor is bound to
- Applications that are able to take advantage of multiple cores will tend to run faster if well designed

However, these are the disadvantages of multi-core processors:

- They require more power than your typical single-core processor
- Cross-core communication is no simple feat; we have multiple different ways of doing this, about which I will go into more detail later in this chapter

# System architecture styles

When designing your programs, it's important to note that there are a number of different memory architecture styles that suit the needs of a range of different use cases. One style of memory architecture could be excellent for parallel computing tasks and scientific computing, but somewhat cumbersome when it comes to your standard home-computing tasks.

When we categorize these different styles, we tend to follow a taxonomy first proposed by a man named Michael Flynn in 1972. This taxonomy defines four different styles of computer architecture. These are:

- SISD: single instruction stream, single data stream
- SIMD: single instruction stream, multiple data stream
- MISD: multiple instruction stream, single data stream
- MIMD: multiple instruction stream, multiple data stream

We will look in more detail at these architectures in the following sections.

# SISD

Single Instruction streams, Single Data streams tend to be your uniprocessor systems. These systems have one sequential stream of data coming into them, and one single processing unit that is used to execute this stream.

This style of architecture typically represents your classical Von Neumann machines, and for a vast number of years, before multi-core processors became popular, this represented your typical home computer. You would have a single processor that handled everything you required. These would, however, be incapable of things such as instruction parallelism and data parallelism, and things such as graphics processing were incredibly taxing on these systems.

The following figure shows an overview of how a uniprocessor system looks. It features one data source that is processed by a single processing unit:

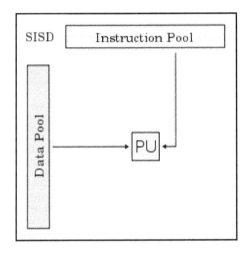

Source: wikipedia.org

This style of architecture features all of the advantages and disadvantages that we outlined earlier in the chapter when we covered single-core processors.

An example of a uniprocessor could be the Intel Pentium 4.

# SIMD

**SIMD (single instruction stream, multiple data streams)** archtecture, multiple data streams architecture is best suited to working with systems that process a lot of multimedia. These are ideal for doing things such as 3D graphics due to the way in which they can manipulate vectors. For instance, say you had two distinct arrays, [10,15,20,25] and [20, 15,10, 5]. In an SIMD architecture, you are able to add these in one operation to get [30,30,30,30]. If we were to do this on scalar architecture, we would have to perform four distinct add operations, as shown in the following figure:

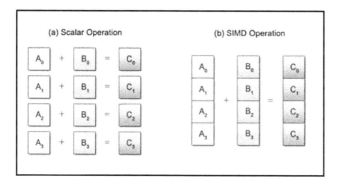

Source: wikipedia.org

The best example of this style of architecture can be found within your graphics processing unit. In OpenGL graphics programming, you have objects called Vertex Array Objects or VAOs, and these VAOs typically contain multiple Vertex Buffer Objects that describe any given 3D object in a game. If someone was to, say, move their character, every element within every Vertex Buffer object would have to be recalculated incredibly quickly in order to allow us to see the character move smoothly across our screens.

This is where the power of SIMD architecture really shines. We pass all of our elements into distinct VAOs. Once these VAOs have been populated, we can then tell it that we want to multiply everything within this VAO with a rotation matrix. This then very quickly proceeds to perform the same action on every element far more efficiently than a non-vector architecture ever could.

The next diagram shows a high-level overview of an SIMD architecture. We have multiple data streams, which could represent multiple vectors, and a number of processing units, all able to act on a single instruction at any given time. Graphics cards typically have hundreds of individual processing units:

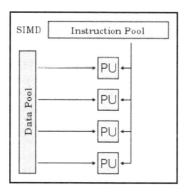

Source: wikipedia.org

The main advantages of SIMD are as follows:

- We are able to perform the same operation on multiple elements using one instruction
- As the number of cores on modern graphics cards increases, so too will the throughput of these cards, thanks to this architecture

We'll be utilizing the full advantages of this style of architecture in `Chapter 11`, *Using the GPU*.

# MISD

Multiple instruction streams, single data streams or MISD is a somewhat unloved style of architecture with no real examples currently available commercially. It's typically quite hard to find a use case in which an MISD architecture style is appropriate, and would lend itself well to a problem.

No real examples of an MISD architecture are available commercially today.

# MIMD

Multiple instruction streams, multiple data streams is the most diverse taxonomy, and encapsulates all modern day multi-core processors. Each of the cores that make up these processors are capable of running independently and in parallel. In contrast to our SIMD machines, MIMD-based machines are able to run a number of distinct operations on multiple datasets in parallel as opposed to a single operation on multiple datasets.

The next diagram shows an example of a number of different processing units, all with a number of different input data streams all acting independently:

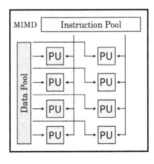

Source: wikipedia.org

A normal multiprocessor typically uses MIMD architecture.

# Computer memory architecture styles

When we start to speed up our programs by introducing concepts such as concurrency and parallelism, we start to face new challenges that must be thought about and addressed appropriately. One of the biggest challenges we start to face is the speed at which we can access data. It's important to note at this stage that if we cannot access data fast enough, then this becomes a bottleneck for our programs, and no matter how expertly we design our systems, we'll never see any performance gains.

Computer designers have been increasingly looking for ways to improve the ease with which we can develop new parallel solutions to problems. One of the ways they have managed to improve things is by providing a single physical address space that all of our multiple cores can access within a processor. This removes a certain amount of complexity away from us, as programmers, and allows us to instead focus on ensuring that our code is thread safe.

There are a number of these different styles of architecture used in a wide range of different scenarios. The main two different architectural styles employed by system designers tend to be those that follow a Uniform Memory Access pattern or a Non-uniform memory access pattern, or UMA and NUMA respectively.

# UMA

**UMA (Uniform Memory Access)** is an architecture style that features a shared memory space that can be utilized in a uniform manner by any number of processing cores. In layman's terms this means that regardless of where that core resides, it will be able to directly access a memory location in the same time no matter how close the memory is. This style of architecture is also known as Symmetric Shared-Memory Multiprocessors or SMP in short.

The following image depicts how a UMA-style system would piece together. Each processor interfaces with a bus, which performs all of the memory accessing. Each processor added to this system increases the strain on the bus bandwidth, and thus we aren't able to scale it in quite the same way we could if we were to use a NUMA architecture:

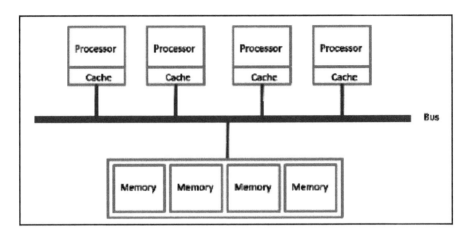

Source: https://software.intel.com/en-us/articles/optimizing-applications-for-numa

The advantages of UMA are as follows:

- All RAM access takes the exact same amount of time
- Cache is coherent and consistent
- Hardware design is simpler

However, there is one disadvantage of UMA:

- UMA systems feature one memory bus from which all systems access memory; unfortunately, this presents scaling problems

# NUMA

**NUMA** (**Non-uniform Memory Access**) is an architecture style in which some memory access may be faster than others depending on which processor requested it--this could be due to the location of the processor with respect to the memory.

Show next is a diagram that shows exactly how a number of processors interconnect in NUMA style. Each has their own cache, access to the main memory, and independent I/O, and each is connected to the interconnection network:

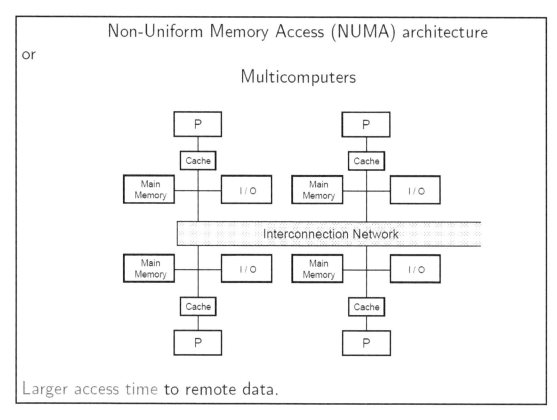

Source: https://virtualizationdeepdive.wordpress.com/deep-dive-numa-vnuma/

There is one major advantage of NUMA:

- NUMA machines are more scalable than their uniform-memory access counterparts

The following are the disadvantages of NUMA:

- Non-deterministic memory access times can lead to either really quick access times if memory is local, or far longer times if memory is in distant memory locations
- Processors must observe the changes made by other processors; the amount of time it takes to observe increases in relation to how many processors are part of it

# Summary

In this chapter, we covered a multitude of topics including the differences between concurrency and parallelism. We looked at how they both leverage the CPU in different ways, and we also branched off into the topic of computer system design and how it relates to concurrent and parallel programming.

By now you should have an appreciation for the two main types of bottlenecks afflicting most software, and also have some idea as to how to combat this. You'll also have an appreciation for some of the different styles of system architecture used, and how we can leverage these different architectures in software design.

In the next chapter, we'll expand more on the life cycle of a thread, and how it lives on your machine.

# 3
# Life of a Thread

In the previous chapter, we looked in depth at the concepts of concurrency and parallelism as well as some of the key issues we face in multithreaded Python applications. Now it's time to look at how we can start working with threads and manipulate them to our will.

In this chapter, we'll be diving into the life of a thread. We'll cover various topics such as:

- The different states a thread can be in
- Different types of threads - Windows vs POSIX
- The best practices when it comes to starting your own threads
- How we can make our lives easier when it comes to working with loads of threads
- Finally, we'll be looking at how we can end threads and the various multithreading models out there

## Threads in Python

Before we jump into more detail about the life of a thread, I feel it's important to know what we are going to be instantiating in real terms. In order to know this, however, we'll need to have a look at Python's Thread class definition which can be found in `threading.py`.

Within this file, you should see the class definition for the Thread class. This has a constructor function which looks something like this:

```
# Python Thread class Constructor
def __init__(self, group=None, target=None, name=None,
        args=(), kwargs=None, verbose=None):
```

This preceding constructor takes in five real arguments, which are defined within that class definition as follows:

- `group`: This is a special parameter which is reserved for a future extension.
- `target`: This is the callable object to be invoked by the `run()` method. If not passed, this will default to `None`, and nothing will be started.
- `name`: This is the thread name.
- `args`: This is the argument tuple for target invocation. It defaults to `()`.
- `kwargs`: This is a dictionary of keyword arguments to invoke the base class constructor.

# Thread state

Threads can exist in five distinct states: running, not-running, runnable, starting, and ended. When we create a thread, we have, typically, not allocated any resources towards this thread as of yet. It exists in no state, as it hasn't been initialized, and it can only be started or stopped. Let's take a quick look at these five states:

- **New Thread**: In the New Thread state, our thread hasn't started, and it hasn't been allocated resources. It is merely an instance of an object.
- **Runnable**: This is the state when the thread is waiting to run, it has all the resources it needs in order to proceed, and the only thing holding it back is the task scheduler having not scheduled it to run.
- **Running**: In this state, the thread makes progress--it executes whatever task it's meant to and has been chosen by the task scheduler to run.
  From this state, our thread can go into either a dead state if we chose to kill, it or it could go into a not-running state.
- **Not-running**: This is when the thread has been paused in some way. This could be caused by a number of reasons such as when waiting for the response of a long running I/O request. Or it could be deliberately blocked until another thread has completed its execution.
- **Dead**: A thread can reach this state through one of two ways. It can, much like us, die of natural causes or be killed unnaturally. The latter poses a significant risk to the murderer, but we'll go into these risks in detail in the ending a thread section of this chapter.

# State flow chart

The following diagram represents the five different states that a thread can be in as well as the possible transitions from one state to another:

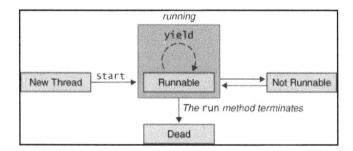

Source: http://www.iitk.ac.in/esc101/05Aug/tutorial/essential/threads/lifecycle.html

# Python example of thread state

So now that we know the various states that our threads can be in, how does this translate into our Python programs? Take a look at the following code:

```python
import threading
import time
# A very simple method for our thread to execute
def threadWorker():
    # it is only at the point where the thread starts executing
    # that it's state goes from 'Runnable' to a 'Running'
    # state
    print("My Thread has entered the 'Running' State")
    # If we call the time.sleep() method then our thread
    # goes into a not-runnable state. We can do no further work
    # on this particular thread
    time.sleep(10)
    # Thread then completes its tasks and terminates
    print("My Thread is terminating")


# At this point in time, the thread has no state
# it hasn't been allocated any system resources
myThread = threading.Thread(target=threadWorker)
# When we call myThread.start(), Python allocates the necessary system
# resources in order for our thread to run and then calls the thread's
# run method. It goes from 'Starting' state to 'Runnable' but not running
myThread.start()
```

```
# Here we join the thread and when this method is called
# our thread goes into a 'Dead' state. It has finished the
# job that it was intended to do.
myThread.join()
print("My Thead has entered a 'Dead' state")
```

# Breaking it down

In this preceding code example, we define a function, `threadWorker`, which will be the invocation target of the thread that we will create. All that this `threadWorker` function does is to print out its current state, and then sleep for 10 seconds by calling `time.sleep(10)`.

After we've defined `threadWorker`, we then go on to create a New Thread object in this line:

```
myThread = threading.Thread(target=threadWorker)
```

At this point in time, our thread object is currently in the New Thread state, and hasn't yet been allocated any system resources that it needs to run. This only happens when we go on to call this function:

```
myThread.start()
```

At this point, our thread is allocated with all of its resources, and the thread's `run` function is called. The thread now enters the "Runnable" state. It goes on to print out its own state, and then proceeds to block for 10 seconds by calling `time.sleep(10)`. During the 10 seconds that this thread sleeps, the thread is considered to be in the "Not-Running" state, and other threads will be scheduled to run over this thread.

Finally, once the 10-second period has elapsed, our thread is considered to have ended and be in the "Dead" state. It no longer needs any of the resources that it was allocated, and it will be cleaned up by the garbage collector.

# Different types of threads

Python abstracts most of the complications of lower-level threading APIs, and allows us to focus on creating even more complex systems on top of it. Not only that, it lets us write portable code that can leverage either POSIX or Windows threads depending on what operating system we execute our code on.

But what do we mean when we mention things like POSIX threads or Windows threads?

## POSIX threads

When we talk about POSIX threads, we are talking about threads that are implemented to follow the IEEE POSIX 1003.1c standard. This standard was registered as a trademark of the IEEE foundation, and was originally developed in order to standardize the implementation of threads across a range of hardware on UNIX systems. Any implementations of threads that follow this standard are, typically, called POSIX threads or PThreads for short.

## Windows threads

When we talk about Windows threads, we are talking about the standard that Microsoft has chosen to implement their own low-level threads against other threads. They feature quite a number of differences when compared to POSIX threads, and the Windows threads API is simpler and overall more elegant than the POSIX threads API.

# The ways to start a thread

In this section of the chapter, we'll take a look at the numerous ways to start threads and processes.

## Starting a thread

In Python, there are a number of different ways we can actually start a thread. When we have a relatively simple task that we wish to multithread, then we have the option of defining this as a single function.

In the following example, we have a very simple function that just sleeps for a random time interval. This represents a very simple piece of functionality, and is ideal for encapsulating a simple function, and then passing this simple function as the target for a new `threading.Thread` object as seen in the following code:

```
import threading
import time
import random
def executeThread(i):
  print("Thread {} started".format(i))
  sleepTime = random.randint(1,10)
  time.sleep(sleepTime)
  print("Thread {} finished executing".format(i))
for i in range(10):
  thread = threading.Thread(target=executeThread, args=(i,))
```

```
thread.start()
print("Active Threads:" , threading.enumerate())
```

# Inheriting from the thread class

Fo scenarios that require more code than can be wrapped up in a single function, we can actually define a class that inherits directory from the thread native class.

This is ideal for scenarios where the complexity of the code is too large for a single function, and, instead, needs to be broken up into multiple functions. While this does give us more flexibility overall when dealing with threads, we do have to take into consideration the fact that we now have to manage our thread within this class.

In order for us to define a New Thread that subclasses the native Python thread class, we need to do the following at a bare minimum:

- Pass in the thread class to our class definition
- Call `Thread.__init__(self)` within our constructor in order for our thread to initialize
- Define a `run()` function that will be called when our thread is started:

```
from threading import Thread
class myWorkerThread(Thread):
    def __init__(self):
    print("Hello world")
    Thread.__init__(self)
    def run(self):
    print("Thread is now running")
myThread = myWorkerThread()
print("Created my Thread Object")
myThread.start()
print("Started my thread")
myThread.join()
print("My Thread finished")
```

# Breaking it down

In the preceding code, we have defined a very simple class called `myWorkerThread`, which inherits from the thread class. Within our constructor, we call the necessary `Thread.__init__(self)` function.

We then also define the `run` function which will be called when we start `myThread.start()`. Within this `run` function, we simply call the `print` function to print our state to the console, and then our thread effectively terminates.

# Forking

To fork a process is to create a second exact replica of the given process. In other words, when we fork something, we effectively clone it and then run it as a child process of the process that we just cloned from.

This newly created process gets its own address space as well as an exact copy of the parent's data and the code executing within the parent process. When created, this new clone receives its own unique **Process IDentifier** (**PID**), and is independent of the parent process from which it was cloned.

Why would you want to clone an existing process though? If you've ever done any form of website hosting, then you've probably run into Apache. Apache heavily utilizes forking in order to create multiple server processes. Each of these independent processes is able to handle their own requests within their own address space. This is ideal in this scenario, as it gives us some protection in the sense that, if a process crashes or dies, other processes running concurrently with it will be unaffected, and able to continue to cater to any new requests.

# Example

Let's see an example of this:

```
import os
def child():
  print "We are in the child process with PID= %d"%os.getpid()
def parent():
  print "We are in the parent process with PID= %d"%os.getpid()
  newRef=os.getpid()
  if newRef==0:
    child()
  else:
    print "We are in the parent process and our child process has PID=
%d"%newRef
parent()
```

# Breaking it down

In the preceding code, we start by importing the os Python module. We then define two distinct functions, one called child and one called parent. The child parent simply prints out the process identifier, otherwise known as the PID.

In the parent function, we first print out the PID of the process that we are in before calling the os.fork() method to fork the current running process. This creates a brand new process, which receives its own unique PID. We then call the child function, which prints out the current PID. This PID, as you should notice, is different from the original PID that was printed out at the start of our script's execution.

This different PID represents a successful forking and a completely new process being created.

# Daemonizing a thread

Firstly, before we look at daemon threads, I feel it is important to know what these are. Daemon threads are 'essentially' threads that have no defined endpoint. They will continue to run forever until your program quits.

"Why is this useful?", you might ask. Say, for example, you have a load balancer that sends service requests to multiple instances of your application. You might have some form of registry service that lets your load balancer know where to send these requests, but how does this service registry know the state of your instance? Typically, in this scenario, we would send out something called a heartbeat or a keep alive packet at a regular interval to say to our service registry, "Hey, I'm still 200!".

This example is a prime use case for daemon threads within our application. We could migrate the job of sending a heartbeat signal to our service registry to a daemon thread, and start this up when our application is starting. This daemon thread will then sit in the background of our program, and periodically send this update without any intervention on our part. What's even better is that our daemon thread will be killed without us having to worry about it when our instance shuts down.

# Example

An example for this is as follows:

```
import threading
import time
def standardThread():
    print("Starting my Standard Thread")
    time.sleep(20)
    print("Ending my standard thread")
def daemonThread():
    while True:
       print("Sending Out Heartbeat Signal")
       time.sleep(2)
if __name__ == '__main__':
   standardThread = threading.Thread(target=standardThread)
   daemonThread = threading.Thread(target=daemonThread)
   daemonThread.setDaemon(True)
   daemonThread.start()

   standardThread.start()
```

# Breaking it down

In the preceding code sample, we define two functions that will act as targets for both our normal, non-daemon thread as well as daemonThread. Our standardThread function essentially just prints out its state and sleeps for 20 seconds to simulate a longer-running program.

The daemonThread function goes into a permanent while loop, and simply prints out Sending Out Heartbeat Signal every 2 seconds. This is simply a placeholder for whatever heartbeat mechanism you choose to go with further down the line.

In our main function, we create two threads, our standard thread and our daemon thread, and we start both using the same start() method. You'll notice that we also use the setDaemon function on our daemonThread object. This simply sets the thread object's daemon flag to whatever we pass into this function, and is only really used for reference.

# Handling threads in Python

In this section of the chapter, we'll take a look at how you can effectively create and manage multiple threads in Python programs.

# Starting loads of threads

The first example we'll look at is how we can start numerous threads all at once. We can create multiple thread objects by using a `for` loop and then starting them within the same `for` loop. In the following example, we define a function that takes in an integer and which sleeps for a random amount of time, printing both when it is starting and ending.

We then create a `for` loop which loops up to 10, and create 10 distinct thread objects that have their target set to our `executeThread` function. It then starts the thread object we've just created, and then we print out the current active threads.

# Example

Let's now look at an example:

```python
import threading
import time
import random
def executeThread(i):
  print("Thread {} started".format(i))
  sleepTime = random.randint(1,10)
  time.sleep(sleepTime)
  print("Thread {} finished executing".format(i))
for i in range(10):
  thread = threading.Thread(target=executeThread, args=(i,))
  thread.start()
  print("Active Threads:" , threading.enumerate())
```

# Breaking it down

In the preceding code, we define a simple function called `executeThread` which takes in `i` as its only parameter. Within this function, we simply call the `time.sleep()` function and pass in a randomly generated `int` between 1 and 10.

We then go on to declare a `for` loop that loops from 1 to 10, which creates a thread object and then starts it while passing in `i` to our thread's args. When you run this script, you should see something like this:

```
$ python3.6 00_startingThread.py
Thread 0 started
Active Threads: [<_MainThread(MainThread, started 140735793988544)>,
<Thread(Thread-1, started 123145335930880)>]
Thread 1 started
```

```
Active Threads: [<_MainThread(MainThread, started 140735793988544)>,
<Thread(Thread-1, started 123145335930880)>, <Thread(Thread-2, started
123145341186048)>]
Thread 2 started
Active Threads: [<_MainThread(MainThread, started 140735793988544)>,
<Thread(Thread-1, started 123145335930880)>, <Thread(Thread-2, started
123145341186048)>, <Thread(Thread-3, started 123145346441216)>]
```

# Slowing down programs using threads

While working with threads, it's important to know that starting hundreds of threads and throwing them all at a specific problem is probably not going to improve the performance of your application. It's highly probable that if you spin up hundreds or thousands of threads, you could, in fact, be absolutely killing performance.

In Chapter 1, *Speed it Up!*, we touched upon how we could use multiple processes in order to speed up a very simple prime factorization program that was computationally intensive. On my machine, I witnessed a good 50-100% speed increase by adding these multiple processes, but what happens is that we try to, instead, make this multithreaded as opposed to multiprocessed. Let's take a look at this example:

# Example

```
import time
import random
import threading
def calculatePrimeFactors(n):
  primfac = []
  d = 2
  while d*d <= n:
    while (n % d) == 0:
      primfac.append(d)
      n //= d
    d |= 1
  if n > 1:
    primfac.append(n)
  return primfac
def executeProc():
  for i in range(1000):
    rand = random.randint(20000, 100000000)
    print(calculatePrimeFactors(rand))
def main():
  print("Starting number crunching")
  t0 = time.time()
```

```
threads = []
for i in range(10):
    thread = threading.Thread(target=executeProc)
    threads.append(thread)
    thread.start()
for thread in threads:
    thread.join()
t1 = time.time()
totalTime = t1 - t0
print("Execution Time: {}".format(totalTime))
if __name__ == '__main__':
    main()
```

# Breaking it down

The preceding sample is almost identical to the *Sequential prime factorization* in Chapter 1, *Speed it Up!*. You should notice, however, that in the main function, instead of defining 10 processes and joining them, we have defined 10 different threads.

If you now run this program, you should see a drastic reduction in the overall performance of our program when compared with both it's single-threaded and multiprocessed counterparts. The results of each are as follows:

| Single-threaded sample: | 3.69 seconds |
|---|---|
| Multi-processing sample: | 1.98 seconds |
| Multi-threaded sample | 3.95 seconds |

As you can see from the results in the preceding table, by starting multiple threads and throwing them at a problem, we've actually managed to achieve a slowdown of around 7% when compared to our single-threaded solution, and almost a 100% slow down when compared against our multiprocessed solution.

# Getting the total number of active threads

Sometimes, for times when you want to, say, query the status of your application, you may want to query the number of active threads currently running within your Python program. Thankfully, Python's native `threading` module easily allows us to get this with a simple call like the one demonstrated in the following code snippet:

# Example

```
import threading
import time
import random
def myThread(i):
  print("Thread {}: started".format(i))
  time.sleep(random.randint(1,5))
  print("Thread {}: finished".format(i))
def main():
  for i in range(random.randint(2,50)):
    thread = threading.Thread(target=myThread, args=(i,))
    thread.start()
  time.sleep(4)
  print("Total Number of Active Threads:
{}".format(threading.active_count()))
if __name__ == '__main__':
  main()
```

# Breaking it down

In the preceding example, all that we are doing is starting a random number of threads between 2 and 50 and have them sleep for a random time interval before conking out. Once all the given threads have been started, we then sleep for 4 seconds, call `threading.active_count()`, and output this in a formatted `print` statement.

# Getting the current thread

For a quick and easy way to determine what thread we are on, we can use the
`threading.current_thread()` function, as shown in the following example:

## Example

```
import threading
import time
def threadTarget():
 print("Current Thread: {}".format(threading.current_thread()))
threads = []
for i in range(10):
 thread = threading.Thread(target=threadTarget)
 thread.start()
 threads.append(thread)
for thread in threads:
 thread.join()
```

## Breaking it down

In the preceding example, we define a function, `threadTarget`, which prints out the
current thread. We then go on to create an empty array for our threads, and we populate
this array with 10 distinct thread objects. We then join each of these threads in turn so that
our program doesn't instantly exit. The output of the preceding program should look
something like this:

```
$ python3.6 10_gettingCurrentThread.py
Current Thread: <Thread(Thread-1, started 123145429614592)>
Current Thread: <Thread(Thread-2, started 123145429614592)>
Current Thread: <Thread(Thread-3, started 123145434869760)>
Current Thread: <Thread(Thread-4, started 123145429614592)>
Current Thread: <Thread(Thread-5, started 123145434869760)>
Current Thread: <Thread(Thread-6, started 123145429614592)>
Current Thread: <Thread(Thread-7, started 123145434869760)>
Current Thread: <Thread(Thread-8, started 123145429614592)>
Current Thread: <Thread(Thread-9, started 123145434869760)>
Current Thread: <Thread(Thread-10, started 123145429614592)>
```

# Main thread

All Python programs feature at least one thread--this sole thread is the main thread. In Python, we are able to call the aptly named `main_thread()` function from wherever we are to retrieve the main thread object. Let's look at this example:

# Example

```
import threading
import time
def myChildThread():
  print("Child Thread Starting")
  time.sleep(5)
  print("Current Thread ----------")
  print(threading.current_thread())
  print("-------------------------")
  print("Main Thread -------------")
  print(threading.main_thread())
  print("-------------------------")
  print("Child Thread Ending")
child = threading.Thread(target=myChildThread)
child.start()
child.join()
```

# Breaking it down

In the preceding code, we define a simple function called `myChildThread`. This will be the target of the thread object that we shall create for demonstration purposes. Within this function, we simply print out the current thread and then the main thread.

We then go on to create a thread object, and then start and join this newly created thread. In the output, you should see something like this:

```
$ python3.6 15_mainThread.py
Child Thread Starting
Current Thread ----------
<Thread(Thread-1, started 123145387503616)>
-------------------------
Main Thread -------------
<_MainThread(MainThread, started 140735793988544)>
-------------------------
Child Thread Ending
```

As you can see, our program prints out first our child thread object, and then goes on to print out the reference of our `MainThread` object.

# Enumerating all threads

There may be a time when you need to enumerate through all active threads in order to do things like query the status of all active threads. Sometimes, however, you may lose track of which threads are at play at a given point of an application.

Thankfully, Python natively allows us to query all the active threads, and then enumerate them easily so that we can obtain the information we need on them, or to properly kill them, and so on. Let's look at an example:

# Example

```python
import threading
import time
import random
def myThread(i):
  print("Thread {}: started".format(i))
  time.sleep(random.randint(1,5))
  print("Thread {}: finished".format(i))
def main():
  for i in range(4):
    thread = threading.Thread(target=myThread, args=(i,))
    thread.start()
  print("Enumerating: {}".format(threading.enumerate()))
if __name__ == '__main__':
  main()
```

# Breaking it down

In the preceding example, we start off by defining a very simplistic function called `myThread`, which will be the target of the threads that we are about to create. Within this function, we simply print that the thread has started, and then we wait for a random interval between 1 and 5 seconds before printing that the thread is terminating.

We have then defined a `main` function which creates four distinct thread objects, and then starts them off. Once we've finished creating and starting these threads, we then print out the results of `threading.enumerate()`, which should output something like this:

```
$ python3.6 07_enumerateThreads.py
Thread 0: started
Thread 1: started
Thread 2: started
Thread 3: started
Enumerating: [<_MainThread(MainThread, started 140735793988544)>,
<Thread(Thread-1, started 123145554595840)>, <Thread(Thread-2,
started 123145559851008)>, <Thread(Thread-3, started
123145565106176)>, <Thread(Thread-4, started 123145570361344)>]
Thread 2: finished
Thread 3: finished
Thread 0: finished
Thread 1: finished
```

# Identifying threads

In certain scenarios, it can be very helpful for us, as developers, to be able to distinguish between different threads. In some scenarios, your application may be made up of hundreds of different threads, and identifying them might help ease your pain when it comes to debugging and identifying issues with your underlying program.

In massive systems, it is a good idea to segregate threads into groups if they are performing different tasks. Say, for instance, you have an application that both listens for incoming stock price changes and also tries to predict where that price will go. You could, for instance, have two different thread groups here: one group listening for the changes and the other performing the necessary calculations.

Having different naming conventions for the threads that do the listening and the threads that do the calculations could make your job of tailing log files a hell of a lot easier.

## Example

In this example, we're going to keep our naming convention really simple; we'll just call our threads Thread-x, where x will be a unique number:

```
import threading
import time
def myThread():
  print("Thread {} starting".format(threading.currentThread().getName()))
```

```
    time.sleep(10)
    print("Thread {} ending".format(threading.currentThread().getName()))
for i in range(4):
    threadName = "Thread-" + str(i)
    thread = threading.Thread(name=threadName, target=myThread)
    thread.start()
print("{}".format(threading.enumerate()))
```

# Breakdown

In the preceding code, what we essentially do is define a function called `myThread`. Within this function, we utilize the `threading.currentThread().getName()` getter in order to retrieve the current thread's moniker, and print this out both when we start our thread's execution, and when it ends.

We then go on to start a `for` loop, and create four thread objects that take in the name parameter, which we define as "`Thread-`" + `str(i)`, as well as the `myThread` function as the target of that thread's execution.

We then, finally, go on to print out all the active threads currently running. This should print out something like the following:

```
$ python3.6 11_identifyingThreads.py
Thread Thread-0 starting
Thread Thread-1 starting
Thread Thread-2 starting
Thread Thread-3 starting
[<_MainThread(MainThread, started 140735793988544)>,
<Thread(Thread-0, started 123145368256512)>, <Thread(Thread-1,
started 123145373511680)>, <Thread(Thread-2, started
123145378766848)>, <Thread(Thread-3, started 123145384022016)>]
Thread Thread-0 ending
Thread Thread-2 ending
Thread Thread-3 ending
Thread Thread-1 ending
```

# Ending a thread

Ending threads is deemed bad practice, and one that I actively advise against. Python doesn't actually provide a native thread function with which to kill other threads, so this should raise flags straight away. These threads that you wish to terminate could be holding a critical resource that needs to be opened and closed properly, or they could also be the parents to multiple child threads. By killing parent threads without killing their child threads, we essentially create orphan threads.

## Best practice in stopping threads

If you require some form of a thread shutdown mechanism, then it is your job to implement a mechanism that allows for a graceful shutdown as opposed to killing a thread outright.

However, there does exist a workaround; while threads might not possess a native mechanism for termination, processes do, in fact, feature such a mechanism. As you should know by now, processes are essentially beefier versions of threads, and while it might not be ideal, in some situations you have to ensure that your programs can gracefully shut down, and this presents itself as a far cleaner solution than implementing your own thread termination. Let's take a look at another example:

## Example

```
from multiprocessing import Process
import time
def myWorker():
 t1 = time.time()
 print("Process started at: {}".format(t1))
 time.sleep(20)
myProcess = Process(target=myWorker)
print("Process {}".format(myProcess))
myProcess.start()
print("Terminating Process...")
myProcess.terminate()
myProcess.join()
print("Process Terminated: {}".format(myProcess))
```

In the preceding example, we define a simple `myWorker()` function which prints out the time at which it was started, and then sleeps for 20 seconds. We then go on to declare `myProcess`, which is a type process, and we pass in our `myWorker` function as the target for its execution.

We kick off the process, and then immediately terminate it using the `terminate` method. You should notice in the output that this program finishes almost instantly, and the `myProcess` process does not block for the full 20 seconds it was meant to.

## Output

```
$ python3.6 09_killThread.py
Process <Process(Process-1, initial)>
Terminating Process...
Process Terminated: <Process(Process-1, stopped[SIGTERM])>
```

# Orphan processes

Orphan processes are threads that have no alive parent process. They take up system resources and provide no benefit, and the only way to kill them is to enumerate alive threads and then kill them.

# How does the operating system handle threads

So now that we've taken a look at the life cycle of a thread, it's important to know how these threads actually work within your machines. Understanding things like the multithreading model and how Python threads map to system threads is important if you are to make the right decisions when designing your high-performance software.

# Creating processes versus threads

A process, as we've seen, is a more heavyweight version of a simple thread in the sense that we can do things like spin up multiple threads within a process. They can perform more CPU-bound tasks better than a standard thread would due to the fact that they each feature their own separate GIL instance.

However, it's important to note that while these might be far better at CPU-bound problems, they are also more resource intensive. Being more resource intensive means that they are also more expensive to spin up on the fly and kill off just as quickly. In this next example, we'll look at the performance impact of spinning up multiple threads, and compare this to the spinning up of multiple processes.

# Example

```
import threading
from multiprocessing import Process
import time
import os
def MyTask():
  print("Starting")
  time.sleep(2)
t0 = time.time()
threads = []
for i in range(10):
  thread = threading.Thread(target=MyTask)
  thread.start()
  threads.append(thread)
t1 = time.time()
print("Total Time for Creating 10 Threads: {} seconds".format(t1-t0))
for thread in threads:
  thread.join()
t2 = time.time()
procs = []
for i in range(10):
  process = Process(target=MyTask)
  process.start()
  procs.append(process)
t3 = time.time()
print("Total Time for Creating 10 Processes: {} seconds".format(t3-t2))
for proc in procs:
  proc.join()
```

# Breaking it down

You'll see in the preceding example that we define a `MyTask` function which will be the target of both the threads and the processes that we'll create.

We first store the starting time in our `t0` variable, and then go on to create an empty array called threads, which will conveniently store the references to all of our thread objects that we create. We then go on to create and then start these threads before recording the time again so that we can calculate the total time needed to perform both the creation and starting.

We then go on to follow the exact same creation and starting process as before, but this time, with processes as opposed to threads. We record the times again, and calculate the difference. When running this script on my machine, the two recorded times for creation and starting were an order of magnitude apart. Creating and starting processes took 10x the amount of time it took to create and start ordinary threads. The output for this particular program looked like this on my machine:

```
[20:08:07] ~/Projects/Python/Chapter 03 master??
$ python3.6 13_forkVsCreate.py
Total Time for Creating 10 Threads: 0.0017189979553222656 seconds
Total Time for Creating 10 Processes: 0.02233409881591797 seconds
```

Now, while the times taken to do both these tasks might be minimal for our relatively lightweight example, consider the performance impact you would see if you were starting hundreds or thousands of processes or threads on huge server racks.

One way we can combat this is to do all our process or thread creation at the start and store them in a pool so that they can sit and wait for further instructions without us having to incur these heavy costs of creation. We'll be looking at this concept of thread pools and process pools in more depth in Chapter 7, *Executors and Pools*.

# Multithreading models

In Chapter 1, *Speed It Up!*, the first section provide a brief introduction to concurrency, where we talked about the two distinct types of threads that we have on a single machine. These were user threads and kernel threads, and it's useful to know how these map to each other, and the different ways that they can be mapped together. In total, there are these three different styles of mapping:

- One user thread to one kernel thread
- Many user-level threads to one kernel thread
- Many user threads to many kernel threads

Within Python, we typically go with the one user thread to one kernel thread mapping, and as such, every thread you create within your multithreaded applications will take up a non-trivial amount of resources on your machine.

However, there do exist some modules within the Python ecosystem that enable you to implement multithreaded-esque functionality to your program while remaining on a single thread. One of the biggest and best examples of this is the asyncio module, which we'll be diving deeper into in Chapter 9, *Event-Driven Programming*.

# One-to-one thread mapping

In this mapping, we see one user-level thread being mapped directly to one kernel-level thread. One-to-one mappings can be expensive due to the inherent costs of creating and managing kernel-level threads, but they provide advantages in the sense that user-level threads are not subject to the same level of blocking as threads that follow a many-to-one mapping are subject to:

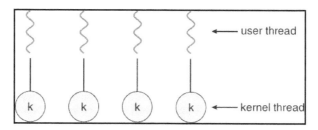

Source: http://www2.cs.uic.edu/~jbell/CourseNotes/OperatingSystems/4_Threads.html

# Many-to-one

In many-to-one mappings, we see many user-level threads being mapped to one solitary kernel-level thread. This is advantageous as we can manage user-level threads efficiently; however, should if the user-level thread is blocked, the other threads that are mapped to kernel-level thread will also be blocked:

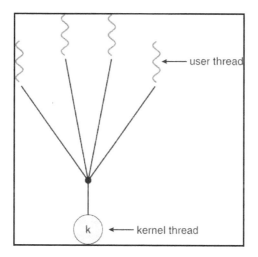

Source: http://www2.cs.uic.edu/~jbell/CourseNotes/OperatingSystems/4_Threads.html

# Many-to-many

In this threading model, we see many user-level threads being mapped to many kernel-level threads. This presents itself as the solution to the shortcomings of the previous two models.

Individual user-level threads can be mapped to a combination of either a single kernel-level thread or multiple kernel threads. It provides us, as programmers, the ability to choose which user-level threads we wish to map to kernel-level threads, and, overall, entitle us to a great deal of power when trying to ensure the very highest of performances when working in a multithreaded environment:

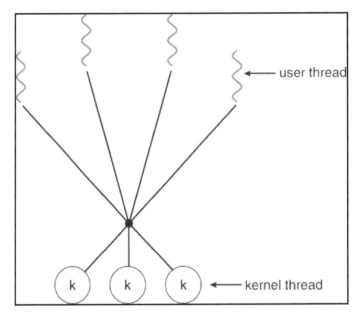

Source: http://www2.cs.uic.edu/~jbell/CourseNotes/OperatingSystems/4_Threads.html

# Summary

In this chapter, we've delved deep into the workings of Python's native threading library. We've looked in depth at how we can effectively work with threads at a very granular level, and take full advantage of everything that the Python threading API has to offer.

We've looked at the numerous different thread types, and how they compare to each other. Not only that, but we've looked in detail at various concepts such as the multithreading model, and the numerous ways in which we can make user threads to their lower level siblings, the kernel threads.

In the next chapter, we'll dive into some of the key concurrency primitives that Python has on offer. Understanding these primitives will pave the way for us when it comes to making thread-safe programs that we can confidently push into production environments.

# 4
# Synchronization between Threads

Now that we've taken a look at threads, and how we can work with and create these threads using various mechanisms in the previous chapter, it's time to look at some of the basic synchronization primitives we can leverage within our multi-threads.

It's not enough to simply add multiple threads to your application in order to improve performance. You also have to take into consideration complexities such as race conditions, and ensure that your code is properly guarded against them.

In this chapter, we'll look at some of the following concepts:

- How we can synchronize our data between threads
- Race conditions--what are they and how to guard against them
- Deadlock, and how it can cripple your systems and bring them to their knees
- An overview of all of the synchronization primitives that Python has to offer

We'll also be introducing some of the key tools that Python developers utilize in order to make the fight against conflicts easier and ensure that our programs remain bug free.

# Synchronization between threads

So you know what threads are and how to properly start and end them in Python, and hopefully, you are starting to realize at least some of the complexity that it takes to implement concurrent programs. But how do we make sure that we are implementing multithreading in a safe way without compromising the flow of our program? In this chapter, we'll be introducing some of the fundamental issues that can plague multithreaded applications if not guarded against.

Before we cover some of the key synchronization primitives, we must first have a look at some of the issues that can occur from using the said primitives. This leads us directly into one of the biggest and most feared issues one can face when designing concurrent systems, that is, deadlock. One of the best ways to illustrate this concept of deadlock is to look at the Dining Philosophers Problem.

## The Dining Philosophers

The Dining Philosophers problem is one of the most famous illustration of some of the problems you can encounter when working in concurrent software systems. It was, originally the famous Edsger Dijkstra, who you were introduced to in `Chapter 1`, *Speed It Up!*, that presented this problem to the world. It was Tony Hoare, however, who gave the problem it's more official formulation.

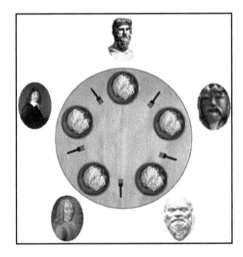

Source: wikipedia.org

In the Dining Philosophers problem, we encounter five famous philosophers sitting at a round table eating from bowls of spaghetti. Between each of these bowls, there are five forks that the philosophers can use to eat their food with. For some strange reason however, these philosophers decide that they each require two of the five forks in order to eat their food.

Each of these philosophers, however, could be either in eating or thinking state, and whenever they choose to dive into the food in front of them, they must first obtain both the left and the right fork. However, when a philosopher takes a fork, they have to wait till they have eaten before they can relinquish said fork.

This method of eating presents a problem when each of the five philosophers manages to pick up their left fork at the same time.

Source: http://www.cs.fsu.edu/~baker/realtime/restricted/notes/philos.html

In the preceding diagram, we see just such a situation arise. Each of the five philosophers has picked up the left fork and is now sitting thinking until such time as the right fork is available. Since every philosopher will never relinquish their fork until they have eaten, the dinner table has reached a deadlocked state, and will never go further.

This problem illustrates a key issue we may run into when we are designing our own concurrent systems that rely on key synchronization primitives (locks) in order to function correctly. Our forks, in this example, are our system resources, and each philosopher represents a competing process.

# Example

In this next example, we are going to implement our own version of the Dining Philosophers problem in Python using RLocks, which we'll cover later on in this chapter. These Rlocks will represent the forks in our problem. We'll start by defining our `Philosopher` class and constructor like this:

```
class Philosopher(threading.Thread):
def __init__(self, leftFork, rightFork):
  print("Our Philosopher Has Sat Down At the Table")
  threading.Thread.__init__(self)
  self.leftFork = leftFork
  self.rightFork = rightFork
```

The `Philosopher` class, which inherits from the Python's native thread class, takes in both a left and a right fork in its constructor function. It then initializes the thread that we can start later on. After we've defined this, we then have to define our thread's `run` function as follows:

```
def run(self):
  print("Philosopher: {} has started
thinking".format(threading.current_thread()))
  while True:
    time.sleep(random.randint(1,5))
    print("Philosopher {} has finished
thinking".format(threading.current_thread()))
    self.leftFork.acquire()
    time.sleep(random.randint(1,5))
    try:
      print("Philosopher {} has acquired the left
fork".format(threading.current_thread()))
      self.rightFork.acquire()
      try:
        print("Philosopher {} has attained both forks, currently
eating".format(threading.current_thread()))
      finally:
        self.rightFork.release()
        print("Philosopher {} has released the right
fork".format(threading.current_thread()))
    finally:
```

```
      self.leftFork.release()
      print("Philosopher {} has released the left
fork".format(threading.current_thread()))
```

In this `run` function, we first think for a random amount of time between 1 and 5 seconds. When our Philosopher finishes thinking, we then attempt to acquire the left fork and again sleep for another 1-5 seconds in order to easily follow the console output.

After we've again finished waiting, we go on to try and acquire the right fork so that we can go into an eating state. We eat only very briefly before releasing both the left and the right fork.

# Output

When you attempt to run this Python program, you should see that some of our Philosophers may get a chance to eat before releasing both locks. However, very quickly, you will see that every fork has been acquired by a Philosopher, and it's now stuck in a state where it's attempting to acquire the right fork.

In the following output, you will see all of our dining philosophers doing a combination of thinking, eating, and acquiring and releasing forks. However, after a certain amount of time, you will, eventually, hit the scenario where all the philosophers have acquired all left forks, and are unable to proceed further, as follows:

```
Marx has started thinking
Russell has started thinking
Aristotle has finished thinking
Marx has finished thinking
Aristotle has acquired the left fork
Aristotle has attained both forks, currently eating
Aristotle has released the right fork
Aristotle has released the left fork
Aristotle has finished thinking
Russell has finished thinking
Kant has finished thinking
Spinoza has finished thinking
Aristotle has acquired the left fork
Marx has acquired the left fork
Russell has acquired the left fork
Kant has acquired the left fork
Spinoza has acquired the left fork
```

# Race conditions

Now that we've had a look at deadlock, it's time to talk about race conditions. Race conditions are an equally troublesome and oft-cursed aspect of concurrent programming that plague hundreds, if not thousands, of programs around the world.

The standard definition of a race condition is as follows:

> *A race condition or race hazard is the behavior of an electronic, software, or other* `system` *where the output is dependent on the sequence or timing of other uncontrollable events.*

Let's break this definition down into simpler terms. One of the best metaphors to describe a race condition is if we imagine writing a banking application that updates your account balance whenever you deposit or withdraw any money from that account.

Imagine, we started with £2,000 in our bank account, and say we are about to receive a bonus of £5,000, because we managed to bug fix a concurrency issue in work that was costing the business millions. Now also imagine that you are also to pay a rent of £1,000 on the same day--this is where a potential race condition could leave you out of pocket.

If our banking application had two processes, one of which dealt with the withdrawing, Process A, and the other which dealt with the depositing, Process B. Say Process B, which deals with deposits into your account, reads your bank balance as £2,000. If Process A was to start its withdrawal for the rent just after Process B starts its transaction, it would see the starting balance as £2,000. Process B would then complete its transaction, and correctly add £5,000 to our starting £2,000, and we'd be left with the grand sum of £7,000.

However, since Process A started its transaction thinking that the starting account balance was £2,000, it would unwittingly leave us bonus-less when it updates our final bank balance to £1,000. This is a prime example of a race condition within our software, and it's a very real danger always waiting to strike us in the most unfortunate ways.

## Process execution sequence

Let's take a look at what happened in closer detail. If we look at the following table, we'll see the ideal flow of execution for both Process A and Process B:

| Thread 1 | Thread 2 | | Integer value |
|---|---|---|---|
| | | | 0 |
| read value | | ← | 0 |
| increase value | | | 0 |
| write back | | → | 1 |
| | read value | ← | 1 |
| | increase value | | 1 |
| | write back | → | 2 |

However, due to the fact we haven't implemented proper synchronization mechanisms to protect our account balance, Process A and Process B actually followed the following execution path and gave us an erroneous result:

| Thread 1 | Thread 2 | | Integer value |
|---|---|---|---|
| | | | 0 |
| read value | | ← | 0 |
| | read value | ← | 0 |
| increase value | | | 0 |
| | increase value | | 0 |
| write back | | → | 1 |
| | write back | → | 1 |

# The solution

Now onto the important part--how do we solve the preceding problem so that we no longer live in fear of losing our bonuses in the future? In this relatively simple example, the answer would be to wrap the code that first reads the account balance, and execute any necessary transactions in a lock, which we'll go into more detail on later in this chapter.

By wrapping the code that performs the read of the account balance and the update in a lock, we ensure that Process A would first have to acquire the lock in order to both read and update our account balance, and likewise, for Process B. This would turn our non-deterministic program deterministic and free of our initial race condition. But by turning it into a deterministic program, we are, essentially, converting this section of code into a single-threaded, serial section of code that could impact performance if we were to have multiple threads.

# Critical sections

We can identify critical sections as any parts of our code that modify or access a shared resource. These critical sections cannot, under any circumstance, be executed by more than one process at any one time. It is when these critical sections are executed simultaneously that we start to see unexpected or erroneous behavior.

Say, for instance, we are writing the code for the banking application example previously defined. We could categorize the part of the code that does the initial reading of the bank account up to the point at which it's updating the accounts bottom line as a critical section.

It was through concurrent execution of this critical section that we first ran into a race condition. By understanding where in our code, we have critical sections, we, as programmers, are able to more accurately protect these sections using some of the primitives that I'll be outlining later on in this chapter.

## Filesystem

It's important to note that race conditions can plague our filesystem as well as our programs. One potential issue could be that two processes simultaneously try to modify a file on the file system. Without appropriate synchronization controls around these files, it's possible that the file could, potentially, become corrupted and useless with two processes writing to it.

## Life-critical systems

One of the worst examples of how race conditions can plague our software is in the software that controlled the Therac-25 radiation therapy machines. This race condition was, unfortunately, enough to cause the death of, at least, three patients who were receiving treatment from the machine.

Most of the time, the software we write will not be as critical as the software that is used within medical devices like this. However, it serves as a very morbid warning to ensure that you try to take every measure in order to prevent your own software from being affected.

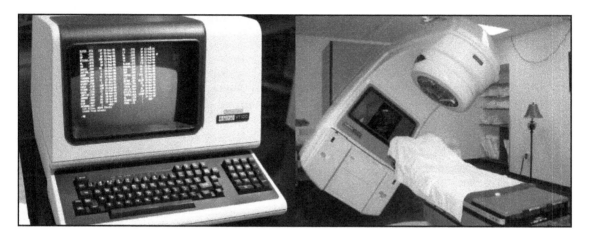

Source: wikipedia.org

# Shared resources and data races

One of the major things we need to guard against when implementing concurrency in your applications is race conditions. These race conditions can cripple our applications, and cause bugs that are hard to debug and even harder to fix. In order to prevent these issues, we need to both understand how these race conditions occur and how we can guard against them using the synchronization primitives we'll be covering in this chapter.

Understanding synchronization and the basic primitives that are available to you is vital if you are to create thread-safe, high-performance programs in Python. Thankfully, we have numerous different synchronization primitives available to us in the threading Python module that can help us in a number of different concurrent situations.

In this section, I'll be giving you a brief overview of all of the synchronization primitives available to you as well as a few simple examples of how you can use these within your programs. By the end of it, you should be able to implement your own concurrent Python programs that can access resources in a thread-safe way.

# The join method

When it comes to developing incredibly important enterprise systems, being able to dictate the execution order of some of our tasks is incredibly important. Thankfully, Python's thread object allow us to retain some form of control over this, as they come with a `join` method.

The `join` method, essentially, blocks the parent thread from progressing any further until that thread has confirmed that it has terminated. This could be either through naturally coming to an end, or whenever the thread throws an unhandled exception. Let's understand this through the following example:

```python
import threading
import time
def ourThread(i):
 print("Thread {} Started".format(i))
 time.sleep(i*2)
 print("Thread {} Finished".format(i))
def main():
 thread1 = threading.Thread(target=ourThread, args=(1,))
 thread1.start()
 print("Is thread 1 Finished?")
 thread2 = threading.Thread(target=ourThread, args=(2,))
 thread2.start()
 thread2.join()
 print("Thread 2 definitely finished")
if __name__ == '__main__':
 main()
```

# Breaking it down

The preceding code example shows an example of how we can make the flow of our threaded programs somewhat deterministic by utilizing this `join` method.

We begin by defining a very simple function called `myThread`, which takes in one parameter. All this function does is print out when it has started, sleep for whatever value is passed into it times 2, and then print out when it has finished execution.

In our `main` function, we define two threads, the first of which we aptly call `thread1`, and pass in a value of 1 as its sole argument. We then start this thread and execute a `print` statement. What's important to note is that this first print statement executes before the completion of our `thread1`.

We then create a second thread object, and imaginatively, call this `thread2`, and pass in 2 as our sole argument this time. The key difference, though, is that we call `thread2.join()` immediately after we start this thread. By calling `thread2`, we can preserve the order in which we execute our `print` statements, and you can see in the output that `Thread 2 Is Definitely Finished` does indeed get printed after `thread2` has terminated.

## Putting it together

While the `join` method may be very useful and provide you with a quick and clean way of ensuring order within our code, it's also very important to note that you could, potentially, undo all the gains we've made by making our code multithreaded in the first place.

Consider our `thread2` object in the preceding example--what exactly did we gain by multithreading this? I know that this is a rather simple program, but the point remains that we joined it immediately after we started it, and essentially, blocked our primary thread until such time as `thread2` completed its execution. We, essentially, rendered our multithreaded application single threaded during the course of the execution of `thread2`.

# Locks

Locks are an essential mechanism when trying to access shared resources from multiple threads of execution. The best way to picture this is to imagine you have one bathroom and multiple flat mates--when you want to freshen up or take a shower, you would want to lock the door so that nobody else could use the bathroom at the same time.

A lock in Python is a synchronization primitive that allows us to essentially lock our bathroom door. It can be in either a "locked" or "unlocked" state, and we can only acquire a lock while it's in an "unlocked" state.

# Example

In `Chapter 2`, *Parallelize It*, we had a look at the following code sample:

```
import threading
import time
import random
counter = 1
def workerA():
 global counter
 while counter < 1000:
   counter += 1
```

```
    print("Worker A is incrementing counter to {}".format(counter))
    sleepTime = random.randint(0,1)
    time.sleep(sleepTime)
def workerB():
 global counter
 while counter > -1000:
    counter -= 1
    print("Worker B is decrementing counter to {}".format(counter))
    sleepTime = random.randint(0,1)
    time.sleep(sleepTime)
def main():
 t0 = time.time()
 thread1 = threading.Thread(target=workerA)
 thread2 = threading.Thread(target=workerB)
 thread1.start()
 thread2.start()
 thread1.join()
 thread2.join()
 t1 = time.time()
 print("Execution Time {}".format(t1-t0))
if __name__ == '__main__':
 main()
```

In this preceding sample, we saw two threads constantly competing in order to increment or decrement a counter. By adding locks, we can ensure that these threads can access our counter in a deterministic and safe manner.

```
import threading
import time
import random
counter = 1
lock = threading.Lock()
def workerA():
 global counter
 lock.acquire()
 try:
    while counter < 1000:
       counter += 1
       print("Worker A is incrementing counter to {}".format(counter))
       sleepTime = random.randint(0,1)
       time.sleep(sleepTime)
 finally:
    lock.release()
def workerB():
 global counter
 lock.acquire()
 try:
    while counter > -1000:
```

```
        counter -= 1
        print("Worker B is decrementing counter to {}".format(counter))
        sleepTime = random.randint(0,1)
        time.sleep(sleepTime)
    finally:
      lock.release()
  def main():
    t0 = time.time()
    thread1 = threading.Thread(target=workerA)
    thread2 = threading.Thread(target=workerB)
    thread1.start()
    thread2.start()
    thread1.join()
    thread2.join()
    t1 = time.time()
    print("Execution Time {}".format(t1-t0))
  if __name__ == '__main__':
    main()
```

# Breaking it down

In the preceding code, we've added a very simple lock primitive that encapsulates both of the while loops within our two worker functions. When the threads first start, they both race to acquire the lock so that they can execute their goal, and try to increment the counter to either 1,000 or -1,000 without having to compete with the other thread. It is only after one thread accomplishes their goal and releases the lock that the other can acquire that lock and try to either increment or decrement the counter.

The preceding code will execute incredibly slowly, as it's mainly meant for demonstration purposes. If you removed the `time.sleep()` calls within the while loop, then you should notice this code executes almost instantly.

# RLocks

Reentrant-locks, or RLocks as they are called, are synchronization primitives that work much like our standard lock primitive, but can be acquired by a thread multiple times if that thread already owns it.

For example, say, thread-1 acquires the RLock, so, for each time that thread-1 then acquires the lock, a counter within the RLock primitive is incremented by 1. If thread-2 tried to come along and acquire the RLock, then it would have to wait until the counter of the RLock drops to 0 before it could be acquired. Thread-2 would go into a blocking state until this 0 condition is met.

Why is this useful, though? Well, it can come in handy when you, for instance, want to have thread-safe access for a method within a class that accesses other class methods.

# Example

Let's see the following example:

```python
import threading
import time
class myWorker():
def __init__(self):
  self.a = 1
  self.b = 2
  self.Rlock = threading.RLock()
 def modifyA(self):
  with self.Rlock:
    print("Modifying A : RLock Acquired:
    {}".format(self.Rlock._is_owned()))
    print("{}".format(self.Rlock))
    self.a = self.a + 1
    time.sleep(5)
def modifyB(self):
  with self.Rlock:
    print("Modifying B : RLock Acquired:
    {}".format(self.Rlock._is_owned()))
    print("{}".format(self.Rlock))
    self.b = self.b - 1
    time.sleep(5)
def modifyBoth(self):
  with self.Rlock:
    print("Rlock acquired, modifying A and B")
    print("{}".format(self.Rlock))
    self.modifyA()
    self.modifyB()
  print("{}".format(self.Rlock))
workerA = myWorker()
workerA.modifyBoth()
```

# Breaking it down

In the preceding code, we see a prime example of the way an RLock works within our single-threaded program. We have defined a class called `myWorker`, which features four functions, these are the constructors which initialize our Rlock and our a and b variables.

We then go on to define two functions that both modify a and b respectively. These both first acquire the classes Rlock using the `with` statement, and then perform any necessary modifications to our internal variables.

Finally, we have our `modifyBoth` function, which performs the initial Rlock acquisition before calling the `modifyA` and `modifyB` functions.

At each step of the way, we print out the state of our Rlock. We see that after it has been acquired within the `modifyBoth` function, its owner is set to the main thread, and its count is incremented to one. When we next call `modifyA`, the Rlocks counter is again incremented by one, and the necessary calculations are made before `modifyA` then releases the Rlock. Upon the `modifyA` function release of the Rlock, we see the counter decrement to 1 before being immediately incremented to 2 again by our `modifyB` function.

Finally, when `modifyB` completes its execution, it releases the Rlock, and then, so does our `modifyBoth` function. When we do a final print out of our Rlock object, we see that the owner has been set to 0, and that our count has also been set to 0. It is only at this point in time that another thread could, in theory, obtain this lock.

## Output

The output would look as follows:

```
$ python3.6 04_rlocks.py
Rlock acquired, modifying A and B
<locked _thread.RLock object owner=140735793988544 count=1 at
0x10296e6f0>
Modifying A : RLock Acquired: True
<locked _thread.RLock object owner=140735793988544 count=2 at
0x10296e6f0>
<locked _thread.RLock object owner=140735793988544 count=1 at
0x10296e6f0>
Modifying B : RLock Acquired: True
<locked _thread.RLock object owner=140735793988544 count=2 at
0x10296e6f0>
<unlocked _thread.RLock object owner=0 count=0 at 0x10296e6f0>
```

# RLocks versus regular locks

If we were to try and perform the same preceding program using a traditional lock primitive, then you should notice that the program never actually reaches the point where it's executing our modifyA() function. Our program would, essentially, go into a form of deadlock, as we haven't implemented a release mechanism that allows our thread to go any further. This is shown in the following code example:

```python
import threading
import time
class myWorker():
def __init__(self):
  self.a = 1
  self.b = 2
  self.lock = threading.Lock()
 def modifyA(self):
  with self.lock:
    print("Modifying A : RLock Acquired: {}".format(self.lock._is_owned()))
    print("{}".format(self.lock))
    self.a = self.a + 1
    time.sleep(5)
def modifyB(self):
  with self.lock:
    print("Modifying B : Lock Acquired: {}".format(self.lock._is_owned()))
    print("{}".format(self.lock))
    self.b = self.b - 1
    time.sleep(5)
def modifyBoth(self):
  with self.lock:
    print("lock acquired, modifying A and B")
    print("{}".format(self.lock))
    self.modifyA()
    print("{}".format(self.lock))
    self.modifyB()
  print("{}".format(self.lock))
workerA = myWorker()
workerA.modifyBoth()
```

RLocks, essentially, allow us to obtain some form of thread safety in a recursive manner without having to implement complex acquiring, and release lock logic throughout your code. They allow us to write simpler code that is easier to follow, and as a result, easier to maintain after our code goes to production.

# Condition

A condition is a synchronization primitive that waits on a signal from another thread. For example, this could be that another thread has finished execution, and that the current thread can proceed to perform some kind of calculation on the results.

# Definition

Let's have a look at the definition of our `condition` object in Python's native library. It's important to understand these fundamental primitives and how they operate at a more granular level, so, I implore you to take a look at the full definition of these objects should you get the time.

```
def Condition(*args, **kwargs):
    """Factory function that returns a new condition variable object.
    A condition variable allows one or more threads to wait until they are
    notified by another thread.
    If the lock argument is given and not None, it must be a Lock or RLock
    object, and it is used as the underlying lock. Otherwise, a new RLock
object
    is created and used as the underlying lock.
```

The most common scenario that is used to highlight the benefits of conditions is that of a producer/consumer. You could have a producer that publishes messages to a queue and notifies other threads, aka the consumers, that there are now messages waiting to be consumed on that queue.

# Example

In this example, we are going to create two different classes that will inherit from the thread class. These will be our Publisher and our subscriber classes. The publisher will do the task of publishing new integers to an integer array, and then notifying the subscribers that there is a new integer to be consumed from the array.

### Our publisher

Our `Publisher` class has two functions defined within it--the constructor which takes in the reference of the integers array and the condition primitive.

The `run` function, essentially, goes into a permanent loop when it is invoked, and then proceeds to generate a random integer between 0 and 1000. Once we have generated this number, we then acquire the condition, and then append this newly generated integer to our integers array.

After we have appended to our array, we then first notify our subscribers that there has been a new item appended to this array, and then we release the condition.

```python
class Publisher(threading.Thread):
  def __init__(self, integers, condition):
    self.condition = condition
    self.integers = integers
    threading.Thread.__init__(self)
  def run(self):
    while True:
      integer = random.randint(0,1000)
      self.condition.acquire()
      print("Condition Acquired by Publisher: {}".format(self.name))
      self.integers.append(integer)
      self.condition.notify()
      print("Condition Released by Publisher: {}".format(self.name))
      self.condition.release()
      time.sleep(1)
```

## Our subscriber

The `subscriber` class, again, has two functions defined within it: the constructor and the `run` function. The constructor takes in two things, the first of which is the reference of array of integers that it will consume from and the second is the condition synchronization primitive.

Within our `run` function, we start a loop that constantly tries to acquire the condition that has been passed into it. When we manage to acquire this lock, we print out the fact that the thread has now acquired it, and then we proceed to try and "pop" the first integer we can from the integers array that we have passed into it. Once we have successfully managed this, we then release the condition primitive, and, once again, start trying to reacquire this condition.

```python
class Subscriber(threading.Thread):
  def __init__(self, integers, condition):
    self.integers = integers
    self.condition = condition
    threading.Thread.__init__(self)
  def run(self):
    while True:
```

```
        self.condition.acquire()
        print("Condition Acquired by Consumer: {}".format(self.name))
        while True:
          if self.integers:
            integer = self.integers.pop()
            print("{} Popped from list by Consumer: {}".format(integer,
  self.name))
            break
          print("Condition Wait by {}".format(self.name))
          self.condition.wait()
        print("Consumer {} Releasing Condition".format(self.name))
        self.condition.release()
```

## Kicking it off

In the `main` function of this program, we first declare the integer array that will act almost like a message queue. We then declare our condition primitive

And finally, we define one publisher and two different subscribers. We then start these publishers and subscribers and join the threads so that our program doesn't instantly terminate before the threads have a chance of executing.

```
def main():
  integers = []
  condition = threading.Condition()
  # Our Publisher
  pub1 = Publisher(integers, condition)
  pub1.start()
  # Our Subscribers
  sub1 = Subscriber(integers, condition)
  sub2 = Subscriber(integers, condition)
  sub1.start()
  sub2.start()
  ## Joining our Threads
  pub1.join()
  consumer1.join()
  consumer2.join()
if  _name__ == '__main__':
  main()
```

# The results

When we run this program, you should see an output that is similar to the following. You should see that when the publisher acquires the condition, it appends a number to the array, and then notifies the condition and releases it.

```
$ python3.6 03_pubSub.py
Condition Acquired by Publisher: Thread-1
Publisher Thread-1 appending to array: 108
Condition Released by Publisher: Thread-1
Condition Acquired by Consumer: Thread-2
108 Popped from list by Consumer: Thread-2
Consumer Thread-2 Releasing Condition
Condition Acquired by Consumer: Thread-2
Condition Wait by Thread-2
Condition Acquired by Consumer: Thread-3
Condition Wait by Thread-3
Condition Acquired by Publisher: Thread-1
Publisher Thread-1 appending to array: 563
. . .
```

At the point of the condition being notified, the battle starts between the two subscribers where they both try to acquire this condition first. When one wins this fight, it then goes on to simply "pop" this number from the array.

# Semaphores

In the first chapter, we touched upon the history of concurrency, and we talked a bit about Dijkstra. Dijkstra was the man that actually took this idea of semaphores from railway systems and translated them into something that we could use within our own complex concurrent systems.

Semaphores have an internal counter that is incremented and decremented whenever either an acquire or a release call is made. Upon initialization, this counter defaults to 1 unless otherwise set. The semaphore cannot be acquired if the counter will fall to a negative integer value.

Say we protected a block of code with a semaphore, and set the semaphore's value to 2. If one thread acquired the semaphore, then the semaphore's value would be decremented to 1. If another thread then tried to acquire the semaphore, the semaphore's value would decrement to 0. At this point, if yet another thread were to come along, the semaphore would deny its acquire request until such point as one of the original two threads called the release method, and the counter incremented to preceding 0.

# Class definition

The class definition for the Python semaphore object looks like this:

```
class _Semaphore(_Verbose):
    # After Tim Peters' semaphore class, but not quite the same (no maximum)
    def __init__(self, value=1, verbose=None):
        if value < 0:
            raise ValueError("semaphore initial value must be >= 0")
        _Verbose.__init__(self, verbose)
        self.__cond = Condition(Lock())
        self.__value = value
```

In the preceding constructor function of the `semaphore` class, you'll notice it takes in a value, which, unless otherwise set, defaults to 1.

In the class definition, the comments define a semaphore as follows:

*Semaphores manage a counter representing the number of* `release()` *calls minus the number of* `acquire()` *calls, plus an initial value. The* `acquire()` *method blocks if necessary until it can return without making the counter negative. If not given, value defaults to 1.*

# Example

This next example is based loosely on a concurrency example from the Stanford computing department. In this example, we'll be creating a simple ticket selling program that features four distinct threads that each try to sell as many tickets of the entire ticket allocation as they can before the tickets are sold out.

# The TicketSeller class

First we'll implement our `TicketSeller` class. This class will contain it's own internal counter for how many tickets that it has sold. In our constructor, we initialize our thread and take in the reference of the semaphore. Within our `run` function, we try to acquire this semaphore if the number of tickets we have available for sale is less than or equal to 0; if it is greater than 0, then we increment the number of tickets our `ticketSeller` has sold, and decrease `ticketsAvailable` by 1. We then release the semaphore and print out our progress.

```
class TicketSeller(threading.Thread):
    ticketsSold = 0
    def __init__(self, semaphore):
```

```
    threading.Thread.__init__(self)
    self.sem = semaphore
    print("Ticket Seller Started Work")
def run(self):
  global ticketsAvailable
  running = True
  while running:
    self.randomDelay()
    self.sem.acquire()
    if(ticketsAvailable <= 0):
      running = False
    else:
      self.ticketsSold = self.ticketsSold + 1
      ticketsAvailable = ticketsAvailable - 1
      print("{} Sold One ({} left)".format(self.getName(),
ticketsAvailable))
    self.sem.release()
  print("Ticket Seller {} Sold {} tickets in total".format(self.getName(),
self.ticketsSold))
def randomDelay(self):
  time.sleep(random.randint(0,1))
```

In the preceding code, we define our `TicketSeller` class. This class features a constructor which takes in the reference of our global semaphore object, and also initializes our thread. Within our `run` function, we define a `while` loop that simulates blocking for anywhere between 0 and 1 seconds, and then tries to acquire the semaphore. Upon successful acquisition of the semaphore, it then checks to see if any tickets are available to sell. If there are, then it increments the number of `ticketsSold` and decrements `ticketsAvailable` before printing it's accomplishment out to the console.

Now that we've defined our `TicketSeller` class, we need to first create our semaphore object which will be passed to all instances of `TicketSerllers`, as follows:

```
# our sempahore primitive
semaphore = threading.Semaphore()
# Our Ticket Allocation
ticketsAvailable = 10
# our array of sellers
sellers = []
for i in range(4):
  seller = TicketSeller(semaphore)
  seller.start()
  sellers.append(seller)
# joining all our sellers
for seller in sellers:
  seller.join()
```

# Output

When you run the preceding program, you should, hopefully, see an output similar to the following. In this particular run, we see an almost even distribution of tickets sold between the four distinct threads. When one of these threads blocks for an indeterminate amount of time, another thread acquires the semaphore and tries to sell their tickets.

```
$ python3.6 06_semaphores.py
Ticket Seller Started Work
Thread-1 Sold One (9 left)
Ticket Seller Started Work
Ticket Seller Started Work
Ticket Seller Started Work
Thread-1 Sold One (8 left)
Thread-3 Sold One (7 left)
Thread-3 Sold One (6 left)
Thread-4 Sold One (5 left)
Thread-2 Sold One (4 left)
Thread-1 Sold One (3 left)
Thread-4 Sold One (2 left)
Thread-2 Sold One (1 left)
Thread-3 Sold One (0 left)
Ticket Seller Thread-4 Sold 2 tickets in total
Ticket Seller Thread-1 Sold 3 tickets in total
Ticket Seller Thread-2 Sold 2 tickets in total
Ticket Seller Thread-3 Sold 3 tickets in total
```

# Thread race

One thing to note with the preceding example is that if you remove the simulated blocking of the thread by commenting out `self.randomDelay` in the `run` function, then, when you run the program, whatever thread acquired the semaphore first will most likely sell all the tickets. This is because the thread that wins the semaphore is in a prime position to reacquire the lock before any other thread is able to.

# Bounded semaphores

Bounded semaphores are almost identical to normal semaphores. Except for the following:

*A bounded semaphore checks to make sure its current value doesn't exceed its initial value. If it does, ValueError is raised. In most situations semaphores are used to guard resources with limited capacity.*

If the semaphore is released too many times, it's a sign of a bug. If a value is not given, the value defaults to 1.

These bounded semaphores could, typically, be found in web server or database implementations to guard against resource exhaustion in the event of too many people trying to connect at once, or trying to perform a specific action at once.

It's, generally, better practice to use a bounded semaphore as opposed to a normal semaphore. If we were to change the preceding code for our Semaphore example to use `threading.BoundedSemaphore(4)` and ran it again, we would see almost exactly the same behavior except that we've guarded our code against some very simple programmatic errors that otherwise would have remained uncaught.

# Events

Events are a very useful, but also a very simple form of communication between multiple threads running concurrently. With events, one thread would, typically, signal that an event has occurred while other threads are actively listening for this signal.

Events are, essentially, objects that feature an internal flag that is either true or false. Within our threads, we can continuously poll this event object to check what state it is in, and then choose to act in whatever manner we want when that flag changes state.

In the previous chapter, we talked about how there were no real mechanisms to kill threads natively in Python, and that's still true. However, we could utilize these event objects and have our threads run only so long as our event object remains unset. While this isn't as useful at the point where a SIGKILL signal is sent, it could, however, be useful in certain situations where you need to gracefully shut down, but where you can wait for a thread to finish what it's doing before it terminates.

An Event has four public functions with which we can modify and utilize it:

- `isSet()`: This checks to see if the event has been set
- `set()`: This sets the event
- `clear()`: This resets our event object
- `wait()`: This blocks until the internal flag is set to true

# Example

In our next example, we are going to show you just how you can control child threads using an event object, and obtain a form of graceful shutdown:

```
import threading
import time
def myThread(myEvent):
  while not myEvent.is_set():
    print("Waiting for Event to be set")
    time.sleep(1)
  print("myEvent has been set")

def main():
  myEvent = threading.Event()
  thread1 = threading.Thread(target=myThread, args=(myEvent,))
  thread1.start()
  time.sleep(10)
  myEvent.set()
if __name__ == '__main__':
  main()
```

# Breaking it down

In the preceding code, we define a `myThread` function; within this function, we have a while loop that only runs while the event object which we pass into this function remains unset. Within this loop, we simply print out that we are waiting for the event to be set at 1 second intervals.

We define our event object that we'll be passing to all our child threads within our `main` function. To do this, we simply call `myEvent = threading.Event()`, and it instantiates a new instance of an event object for us.

We then instantiate our thread object which takes in our `myEvent` object, and start it off. We then go on to sleep for 10 seconds before setting the `myEvent` signal so that our child thread can complete its execution.

# Barriers

Barriers are a synchronization primitive that were introduced in the third major iteration of the Python language, and address a problem that could only be solved with a somewhat complicated mixture of conditions and semaphores.

These barriers are control points that can be used to ensure that progress is only made by a group of threads, after the point at which all participating threads reach the same point.

This might sound a little bit complicated and unnecessary, but it can be incredibly powerful in certain situations, and it can certainly reduce code complexity.

# Example

In the following example, we are going to utilize barriers in order to block the execution of our threads until all of the threads have reached a desired point of execution:

```python
import threading
import time
import random
class myThread(threading.Thread):
  def __init__(self, barrier):
    threading.Thread.__init__(self)
    self.barrier = barrier
  def run(self):
    print("Thread {} working on
something".format(threading.current_thread()))
    time.sleep(random.randint(1,10))
    print("Thread {} is joining {} waiting on
Barrier".format(threading.current_thread(),
self.barrier.n_waiting))
    self.barrier.wait()
    print("Barrier has been lifted, continuing with work")
barrier = threading.Barrier(4)
threads = []
for i in range(4):
  thread = myThread(barrier)
  thread.start()
  threads.append(thread)
for t in threads:
  t.join()
```

# Breaking it down

If we have a look at the preceding code, we have defined a custom class, `myThread`, which inherits from `threading.Thread`. Within this class, we define the standard __init__ function and the `run` function. Our __init__ function takes in our barrier object so that we can reference it later on.

Within our `run` function, we simulate our thread doing some work for a random amount of time between 1 and 10 seconds, and then we start waiting on the barrier.

Out with our class definition, we first create our barrier object by calling `barrier = threading.Barrier(4)`. The 4 that we've passed into this as an argument represents the number of threads that have to be waiting on the barrier before it will be lifted. We then go on to define four distinct threads, and join them all.

## Output

If you run the preceding program on your system, you should, hopefully, see an output similar to the following.

You'll see our four threads printing out that they are working on something, and then, one by one, they randomly start waiting on our barrier object. Once the 4th thread starts waiting, the program almost instantly finishes, as all four threads do their final print statements now that the barrier has been lifted.

```
$ python3.6 08_barriers.py
Thread <myThread(Thread-1, started 123145344643072)> working on
something
Thread <myThread(Thread-2, started 123145349898240)> working on
something
Thread <myThread(Thread-3, started 123145355153408)> working on
something
Thread <myThread(Thread-4, started 123145360408576)> working on
something
Thread <myThread(Thread-1, started 123145344643072)> is joining 0
waiting on Barrier
Thread <myThread(Thread-3, started 123145355153408)> is joining 1
waiting on Barrier
Thread <myThread(Thread-2, started 123145349898240)> is joining 2
waiting on Barrier
Thread <myThread(Thread-4, started 123145360408576)> is joining 3
waiting on Barrier
Barrier has been lifted, continuing with work
Barrier has been lifted, continuing with work
Barrier has been lifted, continuing with work
Barrier has been lifted, continuing with work
```

# Summary

Throughout this chapter, we looked at the various key issues that can impact our concurrent Python applications. We dived into the topic of deadlocks and the famous dining philosophers problem, and how this can impact our own software.

By now, you should have a solid understanding of all of the Python synchronization primitives that are on offer as well as how, and, more importantly, when to use these primitives. In the next chapter, we'll be taking an in-depth look at how we can implement communication between our multithreaded and multiprocess applications.

# 5
# Communication between Threads

Communication is one of the most important parts of your concurrent systems. Without proper communication mechanisms implemented, any performance gains we manage to achieve through the use of concurrency and parallelism could all be for nothing. Communication represents one of the biggest challenges you will have to overcome when it comes to communication between both threads and processes, and it's essential to have a good understanding of all of the options that are available before you dive in.

In this chapter, we'll look at the numerous ways that you can implement your own communication mechanisms, and discuss when and where to use each of these mechanisms.

We'll cover the following topics within this chapter:

- The standard data structures in Python, and how we can interact with them in a thread-safe manner
- Thread-safe communication using queues, and how we can effectively use these queue objects
- Double-ended queues, and how they differ from traditional queues
- How we can utilize all of these new concepts and build our own multithreaded website Crawler

# Standard data structures

Some of Python's traditional data structure features provide various degrees of thread safety by default. However, in most cases, we will have to define some form of a locking mechanism for controlling access to these data structures in order to guarantee thread safety.

# Sets

During my time working with communication between multiple threads in Python, I discovered that one excellent solution to using sets in a thread-safe manner is to actually extend the set class, and to implement my own locking mechanism around the actions that I wish to perform.

## Extending the class

If you are used to working in Python then extending the class should be a somewhat simple operation. We define a `LockedSet` class object, which inherits from our traditional Python `set` class. Within the constructor for this class, we create a `lock` object, which we'll use in subsequent functions in order to allow for thread-safe interactions.

Below our constructor, we define the `add`, `remove`, and `contains` functions. These rely on the `super` class functionality with one key exception. With each of these functions, we use the lock that we initialized in our constructor to ensure that all interactions can only be executed by one thread at any given time, thus ensuring thread safety.

It should be noted that we could use this same technique of extending the existing `set` class with other Python primitives. By implementing our own, we can then, essentially, leverage the underlying functionality of these classes with minimal effort on our part.

The following example is taken from the Stack Overflow question: `http://stackoverflow.com/a/13618333/2903188`. This example does a fantastic job of explaining some of the distinct methods that we'll cover in this chapter:

```
class LockedSet(set):
    """A set where add(), remove(), and 'in' operator are thread-safe"""

    def __init__(self, *args, **kwargs):
        self._lock = Lock()
        super(LockedSet, self).__init__(*args, **kwargs)
```

```
def add(self, elem):
    with self._lock:
        super(LockedSet, self).add(elem)

def remove(self, elem):
    with self._lock:
        super(LockedSet, self).remove(elem)

def __contains__(self, elem):
    with self._lock:
        super(LockedSet, self).__contains__(elem)
```

It should be noted that this tactic of extending the existing classes and adding your own thread-safe logic can be done for most, if not all, Python primitives. It's a great way to leverage some of the excellent features that come with these classes by default, but you need to ensure that the way in which you are implementing thread safety is correct.

## Exercise - extending other primitives

As a means of practice, I would suggest that you try to extend other classes and implement thread-safe actions for them. Look at how you could extend the List primitive in order to provide thread safety when you increment a value within that list by 1. This should give you a good feel for how you can apply this same practice to a whole variety of Python primitives.

## Decorator

While extending existing Python primitives may be the most useful, if not the most desirable, means to provide thread-safe communication, it should be noted that we can also use other techniques.

One of the other key methods that we could leverage is to utilize decorators. With this mechanism, we define our decorator method, locked_method, which takes in a method. This decorator method will then define a new method within it, and call the original method only when it has acquired self._lock.

This allows us to, somewhat effortlessly, turn the potentially erroneous critical sections of our code into thread-safe sections, which can be called without having to worry about race conditions.

In this next example, we look at how we can implement our `decorator` method that returns a race-condition protected version of our passed in method:

```
def lock(method):

  def newmethod(self, *args, **kwargs):
      with self._lock:
          return method(self, *args, **kwargs)
  return newmethod

class DecoratorLockedSet(set):
  def __init__(self, *args, **kwargs):
      self._lock = Lock()
      super(DecoratorLockedSet, self).__init__(*args, **kwargs)

  @locked_method
  def add(self, *args, **kwargs):
      return super(DecoratorLockedSet, self).add(elem)

  @locked_method
  def remove(self, *args, **kwargs):
      return super(DecoratorLockedSet, self).remove(elem)
```

# Class decorator

Class decoration takes our previous example one step further, and instead of protecting one single method, we can protect every function within our class so that all calls are done in a thread-safe manner.

In the following example, we look at how we can implement a class decorator function. The `lock_class` function at the start takes in a list of methods and `lockfactory`, and returns a `lambda` function which takes in the method names specified in the decorator as well as `lockFactory`.

This calls `make_threadsafe`, which initializes an instance of our passed-in class, it then defines a new constructor which also calls `self._lock = lockfactory()`. This `make_threadsafe` function then iterates through all of the methods in `methodnames`, and `locks` each method using the `lock_method` function.

This represents a clean and easy way to add thread safety to an entire class while also giving us the option to choose which functions we wish to lock:

```
from threading import Lock

def lock_class(methodnames, lockfactory):
    return lambda cls: make_threadsafe(cls,
methodnames, lockfactory)

def lock_method(method):
    if getattr(method, '__is_locked', False):
        raise TypeError("Method %r is already locked!" %method)

def locked_method(self, *arg, **kwarg):
    with self._lock:
        return method(self, *arg, **kwarg)
    locked_method.__name__ = '%s(%s)' %
('lock_method', method.__name__)
    locked_method.__is_locked = True
    return locked_method

def make_threadsafe(cls, methodnames,
lockfactory):
    init = cls.__init__
    def newinit(self, *arg, **kwarg):
        init(self, *arg, **kwarg)
        self._lock = lockfactory()
    cls.__init__ = newinit
    for methodname in methodnames:
        oldmethod = getattr(cls, methodname)
        newmethod = lock_method(oldmethod)
        setattr(cls, methodname, newmethod)
    return cls

@lock_class(['add','remove'], Lock)
class ClassDecoratorLockedSet(set):
    @lock_method # if you double-lock a method, a TypeError is raised
    def lockedMethod(self):
        print("This section of our code would be thread safe")
```

# Lists

Lists, by default, are thread safe, but only in the way that we access them. It's important to note that the data represented within this list structure is, in fact, not protected, and if you want to safely modify this data, then you must implement a proper locking mechanism to ensure that multiple threads can't potentially run into race conditions within their execution--this holds true for all thread-safe containers.

The `append()` function is one of the few methods for our list data structure that is atomic, and, as such, thread-safe. Lists, thus, become a very quick and easy structure that we can leverage for temporary, in-memory storage. However, if we were to attempt to modify anything within this list in a concurrent fashion, then it's highly possible that we start to see the side effects most often attributed to race conditions.

One prime example of such a side effect is if we, for instance, try to update the second element in our list at the same time as another thread. If one were to read, and subsequently write, at the same time as a competing thread, then we could see issues where the value is altered incorrectly.

If you wish to utilize lists within your multithreaded applications, then you can do so by extending the class in a similar fashion to how we've previously extended the set primitive.

# Queues

Queues come in a range of different styles. In Python, we have the option to define three different types of queues from the native queue module. These are normal Queues, LifoQueues, and PriorityQueues.

Queues, by default, are thread safe in Python, which means that we do not have to worry about implementing complex locking mechanisms should we wish to utilize queues within our applications. This makes them incredibly powerful when it comes to implementing a quick and easy communication medium through which our numerous threads and processes can communicate.

# FIFO queues

**FIFO (first in first out)** queues to give them their full name, are the standard queue implementation that Python has to offer. They follow the exact same queueing mechanism that you would if you were, say, at the supermarket. The first person to reach the till would be attended to first, the second person waits and is served second, and so on.

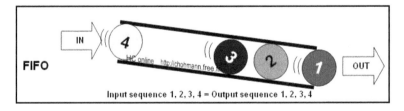

Source: http://javaworldwide.blogspot.co.uk/2015/07/implementing-blocking-queue-in-java.html

Through following this mechanism, we ensure that our customers are treated fairly, and that you'll be able to reasonably estimate roughly how long it will take for you to get served if you were, say, 7th in the queue.

## Example

In this example, we'll utilize the `queue.Queue()` object in order to implement our own FIFO-based queue:

```
import threading
import queue
import random
import time

def mySubscriber(queue):
  while not queue.empty():
    item = queue.get()
    if item is None:
      break
    print("{} removed {} from the queue".format(threading.current_thread(),
item))
    queue.task_done()
    time.sleep(1)

myQueue = queue.Queue()
for i in range(10):
  myQueue.put(i)

print("Queue Populated")

threads = []
for i in range(4):
  thread = threading.Thread(target=mySubscriber, args=(myQueue,))
  thread.start()
  threads.append(thread)

for thread in threads:
  thread.join()
```

## Breaking it down

In the preceding example, we import the necessary queue, Python module. We then go on to define a `mySubscriber` function, which will act as the target for our multiple threads that are going to consume from our queue.

In the following `mySubscriber` function declaration, we then declare our queue by calling `myQueue = queue.Queue()`, and then we proceed to populate the numbers from zero to nine.

Finally, we go on to declare and instantiate our numerous threads which will consume from our thread-safe queue. We start these threads, taking care to pass in our newly declared the `queue` object into their args, and then, subsequently, join them.

## Output

If we now execute the preceding code, you should see that our four distinct threads start grabbing items from the queue one after the other in the order that they were initially put into the queue. So, 0, being the first number to be placed into the queue, is also the first to be taken off the queue:

```
$ python3.6 00_queues.py
Queue Populated
<Thread(Thread-1, started 123145445732352)> removed 0 from the queue
<Thread(Thread-2, started 123145450987520)> removed 1 from the queue
<Thread(Thread-3, started 123145456242688)> removed 2 from the queue
<Thread(Thread-4, started 123145461497856)> removed 3 from the queue
<Thread(Thread-1, started 123145445732352)> removed 4 from the queue
<Thread(Thread-3, started 123145456242688)> removed 5 from the queue
<Thread(Thread-4, started 123145461497856)> removed 6 from the queue
<Thread(Thread-2, started 123145450987520)> removed 7 from the queue
<Thread(Thread-1, started 123145445732352)> removed 8 from the queue
<Thread(Thread-3, started 123145456242688)> removed 9 from the queue
```

# LIFO queues

**LIFO (last in first out)** queues, act in the opposite fashion to that of normal FIFO queues. To extend our supermarket analogy further, in using a LIFO queueing mechanism, we, essentially, serve the last person to join the queue before the existing members of the queue are served. As you can imagine, if this were a real-life supermarket, there would probably be a number of complaints put in by people who were spending hours sitting in the same queue.

In LIFO queues, there is the distinct possibility that a couple of the first people to join the queue could remain in that position indefinitely as more and more people join the queue before they can be served. While this may not make sense as a queueing mechanism in the real world, LIFO has its advantages when it comes to programming.

LIFO queues come in particularly handy when it comes to implementing artificial-intelligence-based algorithms such as depth-first search, depth-limited search, and so on. It also comes in very handy when you want to reverse the order of something--simply populate your LIFO queue with every element, and then pop them off again once you are done. The results of this are more clearly defined in the following illustration:

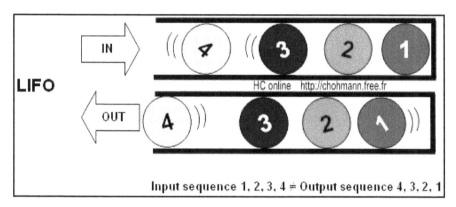

Source: http://www.transtutors.com/homework-help/accounting/inventory-valuation-lifo/

## Example

In the following example, we define `LifoQueue`, which we populate with numbers from `1 -> 10`. We then create a series of subscribers that retrieve all items from this queue until it is empty.

```
import threading
import queue
import random
import time

def mySubscriber(queue):
  while not queue.empty():
  item = queue.get()
  if item is None:
    break
  print("{} removed {} from the queue".format(threading.current_thread(),
item))
  queue.task_done()
```

```
    time.sleep(1)

myQueue = queue.LifoQueue()
for i in range(10):
  myQueue.put(i)

print("Queue Populated")

threads = []
for i in range(2):
  thread = threading.Thread(target=mySubscriber, args=(myQueue,))
  thread.start()
  threads.append(thread)

for thread in threads:
  thread.join()

print("Queue is empty")
```

## Breaking it down

The preceding code isn't that dissimilar to the code that we used for the normal FIFO queue. The only real difference is that when we declare our `myQueue` object, we declare it using `queue.LifoQueue()` instead of the normal `queue.Queue()`.

## Output

If we now run the last program, you should see that it's almost identical to our FIFO queue except for one main distinction--our threads remove the numbers from our queue in the exact opposite order than they were initially put into the queue:

```
$ python3.6 01_lifoQueues.py
Queue Populated
<Thread(Thread-1, started 123145362374656)> removed 9 from the queue
<Thread(Thread-2, started 123145367629824)> removed 8 from the queue
<Thread(Thread-1, started 123145362374656)> removed 7 from the queue
<Thread(Thread-2, started 123145367629824)> removed 6 from the queue
<Thread(Thread-1, started 123145362374656)> removed 5 from the queue
<Thread(Thread-2, started 123145367629824)> removed 4 from the queue
<Thread(Thread-2, started 123145367629824)> removed 3 from the queue
<Thread(Thread-1, started 123145362374656)> removed 2 from the queue
<Thread(Thread-2, started 123145367629824)> removed 1 from the queue
<Thread(Thread-1, started 123145362374656)> removed 0 from the queue
Queue is empty
```

# PriorityQueue

If we move away from our supermarket analogy and now think about an airport security area, there are some people who are more important than the regular customers. These are people like the pilots, the cabin crew, and others. In these exceptional circumstances, we'd typically move them up to the front of the queue so that they could proceed to get the planes in which we are about to fly to get them ready for takeoff.

In other words, we are giving them some form of priority within our queueing mechanism. Sometimes, in the systems that we develop, we need to also accommodate some form of prioritization mechanism so that incredibly important tasks aren't stuck behind millions of relatively unimportant operations for indefinite periods of time. This is where our PriorityQueue object comes into play.

With PriorityQueue, we can give everything that we put into the queue a weight as to how important it is. We can populate our PriorityQueues in much the same way that we populate our normal queue object except that we use tuples, and pass in priority_number as the first value in our tuple: (priority_number, data).

## Example

In the following example, we create PriorityQueue which we will populate with two sets of data, both identical, ranging from (1,1) -> (5,5). We then define a subscriber that will call get on our PriorityQueue until such point as the queue is empty.

```
import threading
import queue
import random
import time

def mySubscriber(queue):
whilenot queue.empty():
  item = queue.get()
  if item is None:
    break
  print("{} removed {} from the queue".format(threading.current_thread(),
item))
  queue.task_done()
  time.sleep(1)

myQueue = queue.PriorityQueue()

for i in range(5):
myQueue.put(i, i)
```

```
for i in range(5):
myQueue.put(i, i)

print("Queue Populated")
threads = []
for i in range(2):
thread = threading.Thread(target=mySubscriber, args=(myQueue,))
thread.start()
threads.append(thread)

for thread in threads:
thread.join()

print("Queue is empty")
```

## Breakdown

Again, the preceding code is pretty much identical to the code that we've seen before, the only difference being that we've changed the way we've initialized our queue object, and we've changed how to populate the queue to this:

```
myQueue = queue.PriorityQueue()

for i in range(5):
myQueue.put(i, i)

for i in range(5):
myQueue.put(i, i)
```

This last piece of code populates our queue with two sets of tuples, both with the same priority_number and the same data, as follows:

| Order of Queue Population | Tuple (priority_number, data) | Execution Order |
|---|---|---|
| 1 | (0, 0) | 1st |
| 2 | (1,1) | 3rd |
| 3 | (2,2) | 5th |
| 4 | (3,3) | 7th |
| 5 | (4,4) | 9th |
| 6 | (0, 0) | 2nd |
| 7 | (1,1) | 4th |

| 8 | (2,2) | 6th |
|---|-------|-----|
| 9 | (3,3) | 8th |
| 10 | (4,4) | 10th |

## Output

If we run this program in our command-line, you should see that the order in which we remove our elements corresponds to the priority of the items within our queue. Our two 0 elements have the highest priority and are removed first, the 1s follow shortly after, and so on until we have removed all the elements from the priority queue:

```
$ python3.6 02_priorityQueue.py
Queue Populated
<Thread(Thread-1, started 123145475166208)> removed 0 from the queue
<Thread(Thread-2, started 123145480421376)> removed 0 from the queue
<Thread(Thread-2, started 123145480421376)> removed 1 from the queue
<Thread(Thread-1, started 123145475166208)> removed 1 from the queue
<Thread(Thread-2, started 123145480421376)> removed 2 from the queue
<Thread(Thread-1, started 123145475166208)> removed 2 from the queue
<Thread(Thread-2, started 123145480421376)> removed 3 from the queue
<Thread(Thread-1, started 123145475166208)> removed 3 from the queue
<Thread(Thread-2, started 123145480421376)> removed 4 from the queue
<Thread(Thread-1, started 123145475166208)> removed 4 from the queue
Queue is empty
```

# Queue objects

With all of these aforementioned queue objects, there comes a range of different public methods with which we can use to work with the queue objects.

# Full/empty queues

We need to be able to limit the size of our queues within our programs; if we let them expand for ever, then we could, in theory, start facing `MemoryErrors`. The amount of memory one Python program could take is limited by the amount of memory we have available on our systems.

By constraining the size of our queues, we are able to, effectively, guard ourselves from hitting these memory constraints. In this example, we'll create a queue, and pass in the `maxsize` parameter, which will be set to zero. We'll then go on to create four distinct threads that will each try and populate this queue with an arbitrary number.

We'll then join all of our newly created threads, and attempt to put as many elements into our queue as possible.

## Example

In the following example, we create a series of publishers that attempt to publish to our `queue` object until it is full:

```
import threading
import queue
import time

def myPublisher(queue):
  while not queue.full():
    queue.put(1)
    print("{} Appended 1 to queue: {}".format(threading.current_thread(),
queue.qsize()))
    time.sleep(1)

myQueue = queue.Queue(maxsize=5)

threads = []
for i in range(4):
  thread = threading.Thread(target=mySubscriber, args=(myQueue,))
  thread.start()
  threads.append(thread)

for thread in threads:
  thread.join()
```

## Output

Upon execution of our code, you should see each thread append at least one item to our queue until the point where the queue has five different elements. At this point, our queue is deemed full, and the execution of our threads terminates:

```
$ python3.6 09_fullQueue.py
<Thread(Thread-1, started 123145399971840)> Appended 1 to queue: 1
<Thread(Thread-2, started 123145405227008)> Appended 1 to queue: 2
<Thread(Thread-3, started 123145410482176)> Appended 1 to queue: 3
<Thread(Thread-4, started 123145415737344)> Appended 1 to queue: 4
<Thread(Thread-1, started 123145399971840)> Appended 1 to queue: 5
```

# The join() function

The `join()` function on our `queue` objects allow us to block our current thread's execution until such point that all elements from the queue have been consumed. This provides us with an excellent stopgap method for when we need to ensure that everything we need to have done is done.

## Example

The following example creates a number of subscribers that subscribe to our queue object. These subscribers then call the get method until such point as our queue is empty:

```python
import threading
import queue
import time

def mySubscriber(queue):
time.sleep(1)
while not queue.empty():
  item = queue.get()
  if item is None:
    break
  print("{} removed {} from the queue".format(threading.current_thread(),
item))
  queue.task_done()

myQueue = queue.Queue()
for i in range(5):
myQueue.put(i)

print("Queue Populated")

thread = threading.Thread(target=mySubscriber, args=(myQueue,))
thread.start()

print("Not Progressing Till Queue is Empty")
myQueue.join()
print("Queue is now empty")
```

## Breakdown

In the preceding code sample, we first define our `mySubscriber` function that takes our `queue` object as its primary argument. Within this, we first sleep for one second, and then enter a `while` loop that runs until our queue is not empty. Within this `while` loop, we first attempt to retrieve an item from our array, and then go on to check to see if this item is none.

If the item isn't none, then we print the current thread and that we've read it from our queue. We then call `task_done()` to signal the end of our blocking get request.

## Output

Upon execution of our last program, you should see that our distinct threads continue to pop elements from the queue until such point as the queue is declared empty. At this point, our join condition is fulfilled, and our program completes it's execution:

```
$ python3.6 10_queueJoin.py
Queue Populated
Not Progressing Till Queue is Empty
<Thread(Thread-1, started 123145410052096)> removed 0 from the queue
<Thread(Thread-1, started 123145410052096)> removed 1 from the queue
<Thread(Thread-1, started 123145410052096)> removed 2 from the queue
<Thread(Thread-1, started 123145410052096)> removed 3 from the queue
<Thread(Thread-1, started 123145410052096)> removed 4 from the queue
Queue is now empty
```

# Deque objects

Deques or double-ended queues are another communication primitive that we can actively leverage in our quest for thread-safe inter-thread communication. It belongs to the `collections` module, and it features functionality much like that of a queue except for the fact that we can pop and push elements into either end of the queue.

# Example

```
import collections

doubleEndedQueue = collections.deque('123456')

print("Dequeue: {}".format(doubleEndedQueue))

for item in doubleEndedQueue:
```

```
print("Item {}".format(item))

print("Left Most Element: {}".format(doubleEndedQueue[0]))
print("Right Most Element: {}".format(doubleEndedQueue[-1]))
```

# Breakdown

In the preceding code example, we first import the `collections` module from which we'll be using the `deque` object. We then go on to define our `deque` object by calling `collections.deque('123456')` and passing in '123456' as a means of populating our newly instantiated the `deque` object.

We then go on to print out our `deque` object, which displays our `deque` object as an array of all of the elements that we have placed into it, and for thoroughness, we then iterate through this `deque` object and print out the values of our array. Finally, we query the left-most and right-most objects, and print these out to our console.

# Output

Our program should first print out our complete `deque` before iterating through each and every element. We then call `doubleEndedQueue[0]` to retrieve the leftmost element of our `queue` object, and then `doubleEndedQueue[-1]` to retrieve the rightmost element of our `queue` object.

```
$ python3.6 03_deque.py
Dequeue: deque(['1', '2', '3', '4', '5', '6'])
Item 1
Item 2
Item 3
Item 4
Item 5
Item 6
Left Most Element: 1
Right Most Element: 6
```

# Appending elements

Being able to query and view all of the elements in our deque object might be useful in some situations, but, typically, you will want to interact with these objects. In this next example, we are going to introduce the append() and appendLeft() functions that enable us to publish new items into our deque object at either the first or the last position of our queue object.

## Example

The following code example will show you how we can append to both the start and the end of our deque object:

```
import collections

doubleEndedQueue = collections.deque('123456')

print("Deque: {}".format(doubleEndedQueue))

doubleEndedQueue.append('1')
print("Deque: {}".format(doubleEndedQueue))

doubleEndedQueue.appendleft('6')
print("Deque: {}".format(doubleEndedQueue))
```

## Breaking it down

In the last code example, we first create doubleEndedQueue a deque object. We then print out the current state of this deque, and then append 1 to the end of this queue using the append() function. We then again print out the state of our deque object, and see that this has accurately appended our 1 to the right-hand side. We then utilize the appendleft() function in order to append a 6 to the front of our queue object.

# Output

When we run the preceding program, we should see our original deque with elements 1-6. After we have appended 1 using the append(1) function, we then see deque printing out with 1 at the end of our deque object. We then call the appendLeft(6) function, and again print out our deque object, and see 6 appear at the at the start of our deque object.

```
$ python3.6 04_addRemoveDeque.py
Deque: deque(['1', '2', '3', '4', '5', '6'])
Deque: deque(['1', '2', '3', '4', '5', '6', '1'])
Deque: deque(['6', '1', '2', '3', '4', '5', '6', '1'])
```

# Popping elements

Conversely, we may have to retrieve some of the elements that we publish to our deque object. The way to do this is to utilize the pop() and the popleft() public functions that come with our deque object.

# Example

The following code example will show you how we can pop items from both the start and the end of our queues using pop() and popleft():

```
import collections

doubleEndedQueue = collections.deque('123456')

print("Deque: {}".format(doubleEndedQueue))

# Removing Elements from our queue
rightPop = doubleEndedQueue.pop()
print(rightPop)
print("Deque: {}".format(doubleEndedQueue))

leftPop = doubleEndedQueue.popleft()
print(leftPop)
print("Deque: {}".format(doubleEndedQueue))
```

# Breaking it down

In the preceding code sample, we again declare our standard `doubleEndedQueue` object, and pass in our 1-6 values. We then print out the current state of our deque immediately after this so we know how our base deque looks.

We then first declare a `rightPop` variable, and call `doubleEndedQueue.pop()` in order to retrieve the rightmost value from our `deque` object. Immediately after this, we print the value we've just pop-ed and then the state of our `deque` object.

Following the same process as we did for retrieving the last value of our `deque` object, we can retrieve the first value of our `deque` object by utilizing the `popleft()` method. We call this and instantiate our `leftPop` variable with it, and again print out the current state of our `deque` object.

# Output

The output from the preceding program confirms that our `pop()` and `popleft()` work as expected. We print out our original `deque`, `pop()`, which pops the last element of our `deque` object from the `queue` object and prints it out onto the console.

We then call `popleft()`, which pops the frontmost element from our `deque` object, and again prints it out onto the console:

```
$ python3.6 05_removeDeque.py
Deque: deque(['1', '2', '3', '4', '5', '6'])
6
Deque: deque(['1', '2', '3', '4', '5'])
1
Deque: deque(['2', '3', '4', '5'])
```

# Inserting elements

Being able to populate a `deque` object is important, as without this mechanism, our `deque` object wouldn't be very useful.

# Example

In this example, we are going to take a quick look at how you can insert elements into an array at specific points:

```
import collections

doubleEndedQueue = collections.deque('123456')

print("Deque: {}".format(doubleEndedQueue))

doubleEndedQueue.insert(5,5)

print("Deque: {}".format(doubleEndedQueue))
```

# Breaking it down

In the preceding code snippet, we utilize the `insert(n, n)` function in order to insert the element 5 at position five of our `deque` object.

# Output

This output of the last program shows us that it successfully inserts a 5 to the fifth location of our `deque` object:

```
$ python3.6 06_insertDeque.py
Deque: deque(['1', '2', '3', '4', '5', '6'])
Deque: deque(['1', '2', '3', '4', '5', 5, '6'])
```

# Rotation

Deques give us the ability to rotate our `queue` object by *n* steps to either the right or the left depending on whether the number passed in is positive or negative.

# Example

The following example shows how we can perform rotation on our `deque` object by both a positive and negative value to rotate all the elements both forwards and backwards:

```
import collections

doubleEndedQueue = collections.deque('123456')

print("Deque: {}".format(doubleEndedQueue))

doubleEndedQueue.rotate(3)

print("Deque: {}".format(doubleEndedQueue))

doubleEndedQueue.rotate(-2)

print("Deque {}".format(doubleEndedQueue))
```

# Breaking it down

In the preceding example, we create our standard `deque` and pass in our regular one to six values. We then print out our default `deque`, and then rotate it three places to the right.

Upon rotation, all of the elements in our `deque` object move three places to the right; the last element in our queue becomes the first, and then the second, and subsequently, the third.

This diagram succinctly shows how we can rotate both forward and backwards using positive and negative values:

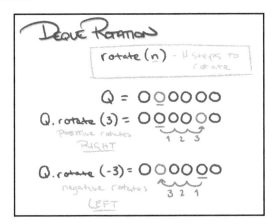

Source: http://www.transtutors.com/homework-help/accounting/inventory-valuation-lifo/

# Output

As you can see from the output of our sample application, we start off with our `deque` object with values 1 to 6 in the correct order. We then rotate forward by three places, and all of our elements correctly move three places forward.

We then attempt to rotate backwards by two, and again, we see that all of the elements within our array move back two spaces correctly:

```
$ python3.6 08_rotateDeque.py
Deque: deque(['1', '2', '3', '4', '5', '6'])
Deque: deque(['4', '5', '6', '1', '2', '3'])
Deque deque(['6', '1', '2', '3', '4', '5'])
```

# Defining your own thread-safe communication structures

Sometimes, standard communication primitives don't quite cut it, and we have to implement our own composite objects in order to communicate between threads.

# A web Crawler example

Now that we've got a good handle of both our communication primitives as well as the synchronization primitives that we dealt with in the previous chapter, it's time to start putting these to good use.

What better way to put into practice our newfound knowledge than to build something interesting with it?

In this section of the chapter, we are going to build a very simple multithreaded web Crawler.

# Requirements

Just like any real project, we first need to define a set of requirements. In other words, we need to know the general direction that we'll be working towards. For this project, we have the following requirements:

- The web Crawler needs to utilize multiple threads
- It should be able to crawl all the particular web pages of a website
- It should be able to report back any 404 links
- It should take in a domain name from the command-line
- It should avoid cyclic traversal

That last point about cyclic traversal is important--in order to prevent our program endlessly crawling two or more pages that all interlink each other, we must track exactly what pages we've already crawled. We'll be able to leverage here one of the synchronization primitives that we've learned about in the previous chapter.

# Design

In our program, we are going to need a something to do our heavy lifting--this will be the requesting of web pages and the parsing of these web pages for new links to crawl.

We'll separate this worker out into a class that we'll call a Crawler; this will have a few different functions--its constructor function, a run function, and an auxiliary `processLink` function.

# Our Crawler class

The first thing we want to build out in this Crawler is our Crawler class. This will contain the static methods which will perform any crawling and enqueueing of links to the crawled list.

At the top, we import all of the modules that we'll need; this is a mix of things from the `urllib.request` module and the `urllib.parse` module as well as `ssl` so that we can successfully make the HTTPs requests and the `BeautifulSoup` module. This `BeautifulSoup` module will do the bulk of our heavy lifting when it comes to parsing our HTML for new links to crawl.

At the top of our class, we declare several variables, this first of which is `base_url` which will be used to check and see that we haven't left the site we originally intended to crawl. If we were to crawl say `https://tutorialedge.net`, then this would be set as `base_url`, and we would only proceed to crawl links from this domain.

Below that, we declare the `myssl` context, which we'll pass in as the context for our HTTPS requests. And finally, we instantiate a new set called `errorLinks`, which will be populated with any links that throw less than favorable 200 status codes.

```
from urllib.request import Request, urlopen, urljoin, URLError
from urllib.parse import urlparse
import ssl
from bs4 import BeautifulSoup

class Crawler:

  base_url = ''
  myssl = ssl.create_default_context()
  myssl.check_hostname=False
  myssl.verify_mode=ssl.CERT_NONE
  errorLinks = set()
```

We then go on to declare our Crawler's `constructor` function which will set `base_url`.

After this, we declare `crawl` static method and `enqueueLinks` static method. This takes in a list of links and `linksToCrawl`, a `queue` object. It iterates through them and if the link has not already been crawled, and if it is not already `enqueued` in `linksToCrawl`, then we add it to the `queue` object.

```
def __init__(self, base_url):
  Crawler.base_url = base_url

@staticmethod
def crawl(thread_name, url, linksToCrawl):
  try:
    link = urljoin(Crawler.base_url, url)

    if (urlparse(link).netloc == 'tutorialedge.net') and (link not in
Crawler.crawledLinks):
      request = Request(link, headers={'User-Agent': 'Mozilla/5.0'})
      response = urlopen(request, context=Crawler.myssl)
      Crawler.crawledLinks.add(link)
      print("Url {} Crawled with Status: {} : {} Crawled In
Total".format(response.geturl(), response.getcode(),
len(Crawler.crawledLinks)))
      soup = BeautifulSoup(response.read(), "html.parser")
```

```
        Crawler.enqueueLinks(soup.find_all('a'), linksToCrawl)
    except URLError as e:
      print("URL {} threw this error when trying to parse: {}".format(link,
e.reason))
      Crawler.errorLinks.add(link)

  @staticmethod
  def enqueueLinks(links, linksToCrawl):
    for link in links:
      if (urljoin(Crawler.base_url, link.get('href')) not in
Crawler.crawledLinks):
        if (urljoin(Crawler.base_url, link.get('href')) not in linksToCrawl):
          linksToCrawl.put(link.get('href'))
```

# Our starting point

The next thing we need to do is implement our `main.py` file. This will be our main entry point for our web Crawler program.

We begin by importing all the necessary modules as well as `CheckableQueue`, which we'll be defining later on. Below our imports, we define the number of threads upon which we want our code to execute upon. Due to the highly I/O bound nature of web Crawlers, having multiple threads of execution allows us to perform multiple I/O-bound HTTP requests concurrently.

Below this, we define the `createCrawlers` function, which is, essentially, a thread factory. Next, we define our run function which will feature as the target of all the threads that we'll create. In this function, we constantly loop round and attempt to call the `get()` method on our `linksToCrawl` queue. If the item that we retrieve from the `get()` is `None`, then we terminate our thread, if not, then we crawl the URL by calling our static `Crawler.crawl()` function and passing in our `current_thread`, our URL, and the `linksToCrawl` queue.

Finally, we define our main function. This first takes in the URL that we wish to crawl--in my example, we use `https://tutorialedge.net`, but I implore you to try your own sites and have mercy on my web server. We then instantiate an instance of our Crawler, and pass in the `base_url` that will constrain our Crawler from crawling other websites.

Finally, within our `main` function, we call our factory function, `createCrawlers()`, and join our `linksToCrawl` queue so that our program doesn't finish execution until everything on the queue has been processed.

```
import threading
import queue
from Crawler import *
from CheckableQueue import *

THREAD_COUNT = 20
linksToCrawl = CheckableQueue()

def createCrawlers():
  for i in range(THREAD_COUNT):
    t = threading.Thread(target=run)
    t.daemon = True
    t.start()

def run():
  while True:
    url = linksToCrawl.get()
    try:
      if url is None:
        break
      Crawler.crawl(threading.current_thread(), url, linksToCrawl)
    except:
      print("Exception")
    linksToCrawl.task_done()

def main():
  url = input("Website > ")
  Crawler(url)
  linksToCrawl.put(url)
  createCrawlers()
  linksToCrawl.join()
  print("Total Links Crawled: {}".format(len(Crawler.crawledLinks)))
  print("Total Errors: {}".format(len(Crawler.errorLinks)))

if __name__ == '__main__':
  main()
```

# Extending the queue object

In our example, we will want to utilize the atomicity of the `queue` object that we've covered previously. However, we also want to extend this further, as we'll need to check if a new-found link has already been crawled, and also that it isn't enqueued to be crawled again in the future.

```python
import queue

class CheckableQueue(queue.Queue):
  def __contains__(self, item):
    with self.mutex:
      return item in self.queue

  def __len__(self):
    return len(self.queue)
```

## Breaking it down

So, in the preceding example, we import the `queue` module, and then go on to define our `CheckableQueue` object that inherits from `queue.Queue`.

Below this, we define the `__contains__` method, which will take in an item, and, utilizing a mutex, will safely traverse the queue to check whether or not the passed-in item exists in that queue.

We also define the `__len__` function, which simply returns the length of our queue. This is not that vital, but it can give us a nice indication as to how much work our Crawler has yet to do at various points throughout our program.

## Output

Upon running our Crawler program and inputting `https://tutorialedge.net`, our program then goes off and works through each and every page of `tutorialedge.net` that it can find.

Every time a new page is found, it is added to our `linksToCrawl CheckableQueue` object, and a thread then proceeds to pick it up and index it. We then print the status of our Crawler every time it makes a request indicating the URL that we've crawled, the HTTP status that was returned, and finally, how many pages we've crawled in total.

```
$ python3.6 main.py
Website > https://tutorialedge.net
Url https://tutorialedge.net Crawled with Status: 200 : 1 Crawled In Total
```

```
Url https://tutorialedge.net/series/blog/ Crawled with Status: 200 : 2
Crawled In Total
Url
https://tutorialedge.net/post/webdev/difference-between-class-id-selector-c
ss/ Crawled with Status:
200 : 3 Crawled In Total
....
Url https://tutorialedge.net/page/9/ Crawled with Status: 200 : 216 Crawled
In Total
Url https://tutorialedge.net/page/10/ Crawled with Status: 200 : 217
Crawled In Total
Url https://tutorialedge.net/page/11/ Crawled with Status: 200 : 218
Crawled In Total
Total Links Crawled: 218
Total Errors: 11
```

# Future enhancements

This was just an example of a relatively simple website Crawler that could be improved in quite a number of different ways. You could expand this into a full-blown web spider that indexes everything it can, or you could use this to constantly monitor the health of your sites.

One of the best ways you could, potentially, improve this is by wrapping an API around it so that you could run this constantly on a server and test multiple websites through a web interface.

# Conclusion

Hopefully, this gave you some idea of how you can construct more and more complex programs using some of the primitives and concepts that we've learned about in the last few chapters.

In this example, we were able to construct a multithreaded website Crawler that was able to determine the health of all the linked content on a given site. It takes in a single URL as a starting point, parses it for every link within that page, and then proceeds to parse those. It continues to do that until it has scanned every linked page on your website.

We've touched upon a few topics within this example, such as the following:

- Multiple threads improving the performance of our I/O-bound application: By utilizing multiple threads, we were able to request multiple website pages concurrently.
- Communication between multiple threads: In this example, we utilized both Queues and Sets in order to obtain thread-safe communication. We utilized a queue object for storing all of the URLs that we wanted to parse, and sets in order to store the links that we parsed.

## Exercise - testing your skills

As a means of testing your new-found thread communication skills, I would suggest trying to add some of the new functionality to the web Crawler, similar to what we talked about in the future enhancements section. One of the best ways to improve your skills when it comes to thread-safety is, in my opinion, to get your hands dirty and dive deeper into ever more complex problems.

Or, if this doesn't tickle your fancy, then there are a number of different applications that you could potentially try your hand at building.

**Web Server**: You could try to build your own web server that is able to handle more than one connection at a time. This poses an interesting challenge, and is quite rewarding, as it gives you a little bit of insight into how some of the bigger Python frameworks have come to be.

# Summary

In this chapter, we looked at quite a number of different mechanisms that we can employ when it comes to implementing communication in our multithreaded systems. We took a deep dive into the thread-safe queue primitives that Python features natively, and how we can implement solutions around these primitives that we can be confident with.

In the last section, we pulled all of the concepts that we covered in the previous two chapters together, and created a useful tool for checking the health of all the links on a given website.

In the next chapter, we'll look in depth at the various debugging and benchmarking techniques that one can use in order to ensure that their systems are production ready and bug free.

# 6
# Debug and Benchmark

Programming is never just about crafting a solution to a problem and leaving it once it's reached a somewhat *finished* state. More often than not, it's also about maintaining the existing solutions so that businesses can continue to run and make money. Maintaining these existing solutions, typically, means doing things like debugging and adding new features, and in order to do these things, it's important to have a working knowledge of some of the tools that exist within the Python ecosystem.

In this chapter, we'll be looking at the various testing strategies we can follow in order to ensure that we can continue to add new features and perform refactoring of our code with minimal risk to the existing features.

We'll also be diving deep into some of the tools available that allow us to gain a better understanding of our Python applications at a far more granular level. To that end, in this chapter, we'll be covering the following topics:

- Test strategies for your code
- The Python debugger
- Pdb
- The `line_profiler` tool.
- The `memory_profiler` tool

By the end of this chapter, you should have an appreciation of the value of testing your systems as well as a handle on how you can perform your own benchmarking and profiling. Let's get started by looking at some testing strategies we can use to improve our code.

# Testing strategies

While this chapter might be titled *Debugging and Benchmarking*, I've often found that one of the best ways to debug your codebases is to build up a range of integration tests that cover as much of your codebase as is practical. We'll begin by looking at the main reason as to why we test our code bases.

# Why do we test?

So, we've gotten roughly halfway through this book, and not once have we defined any sort of tests, or ensured that the programs that we have written are verifiably correct. Up until this point, you've taken my word that the programs I have shown you do everything that I've said they do. But how can we guarantee that they give us the same results every time regardless of how many changes we make to them?

This is where your testing strategy comes into play.

In professional software development, testing your software to try and limit the bugs is one of the most important things you can do. All great software developers implement a decent testing strategy surrounding the systems they build, and this, actually, enables them to make changes faster and with more confidence.

Say we had a legacy system that had 100,000 lines of code, and had no test suite and no testing strategy implemented. How would you test that what you were doing wasn't breaking something further down the chain? How could you confidently say that a code change you implemented wasn't going to bring down $X$, $Y$, and $Z$ other applications in production, and, potentially, cost your business money? The answer is it's next to impossible; every change you make will make you nervous when the change is deployed, and you'll be on support for potentially catastrophic breaks 24x7.

Conversely, say you were in charge of developing a new feature on a legacy system that has 100,000 lines of code. If you made any changes to specific parts of the code base, the suite of tests that your team has built up would catch any potentially catastrophic breaks, and you would be confident that this new feature would be able to go into production without impacting anything existing. This is a huge advantage for development teams that follow an agile methodology, and iteratively implements lots of changes to their software systems. It also means that the chance for your business to be impacted by an issue in production is far lower, and you don't have to worry about being on support all the time.

# Testing concurrent software systems

One of the most important things to take away from this book is that you need to ensure that all of your concurrent programs are tested and proven to be valid before you implement multiple threads. If you have a single-threaded application that has a bug, and you add multiple threads to that application, you now have multiple bugs and your life becomes a hell of a lot more complex.

All software systems should be designed in a way that ensures their correctness before any optimizations are implemented.

# What should we test?

Now that you have some appreciation as to why we should test, it's important to know exactly what you should and shouldn't be testing. One metric I've often seen used as a quality sticker is code coverage. This, essentially, boils down to how many lines of code your tests hit, and I've seen people boost this metric by writing almost pointless tests like testing getters and setters on your Python objects. This is something which I would absolutely avoid, as it provides no real value to your system.

Instead of focusing on a metric like code coverage, you should, instead, be focusing on testing only the most important parts of your code, and then expand your tests to include your less important parts later on. In your typical project environment, trying to test everything could drastically decrease the time taken to reach the market, so, you need to try and come up with a blend of testing that does just enough to ensure platform stability while also meeting business demands.

I would recommend trying to come up with a multitude of different tests that push your software to the limit. Intentionally try and break your logic, and ensure that the majority of it is up to scratch.

# Unit tests

A unit test can be defined as a programmatic test that tests a single logical unit of your code. When we say unit, we, typically, mean a function within our codebase.

When it comes to writing unit tests in Python, typically, the first thing to come to mind is the `unittest` module that is included by default in Python 3.6.

# PyUnit

PyUnit is to Python what JUnit is to Java. It's the standard unit testing module that provides, basically, everything you need in order to define an automated testing strategy.

## Example

The first thing we need to do within our test program is to import the `unittest` module. This will contain everything we need in order to test our simple function.

Below this import, we define our `simpleFunction`, which takes in a single argument and increments it by one. Nothing overly complex, I'm sure you'll agree, but the key point here is that if other parts of our codebase start to rely on the output of this function, then we need to have some form of a checking mechanism to ensure we don't break everything if we make some changes.

In the function code given next, we define our `SimpleFunctionTest` class which inherits from `unittest.TestCase`. Within this, we define our `setUp` and `tearDown` functions. These will run before and after all of the tests in our test suite.

Finally, we kick off this newly defined, but somewhat barebones, test suite by calling `unittest.main()`.

```python
import unittest

def simpleFunction(x):
  return x + 1

class SimpleFunctionTest(unittest.TestCase):

  def setUp(self):
    print("This is run before all of our tests have a chance to execute")

  def tearDown(self):
    print("This is executed after all of our tests have completed")

  def test_simple_function(self):
    print("Testing that our function works with positive tests")
    self.assertEqual(simpleFunction(2), 3)
    self.assertEqual(simpleFunction(234135145145432143214321432),
234135145145432143214321433)
    self.assertEqual(simpleFunction(0), 1)

if __name__ == '__main__':
  unittest.main()
```

# Output

If we were to run the preceding program, we will see that our `setUp` function executes first, followed swiftly by our single test case, and finally, we see our `tearDown` function executing.

It then prints out how many tests were run, how long these tests took, and finally, an overall status:

```
$ python3.6 00_unittest.py
This is run before all of our tests have a chance to execute
Testing that our function works with positive tests
This is executed after all of our tests have completed
.
-------------------------------------------------------------------
Ran 1 test in 0.000s

OK
```

# Expanding our test suite

So, in the previous section, we looked at how we could test a very simple function with a few positive tests. This has told us that one path in our code works the way we intended, which is good; however, it could be far better.

In our current situation, we have no idea how our code will handle, say, a string input, a negative value, or an object.

One of the most popular trends for writing stable production-ready code these days is to, actually, define a range of failing tests before you've written any of your code. This is called test-driven development, and it could save you a hell of a lot of time further down the road when it comes to finding bugs and making changes with confidence.

The idea behind test-driven development is that you start by writing failing tests that accurately test how your system should work. You then write your code until you have a set of passing tests.

# Unit testing concurrent code

Unfortunately, when it comes to unit testing concurrent code, there is no silver bullet solution that will work for everything. You'll have to use your own discretion in order to come up with a strategy, or strategies, that will work for the systems that you are developing.

You will likely never be able to test every possible scenario of your codebase if you introduce multiple threads. Ideally, you should try to follow a blend of different strategies like these:

- Unit test the parts of your code that don't run on multiple threads.
- Create a test suite that probes your multithreaded code in a variety of different ways. If possible, try and include load tests on these specific sections of code to give you confidence that your multithreaded logic stands up to constant pressure.

There are, of course, more strategies that you can follow, but adequately testing your codebase is a complex blend of both science and art that hugely depends on what you are developing and the complexities of your system.

One rule of thumb I would tend to agree with is that if your code is so complex that testing becomes near impossible, then it could be time to rethink your initial approach, and come up with a simpler design. This isn't always possible, but it is something I would actively recommend you do if you have the time and resources available to do so.

# Integration tests

While unit tests represent tests that ensure the correctness of a single unit of your code, integration tests are used to ensure the correctness of multiple sections of code or different parts of your systems.

Integration tests are a lot more complex in nature, but the reward for doing them is that you know your system works well as a piece of a bigger puzzle. Like your unit tests, integration tests give you that extra bit of insight to see how your system will run when synced up with everything else.

Integration tests could be a complete chapter on their own, but, unfortunately, they are somewhat outside the remit of this book. I do, however, encourage you to research different integration testing strategies, as they can help to ensure that your code is less likely to contain errors, and with a good integration testing strategy, the art of debugging becomes a lot easier for developers.

# Debugging

Being able to debug your code is a key skill that any software developer must be able to do. As our systems grow ever more complex, the potential for bugs within our code grows exponentially, and knowing the best practices for debugging in certain scenarios could save you a substantial amount of time.

The techniques I'll be showing you next will work for both single-threaded and multithreaded applications. For brevity, I'll only be demonstrating these techniques on simple, single-threaded applications, but I implore you to try and become as familiar with these tools as possible, and practice using them in multithreaded scenarios.

# Make it work as a single thread

Imagine you were writing a new AI-based system that would drastically improve the sales that your website makes, or be able to place trades that would make you a multi-millionaire overnight. You've spent months working on this system, and you are very close to cracking it and making it work perfectly, but you think it's running very slowly. This could be because it's running through millions of calculations per second in order to crank out accurate predictions.

You may think, in this scenario, that you could optimize the code based off some of the previous examples in this book we've given. You start to add multiple processes to handle the number crunching more effectively, and see some noticeable improvements in the speed.

However, you've not yet cracked the final problem, and, suddenly, you see that following the logical flow of your system is exponentially harder. You have to follow the flow across multiple threads and processes, and could, potentially, have introduced more bugs into your system.

The moral of this theoretical story is to ensure that you get your applications fully working in a deterministic manner before you set about increasing the complexity of the codebase, and try to optimize things. Single-threaded programs are far easier to debug and work through, and catching logical errors at this stage is far easier than trying to debug a system that's running across multiple threads in a non-deterministic manner.

However, sometimes, this may not be possible--you could be trying to debug a system that has already been in production for months or even years before these bugs rear their ugly heads. In this case, you'll have to utilize some of the following tools in order to debug these complex systems.

Again, I will point you to the talk done by Raymond Hettinger at PyCon. He eloquently goes over some of the reasons why you should get things working in a single-threaded manner before adding concurrency, and overall, the talk is excellent. You can watch it at `ht tps://www.youtube.com/watch?v=Bv25Dwe84g0&t=640s`.

# Pdb

Pdb or the Python Debugger is the standard debugger included in Python. It's an excellent fallback tool for when the more standard methods of debugging are found to be lacking. Pdb gives you complete control, and allows you to check the values of variables at runtime, and perform other very handy tasks, such as stepping through code and setting breakpoints.

With Pdb, we can do either postmortem debugging, which can be done through the command-line, or we can interactively run our Pdb. If we were to work through our script using the interactive command-line, then we'll need to familiarize ourselves with a series of commands such as the following:

- l (list)
- n (next)
- c (continue)
- s (step)
- r (return)
- b (break)
- Python

If you ever forget these commands, then you can simply type ? while running Pdb, and you should see a table of all the commands available to you. Quite a number of these will be duplicates, so don't feel overwhelmed by the number of commands it presents to you:

```
(Pdb) ?
Documented commands (type help <topic>):
========================================
… A table with all of the commands – not shown for brevity
```

# An interactive example

Say, we wanted to start debugging this following script, and see what the values of certain variables are during runtime. In order to do this, we could utilize the following line in order to set a breakpoint within our code:

```
Import pdb; pdb.set_trace()
```

By setting this, we can then execute our program normally, and it will execute up until the point that this line has been set. Upon reaching this line, the Pdb interactive terminal will start up, and we'll be able to utilize the various commands outlined previously in order to debug the current state of our program.

```
from timer import Timer
from urllib.request import Request, urlopen
import ssl

def myFunction():
    # We create this context so that we can crawl
    # https sites
    myssl = ssl.create_default_context()
    myssl.check_hostname=False
    myssl.verify_mode=ssl.CERT_NONE
    with Timer() as t:
        import pdb; pdb.set_trace()
        req = Request('https://tutorialedge.net', headers={'User-Agent':
'Mozilla/5.0'})
        response = urlopen(req, context=myssl)

print("Elapsed Time: {} seconds".format(t.elapsed_secs))

myFunction()
```

Let's try executing this preceding script now. You should see that upon execution, the Pdb kicks in and our code breaks at the point that we placed our `set_trace()` function. In the preceding program, we put the `set_trace()` function call on line 12 of our code, so you should see that the code breaks at line 13. In order to see the current code that we are executing, type `l` or `list` into (Pdb), and you should see all the code surrounding our current line of execution.

The current line that we are executing can be determined by the `->` arrow that features next to the line number.

```
$ python3.6 04_timeitContext.py
> /Users/elliotforbes/Projects/Python/Chapter
06/04_timeitContext.py(13)myFunction()
```

```
-> req = Request('https://tutorialedge.net', headers={'User-Agent':
'Mozilla/5.0'})
(Pdb) l
  8          myssl = ssl.create_default_context();
  9          myssl.check_hostname=False
 10          myssl.verify_mode=ssl.CERT_NONE
 11          with Timer() as t:
 12              import pdb; pdb.set_trace()
 13  ->          req = Request('https://tutorialedge.net', headers={'User-Agent':
'Mozilla/5.0'})
 14              response = urlopen(req, context=myssl)
 15
 16          print("Elapsed Time: {} seconds".format(t.elapsed_secs))
 17
 18
```

If we then wanted to try and check on, say, the value of our `http` response object, we could continue the execution of our code until the next line using the n command. This then takes us to `response = urlopen(req, context=myssl)`.

In order to obtain the value of our response object, we'll have to run this line again using the n command, and then we'll be able to do `print(response)` which prints out our response object. We can then treat the object as if we were inside our script, and call it's `geturl()` function in order to see what the value of the URL is at runtime.

```
$ python3.6 04_timeitContext.py
> /Users/elliotforbes/Projects/Python/Chapter
06/04_timeitContext.py(13)myFunction()
-> req = Request('https://tutorialedge.net', headers={'User-Agent':
'Mozilla/5.0'})
(Pdb) n
> /Users/elliotforbes/Projects/Python/Chapter
06/04_timeitContext.py(14)myFunction()
-> response = urlopen(req, context=myssl)
(Pdb) n
> /Users/elliotforbes/Projects/Python/Chapter
06/04_timeitContext.py(16)myFunction()
-> print("Elapsed Time: {} seconds".format(t.elapsed_secs))
(Pdb) print(response)
<http.client.HTTPResponse object at 0x1031e2588>
(Pdb) print(response.geturl())
https://tutorialedge.net
```

While I was still learning the language, I would constantly rerun applications after modifications in order to try and achieve the results I wanted. However, as the programs I worked on became bigger and took longer to execute, this simple method of debugging was no longer sufficient.

Through learning about these excellent debugging methods, I was able to drastically improve the speed at which I found errors, and subsequently, the speed at which I was able to fix them, so, I would encourage you to spend a lot of time combing the documentation and practice using the Pdb.

Official documentation

Before we go any further, I implore you to take a look at the official documentation of Pdb for Python 3.6, as it'll show you all the different commands you can utilize in your debugging adventures. That documentation can be found at `https://docs.python.org/3.6/library/pdb.html`.

# Catching exceptions in child threads

An important point to consider when writing multithreaded applications is how do we handle any exceptions thrown in child threads? We looked at cross-thread communication in the previous chapter, so a logical method for catching and communicating exceptions between child and parent threads could be to use one or more of the techniques we have already discussed.

In this next code sample, we'll look at exactly how you can communicate any exceptions thrown from a child thread to the parent thread. We'll be utilizing the sys module to extract the information we need about the exception, and then place this within the confines of our thread-safe queue primitive:

```python
import sys
import threading
import time
import queue

def myThread(queue):
 while True:
   try:
     time.sleep(2)
     raise Exception("Exception Thrown In Child Thread
{}".format(threading.current_thread()))
   except:
     queue.put(sys.exc_info())
```

```
queue = queue.Queue()
myThread = threading.Thread(target=myThread, args=(queue,))
myThread.start()

while True:
 try:
   exception = queue.get()
   except Queue.Empty:
   pass
 else:
   print(exception)
   break
```

When you run this preceding Python program, you'll see that the child thread throws an error two seconds after it starts; this error is put into the thread-safe queue object which our parent thread then reads from. We are then able to handle the exception in any way we wish within our parent thread.

```
[20:22:31] ~/Projects/Python/Chapter 06 master⏎
 $ python3.6 07_threadException.py
(<class 'Exception'>, Exception('Exception Thrown In Child Thread
<Thread(Thread-1, started 123145552101376)>',), <traceback object at
0x102320548>)
```

# Benchmarking

When we talk about benchmarking our code, we are talking about measuring how quickly it can perform one complete operation. For instance, take the web crawler that we built in the last chapter--if we benchmarked this program, we would typically measure the number of pages we could index per second.

When doing performance optimizations, we take a starting benchmark that represents the current state of our program as a whole, and then use a combination of micro benchmarking and profiling in order to optimize these programs and achieve higher throughput.

Micro benchmarking is, essentially, decomposing our application into a series of steps, and then, benchmarking each of these steps individually in order to determine the bottlenecks within our code. We break, what is essentially a hard problem to optimize as a whole, into a series of smaller problems that become easier to optimize and tune.

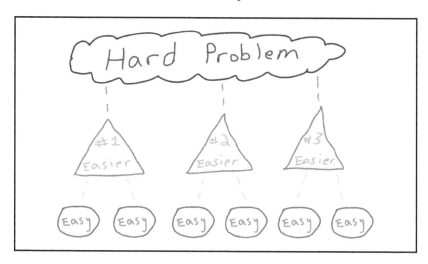

Source: https://nickjanetakis.com/blog/breaking-down-problems-is-the-number-1-software-developer-skill

So, how can we perform benchmarks upon our code? Well, thankfully, we have a number of different options that we can leverage, which come as part of Python.

# The timeit module

The `timeit` module in Python happens to be one such tool that we can utilize. Python, by default, comes with this `timeit` module which provides an excellent way to measure the performance of small bits of Python code within your main application.

The `timeit` module gives us the flexibility to either have our benchmarks included within our codebase, or, conversely, we can call it through the command-line and feed in sections of code that we wish to time.

 The official documentation for the `timeit` module can be found at `https ://docs.python.org/3/library/timeit.html`.

The first method of using the `timeit` module that we'll cover will be through the command-line interface.

# Timeit versus time

It's worthwhile to note that there are a number of advantages when using the `timeit` module as opposed to the time module. `timeit` is specifically designed to obtain far more accurate measurements of time as opposed to the time module.

With `timeit`, we can tell our programs to run things multiple times, and then give us a precise measurement that is far less likely to be impacted by extraneous factors within our OS, which we have no direct control over.

# Command-line example

To quickly come to grips with the command-line `timeit` module, I suggest that you try profiling some of the code that we've previously featured within this book. The multitude of samples that are available in the Concurrency with Python GitHub repo can give us a detailed spread of how fast or slow each of the different concurrency concepts we've covered truly is.

# Importing timeit into your code

This next sample will cover a very simple way we can utilize the `timeit` module to measure the time taken to execute two distinct functions:

```python
import timeit
import time

def func1():
  print("Function 1 Executing")
  time.sleep(5)
  print("Function 1 complete")

def func2():
  print("Function 2 executing")
  time.sleep(6)
  print("Function 2 complete")

start_time = timeit.default_timer()
func1()
print(timeit.default_timer() - start_time)

start_time = timeit.default_timer()
func2()
print(timeit.default_timer() - start_time)
```

The preceding code takes a start, then executes each function, and then records an end time before printing the precise difference between the two times.

It should be noted that while we've managed to measure the time taken for each function, we've not actually utilized the `timeit` module to its full potential.

```
import timeit
import time

def func1():
    print("Function 1 Executing")
    time.sleep(3)
    print("Function 1 complete")

def func2():
    print("Function 2 executing")
    time.sleep(2)
    print("Function 2 complete")

t1 = timeit.Timer("func1()", setup="from __main__ import func1")
times = t1.repeat(repeat=2, number=1)
for t in times:
print("{} Seconds: ".format(t))

t2 = timeit.Timer("func2()", setup="from __main__ import func2")
times = t2.repeat(repeat=2, number=1)
for t in times:
    print("{} Seconds: ".format(t))
```

In the last code, we instantiate two `Timer` objects, each taking in the function that they are going to be timing as well as the imports needed in order to run them within `timeit`.

We then call `.repeat()` on these two `Timer` objects, passing in `repeat = 2` to determine how many times we want to time our code, and `number = 1` to determine how many times we want to run these tests.

Executing the preceding code should provide the following output:

```
$ python3.6 timeitCode.py
Function 1 Executing
Function 1 complete
Function 1 Executing
Function 1 complete
3.002750840038061 Seconds:
3.0001289139618166 Seconds:
Function 2 executing
Function 2 complete
```

```
Function 2 executing
Function 2 complete
2.0005433409824036 Seconds:
2.00145923596574 Seconds:
```

# Utilizing decorators

Sometimes, however, manually inserting the last code can be somewhat of an overkill, and may end up bloating your codebase when it's unnecessary. Thankfully, Python offers a solution to this.

We can define our own `decorator` function, which will automatically wrap our function's execution with two calls to `timeit.default_timer()`. We'll then retrieve the differences between these two calls and display this on the console.

```python
import random
import timeit
import time
def timethis(func):

    def function_timer(*args, **kwargs):
        start_time = timeit.default_timer()
        value = func(*args, **kwargs)
        runtime = timeit.default_timer() - start_time
        print("Function {} took {} seconds to run".format(func.__name__,
runtime))
        return value
    return function_timer


@timethis
def long_runner():
    for x in range(3):
        sleep_time = random.choice(range(1,3))
        time.sleep(sleep_time)

if __name__ == '__main__':
    long_runner()
```

This preceding code will print out any function we pass into it with the exact time it took to run it. When you run it, you should see the following output on the console:

```
$ python3.6 05_timeitDecorator.py
Function long_runner took 5.008787009981461 seconds to run
```

# Timing context manager

Context managers are objects that define the runtime context to be established when executing a `with` statement.

In Python, we can define our own `Timer` context manager object, which we can then use in order to time specific sections of our code without too detrimental an impact on our codebase.

This time, the context manager object will look something this:

```python
from timeit import default_timer

class Timer(object):
  def __init__(self, verbose=False):
      self.verbose = verbose
      self.timer = default_timer
  def __enter__(self):
      self.start = default_timer()
      return self
  def __exit__(self, *args):
      end = default_timer()
      self.elapsed_secs = end - self.start
      self.elapsed = self.elapsed_secs * 1000  # millisecs
      if self.verbose:
          print('elapsed time: %f ms' % self.elapsed)
```

We define a `Timer` class which features a constructor, an entry point, and an exit point. Upon entry, we start the `Timer`, and upon exit, we calculate the elapsed time.

We can then utilize this class like this within our Python programs:

```python
from timer import Timer
from urllib.request import Request, urlopen
import ssl

def myFunction():
  # We create this context so that we can crawl
  # https sites
  myssl = ssl.create_default_context()
  myssl.check_hostname=False
  myssl.verify_mode=ssl.CERT_NONE
  with Timer() as t:
    req = Request('https://tutorialedge.net', headers={'User-Agent':
'Mozilla/5.0'})
    response = urlopen(req, context=myssl)
```

```
print("Elapsed Time: {} seconds".format(t.elapsed))
myFunction()
```

# Output

If we were to execute the preceding code, then you should see that it executes and then prints out the total elapsed time taken for the request as follows:

```
$ python3.6 04_timeitContext.py
Elapsed Time: 0.5995572790270671 seconds
```

# Profiling

When we talk about profiling our code, what we intend to do is measure some key attributes about our programs, such as how much memory they use, the time complexity of our programs, or the usage of particular instructions. It's a vital tool in a programmer's arsenal when it comes to squeezing the highest performance out of their systems.

Profiling, typically, uses a technique called Dynamic program analysis to achieve its measurements, and this involves running our programs on a real or virtual processor. The technique goes all the way back to IBM/360 and IBM/370 platforms in the early 1970s.

# cProfile

cProfile is a C-based module that comes as part of Python as standard. We can use it to understand the following characteristics of our code:

- `ncalls`: This is the number of times a line/function is called throughout the execution of our program.
- `tottime`: This is the total time that the line or function took to execute.
- `percall`: This is the total time divided by the number of calls.
- `cumtime`: This is the cumulative time spent executing this line or function.
- `percall`: This is the quotient of `cumtime` divided by the number of primitive calls.
- `filename`: `lineno`(function): This represents the actual line or function that we are measuring.

Let's take a quick look at how we can utilize the `cProfile` module in order to attain these attributes on some of our previous Python samples.

# Simple profile example

For this example, I'm going to use a program from the previous chapter, which showed us how to append things to a double-ended queue. It's a rather simplistic script which doesn't do a hell of a lot, so, it's perfect for showing you the results without too much noise.

```
import collections

doubleEndedQueue = collections.deque('123456')

print("Deque: {}".format(doubleEndedQueue))

doubleEndedQueue.append('1')
print("Deque: {}".format(doubleEndedQueue))

doubleEndedQueue.appendleft('6')
print("Deque: {}".format(doubleEndedQueue))
```

When we call `cProfile` on the preceding program, it should first run through the entire program for us and display the output on the console before displaying the tabled stats that it's recorded for this particular bit of code.

```
$ python3.6 -m cProfile 04_appendDeque.py
Deque: deque(['1', '2', '3', '4', '5', '6'])
Deque: deque(['1', '2', '3', '4', '5', '6', '1'])
Deque: deque(['6', '1', '2', '3', '4', '5', '6', '1'])
        11 function calls in 0.000 seconds

   Ordered by: standard name

   ncalls  tottime  percall  cumtime  percall filename:lineno(function)
        1    0.000    0.000    0.000    0.000 04_appendDeque.py:1(<module>)
        1    0.000    0.000    0.000    0.000 {built-in method
builtins.exec}
        3    0.000    0.000    0.000    0.000 {built-in method
builtins.print}
        1    0.000    0.000    0.000    0.000 {method 'append' of
'collections.deque' objects}
        1    0.000    0.000    0.000    0.000 {method 'appendleft' of
'collections.deque' objects}
        1    0.000    0.000    0.000    0.000 {method 'disable' of
'_lsprof.Profiler' objects}
        3    0.000    0.000    0.000    0.000 {method 'format' of 'str'
objects}
```

As you can see, the preceding code takes next to no time to execute. We can see from this that the method `append` and `appendleft` were called a grand total of once each, and that they took a miniscule amount of time to execute. You can also see on the last line of our table that we called the `format` function thrice, and that it again took a minimal amount of time.

Let's see what happens if we try using the cProfile on a slightly more advanced program like this:

```
import threading
import random
import time

def myWorker():
for i in range(5):
  print("Starting wait time")
  time.sleep(random.randint(1,5))
  print("Completed Wait")

thread1 = threading.Thread(target=myWorker)
thread2 = threading.Thread(target=myWorker)
thread3 = threading.Thread(target=myWorker)

thread1.start()
thread2.start()
thread3.start()

thread1.join()
thread2.join()
thread3.join()
```

If we were to execute `cProfile` on the last program, which doesn't look too mind bogglingly complex compared to our first program, then you should see a far bigger table rendered out to your console.

For this particular example, the output is far more insightful, and gives us an indication of where some of the slowdowns occur within our codebase so that we can further optimize and improve these speeds.

```
5157 function calls (5059 primitive calls) in 17.354 seconds

   Ordered by: standard name

   ncalls  tottime  percall  cumtime  percall filename:lineno(function)
        1    0.000    0.000   17.354   17.354 01_timeit.py:1(<module>)
   ...
```

You should notice that the number of function calls in the preceding output is exponentially higher than that of our first program--a staggering 5157 function calls as opposed to 10.

This should give you some indication as to how drastically the performance of two programs can differ, and the sheer magnitude of the work that goes on in the background without our knowledge. cProfile, and other tools like this, give us an incredibly important insight into the inner workings of our systems, and arming ourselves with this knowledge allows us to actively start improving performances across all of our systems.

# The line_profiler tool

Using the traditional methods of wrapping every line with a time calculation can, at times, be unrealistic, as the number of lines in your functions may be quite substantial. Fortunately, there are tools available to us that automate this task, and allow us to obtain that finer-grained analysis of our codebase that could lead us to spot potential hotspots.

The line_profiler is one such tool that allows us to do line-by-line analysis of how long our programs take to execute. This saves us from doing the standard time calculations around every line of our code. Unfortunately, this doesn't come as standard with Python, but it's easily attainable through our friend pip.

In order to install the line_profiler tool with pip, run the following line:

```
pip install line_profiler
```

 If you are interested in seeing how this tool works, then the good news is that the line_profiler tool is open source. You can find the complete codebase for this tool at https://github.com/rkern/line_profiler.

# Kernprof

Kernprof comes with the line_profiler tool, by default, and allows us to easily get started using the line_profiler tool. With line_profiler, we need to explicitly state the functions that we need to profile within our codebase. This is typically done using the @profile decorator.

For the purpose of this example, let's create a very simple program that features two functions, a slow function and a fast function. We somewhat suspect that slowFunction() might be the one that is causing our program to be inefficient, and due to its colossal size, we are unable to wrap every line of it with a time calculation.

If we wanted a line-by-line analysis of exactly how long everything takes, then we can add the @profile decorator in order to see what has gone wrong, as follows:

```
import random
import time

@profile
def slowFunction():
    time.sleep(random.randint(1,5))
    print("Slow Function Executed")

def fastFunction():
    print("Fast Function Executed")

def main():
    slowFunction()
    fastFunction()

if __name__ == '__main__':
    main()
```

In order to run our tool, we first have to call the kernprof tool in order to generate an .lprof file. It's this file that we've just generated that we'll be passing into our line_profiler tool in order to see the exact output.

```
$ python3.6 -m kernprof -l profileTest.py
Slow Function Executed
Fast Function Executed
Wrote profile results to profileTest.py.lprof

$ python3.6 -m line_profiler profileTest.py.lprof
Timer unit: 1e-06 s

Total time: 3.00152 s
File: profileTest.py
Function: slowFunction at line 4

Line #      Hits         Time  Per Hit   % Time  Line Contents
==============================================================
     4                                           @profile
     5                                           def slowFunction():
     6         1      3001412 3001412.0    100.0
time.sleep(random.randint(1,5))
     7         1          106    106.0      0.0   print("Slow Function
Executed")
```

As you can see, we first run our `kernprof`, which runs through our program, and successfully generates our `profileTest.py.lprof` file. We then pass this file into our `line_profiler` tool, and it outputs a table that features the line numbers of the code we've executed, the number of times that line was hit, and the time per hit.

As you can see, line 6 was deemed to have taken up 100.0 percent of the time rounded up. It took just slightly over 3 seconds, and has crippled the execution time of our program. Armed with this knowledge, we can try to refactor our app to possibly remove this unnecessary line, and greatly improve the speed at which our program executes.

# Memory profiling

Being able to profile your program's memory usage is yet another key skill that most senior developers will need in order to effectively debug issues with their systems. I've often seen developers pay little or no attention to the limitations of the hardware that they are developing on--I've also been one of the biggest perpetrators of this heinous crime.

I've loaded a server with a `jenkins` instance along with multiple heavy JVM-based systems as well as multiple cron jobs and whatever else I could fit in there, and seen it all come tumbling down after one particularly memory hungry program gobbled up all of the remaining memory available on that server. The main cause of the issue? I'd not paid attention to appropriate garbage collection within one of my applications, and over time it started throwing exceptions and dying on me slowly.

It was only once I'd been burned by this kind of issue that I started to seriously analyze the memory usage of the programs that I create. Within the Python ecosystem, we have a tool aptly called `memory_profiler`, which, very much like our `line_profiler`, generates informative tables based on the memory usage of each of the lines of our explicitly chosen functions.

In order to install the memory profiler, run the following command:

```
pip install -U memory_profiler
```

Again, we'll take the following program as our test bed:

```
import random
import time

@profile
def slowFunction():
    time.sleep(random.randint(1,5))
    print("Slow Function Executed")
```

```
def fastFunction():
  print("Fast Function Executed")

def main():
  slowFunction()
  fastFunction()

if __name__ == '__main__':
  main()
```

Thankfully, we are able to reuse the `@profile` annotation when it comes to memory profiling our slower function. In order to perform a memory profile, we can execute this:

```
$ python3.6 -m memory_profiler profileTest.py
```

Upon execution of this, you should then see a table, much the same layout as our `line_profiler` display in the console. This gives us the line numbers of the code that we are actively profiling, their associated memory usage, and the amount by which memory usage incremented when executing that line.

As you can see, our slowFunction in this particular program isn't exactly too demanding on our system, and thus, no real action needs to be taken.

```
Line #    Mem usage    Increment   Line Contents
================================================
    4    33.766 MiB   0.000 MiB    @profile
    5                              def slowFunction():
    6    33.777 MiB   0.012 MiB      time.sleep(random.randint(1,5))
    7    33.785 MiB   0.008 MiB      print("Slow Function Executed")
```

# Memory profile graphs

If you want to be able to view your memory usage over a set period of time, then there is the option of using the mprof tool that comes with `memory_profiler`. The mprof tool takes a series of memory usage samples at a 0.1-second intervals, and then plots this usage into a series of `.dat` files.

These .dat files can then be used in conjunction with matplotlib in order to show the memory usage of your program over a set period of time.

```
python -m pip install matplotlib
```

Now, if you are like me, and you have multiple versions of Python installed on your machine, you might find it a little tricky to get mprof to work. I'm working off macOS, and managed to run mprof using the following command:

```
$ python3.6 /Library/Frameworks/Python.framework/Versions/3.6/bin/mprof run profileTest.py
```

This was run against the following code that we've used previously except without the @profile decoration on our slowFunction():

```
import random
import time

def slowFunction():
  time.sleep(random.randint(1,5))
  print("Slow Function Executed")

def fastFunction():
  print("Fast Function Executed")

def main():
  slowFunction()
  fastFunction()

if __name__ == '__main__':
  main()
```

Upon completion, we can then run the following command in order to plot our memory usage over time:

```
$ python3.6 /Library/Frameworks/Python.framework/Versions/3.6/bin/mprof
plot
```

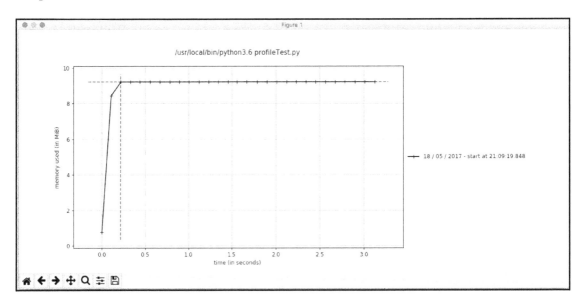

For a very simple program like the preceding one, the graph outputted is somewhat basic, but still, it's a good, simple demonstration for us to pick apart.

On the *y*-axis, we have the total memory used measured (in MiB), and on the *x*-axis, we have the time (in seconds). With longer running programs, you should see far more interesting variations in the total memory used, and it should stand you in good stead for trying to identify any memory issues you face further down the line.

# Summary

In this chapter, we took a comprehensive look at some of the techniques that you can utilize in order to ensure your concurrent Python systems are as free as practically possible from bugs before they plague your production environment. We covered testing strategies that help to ensure the soundness of your code's logic, and provide you with that extra peace of mind when bug fixing.

We then looked at the various ways that you can debug your Python codebase, touching upon the inbuilt Pdb, and how you can interactively use that in the command-line.

Finally, we looked at the various techniques that you can employ in order to benchmark and profile your Python applications, and ensure that they are as efficient as possible.

In the next chapter, we are going to look at Python's Asyncio library, and explain how we can utilize executors and pools in order to improve the performance of our Python applications.

# 7

# Executors and Pools

In this chapter, we will look in depth at concepts such as Thread pools and Process pools, and how we can work with Python's implementation of these concepts in order to speed up the execution of our programs.

We'll be looking at the following topics in some detail:

- Concurrent Futures
- Future Objects
- Process Pool Executors

We'll also continue with our progress on the website crawler that we created in `Chapter 5`, *Communication between Threads*, by adding functionality, such as writing the results to a CSV file and refactoring our code, to use the new techniques you'll be learning about in more detail within this chapter.

By the end of this chapter, you should have an appreciation as to how we can improve the performance of our Python program by leveraging executor objects as well as how they can help to simplify the amount of work we have to do with regard to handling threads and processes.

## Concurrent futures

Concurrent futures are a new feature added to Python in version 3.2. If you come from a Java-based background, then you may be familiar with `ThreadPoolExecutor`. Well, concurrent futures are Python's implementation of this `ThreadPoolExecutor` concept.

When it comes to running multithreaded tasks, one of the most computationally expensive tasks is starting up threads. `ThreadPoolExecutors` get around this problem by creating a pool of threads that will live as long as we need them to. We no longer have to create and run a thread to perform a task and continue to do this for every task we require; we can, instead, just create a thread once, and then constantly feed it new jobs to do.

A good way to think about this is to imagine you were in an office that had numerous workers. We wouldn't hire an employee, train them up, and then allocate one and only one job to them before firing them. We would, instead, only incur this expensive process of training them up once, and then allocate them numerous jobs throughout the term of their employment, and thus, achieve greater efficiency.

This is analogous to our thread pool. We hire a number of threads once, and incur the cost of creating them once before delegating them numerous tasks throughout their lifespan.

# Executor objects

The Executor class falls within the `concurrent.futures` module, and provides us with the ability to execute a number of different calls in a concurrent fashion. It can be used in a number of different ways, such as by itself or as a context manager, and it can drastically improve the legibility of our code by handling tedious tasks such as thread creation, start, and joining, all in one go.

## Creating a ThreadPoolExecutor

The first step we need to know is how to define our own `ThreadPoolExecutors`. This is a rather simple one-liner, which looks something like this:

```
executor = ThreadPoolExecutor(max_workers=3)
```

In the preceding command, we instantiate an instance of our `ThreadPoolExecutor`, and pass in the maximum number of workers that we want it to have. In this case, we've defined it as 3, which, essentially, means that this thread pool will only have three concurrent threads that can process any jobs that we submit to it.

In order to give the threads within our `ThreadPoolExecutor` something to do, we can call the `submit()` function, which takes in a function as its primary parameter like this:

```
executor.submit(myFunction())
```

# Example

In this example, we'll put together both the creation of our `ThreadPoolExecutor` object and the submission of tasks to this newly instantiated object. We'll have a very simple task function that will simply sum up the numbers from 0 to 9, and then print out the result. Not the most cutting edge software, I'm sure you'll agree, but it serves as a fairly adequate example.

Following we defined the `task` function, we have our standard `main` function. It's within this that we define our `executor` object in a similar fashion to the aforementioned before then submitting two tasks to this new pool of threads:

```python
from concurrent.futures import ThreadPoolExecutor
import threading
import random

def task():
    print("Executing our Task")
    result = 0
    i = 0
    for i in range(10):
        result = result + i
    print("I: {}".format(result))
    print("Task Executed {}".format(threading.current_thread()))

def main():
    executor = ThreadPoolExecutor(max_workers=3)
    task1 = executor.submit(task)
    task2 = executor.submit(task)

if __name__ == '__main__':
    main()
```

# Output

If we were to execute the preceding Python program, we would see the rather bland output of both our tasks being executed, and the result of our computation being printed out on the command-line.

We then utilize the `threading.current_thread()` function in order to determine which thread has performed this task. You will see that the two values given as outputs are distinct daemon threads.

```
$ python3.6 05_threadPool.py
Executing our Task
I: 45
Executing our Task
I: 45
Task Executed <Thread(<concurrent.futures.thread.ThreadPoolExecutor object
at 0x102abf358>_1, started daemon 123145333858304)>
Task Executed <Thread(<concurrent.futures.thread.ThreadPoolExecutor object
at 0x102abf358>_0, started daemon 123145328603136)>
```

# Context manager

The second, and possibly the most popular, method of instantiating `ThreadPoolExecutor` is to use it as a context manager as follows:

```
with ThreadPoolExecutor(max_workers=3) as executor:
```

The preceding method does much the same job as the previous method we looked at, but, syntactically, it looks better and can be advantageous to us as developers in certain scenarios.

Context managers, if you haven't encountered them before, are an incredibly powerful concept with Python that allow us to write more syntactically beautiful code.

### Example

This time, we'll define a different task that takes in a variable n as input just to give you a simple demonstration of how we can do this. The `task` function just prints out that it's processing 'n', and nothing more.

Within our main function, we utilize our `ThreadPoolExecutor` as a context manager, and then call `future = executor.submit(task, (n))` three times in order to give our thread pool something to do:

```
from concurrent.futures import ThreadPoolExecutor

def task(n):
    print("Processing {}".format(n))

def main():
```

```
print ("Starting ThreadPoolExecutor")
with ThreadPoolExecutor (max_workers=3) as executor:
    future = executor.submit(task, (2))
    future = executor.submit(task, (3))
    future = executor.submit(task, (4))
print ("All tasks complete")

if __name__ == '__main__':
    main()
```

## Output

When we execute the last program, you will see that it prints out that we are starting out `ThreadPoolExecutor` before going on to execute the three distinct tasks we submit to it, and then, finally, prints out that all tasks are complete:

```
$ python3.6 01_threadPoolExe.py
Starting ThreadPoolExecutor
Processing 2
Processing 3
Processing 4
All tasks complete
```

# Maps

Maps in Python allow us to do cool things such as apply a certain function to every element within `iterables`:

```
map(func, *iterables, timeout=None, chunksize=1)
```

Thankfully, within Python, we can actually map all the elements of an iterator to a function, and submit these as independent jobs to our `ThreadPoolExecutor`:

```
results = executor.map(multiplyByTwo, values)
```

This, essentially, saves us from doing something far more verbose like the following example:

```
for value in values:
    executor.submit(multiplyByTwo, (value))
```

## Example

In this example, we'll use this new map function in order to apply our `multiplyByTwo` function to every value in our values array:

```
from concurrent.futures import ThreadPoolExecutor
from concurrent.futures import as_completed

values = [2,3,4,5,6,7,8]

def multiplyByTwo(n):
    return 2 * n

def main():
    with ThreadPoolExecutor(max_workers=3) as executor:
        results = executor.map(multiplyByTwo, values)

        for result in results:
            print(result)

if __name__ == '__main__':
    main()
```

## Output

As you can see, when we execute this preceding program on our computer, it does exactly what we expected it to, and prints out all of the multiplied results in our array after our map function has finished computing them:

```
$ python3.6 03_threadPoolMap.py
4
6
8
10
12
14
16
```

# Shutdown of executor objects

Being able to shut down your executor objects in a graceful manner can be quite important in a number of different situations. It gives you that added bit of flexibility when you may need it the most.

When we shut down an executor object, what we are essentially doing is saying that it can't accept any further tasks. The tasks that were already underway by the executor object will still be finished after the call to shut down, but trying to submit any further tasks to the said executor object will result in an error being thrown.

## Example

In this example, we are going to demonstrate a shutdown of a running executor. We'll first define a function which will essentially "work" for *n* number of seconds. We'll submit a number of tasks, and then call the shutdown method on our executor. After this point, we will attempt to submit yet more tasks to the executor:

```python
import time
import random
from concurrent.futures import ThreadPoolExecutor

def someTask(n):
    print("Executing Task {}".format(n))
    time.sleep(n)
    print("Task {} Finished Executing".format(n))

def main():
    with ThreadPoolExecutor(max_workers=2) as executor:
        task1 = executor.submit(someTask, (1))
        task2 = executor.submit(someTask, (2))
        executor.shutdown(wait=True)
        task3 = executor.submit(someTask, (3))
        task4 = executor.submit(someTask, (4))

if __name__ == '__main__':
    main()
```

## Output

If we were to run the preceding Python program, we will see that both task 1 and task 2 are successfully picked up and executed by our ThreadPoolExecutor. After our call to executor.shutdown(wait=True), we should then see that a stack trace is printed out in our console, as our executor object does not accept any further tasks.

In this example, we don't attempt to handle the exception in any way, and our program fails rather ungracefully. It's important to note that if you start implementing features like shutdown in order to handle certain events, then you should also implement some form of exception handling:

```
$ python3.6 11_shutdownExecutor.py
Executing Task 1
Executing Task 2
Task 1 Finished Executing
Task 2 Finished Executing
.. stack trace removed for brevity
RuntimeError: cannot schedule new futures after shutdown
FAIL
```

# Future objects

Future objects are instantiated whenever we submit a task to an executor, such as how we submitted tasks to `ThreadPoolExecutor` in previous examples within this chapter. Future objects are objects that will, eventually, be given a value sometime in the future.

# Methods in future objects

The future objects have the following methods with which we can access and modify them. Each of these methods will be covered in a full code sample further on in the chapter.

# The result() method

The `result()` method gives us any returned values from the future object. This `result` method can be called like this:

```
futureObj.result(timeout=None)
```

By specifying the `timeout` parameter, we, basically, put a time limit on our future object. If the future object fails to complete in the given time frame, then a `concurrent.futures.` The `timeout` error is raised. This is quite useful, as it gives us more control in terms of capping the amount of time erroneous threads can execute for, and limiting the damage they can do to our program's performance.

# The add_done_callback() method

When dealing with futures, we can specify a callback function which will be executed at the point of the future's completion. This saves us from tracking the state of all of our future objects, and simplifies our code. We can add callbacks to our future objects by utilizing the `add_done_callback` method.

```
futureObj.add_done_callback(fn)
```

# The .running() method

If, at some point in time within your Python program, you need to determine if $x$ future object is currently executing, then you can call the `.running()` method in order to check its current status:

```
futureObj.running()
```

This last method will return either true or false depending on the current running status of our future object.

# The cancel() method

The `cancel()` method attempts to cancel a future object, and can only be called before the point at which the future object commences execution:

```
futureObj.cancel()
```

# The .exception() method

We can retrieve any exceptions thrown by futures using the `.exception()` function. By specifying the `timeout` parameter, we can, essentially, dictate that if this future does not complete in $x$ seconds, then throw a `concurrent.futures.TimeoutError`.

```
futureObj.exception(timeout=None)
```

# The .done() method

The `.done()` method returns either true or false depending on whether the future object has successfully completed or been cancelled:

```
futureObj.done()
```

# Unit testing future objects

Unit testing concurrent applications can be a somewhat difficult task, but thankfully, the concurrent.futures. The future object comes with the following three methods that are designed explicitly for the purpose of unit testing.

## The set_running_or_notify_cancel() method

The set_nofity_or_nofity_cancel() method is utilized to mock a future completing or being cancelled:

```
futureObj.cancel() # cancel future before it's started
futureObj.set_notify_or_notify_cancel() # This call would return False
...
futureObj.running() # if this returns true
futureObj.set_notify_or_notify_cancel() # this would also return true
```

## The set_result() method

The aptly named set_result() method can set the result of a future object within your unit tests. This can be used in a variety of situations such as mocking the output of your executors.

It's intended to be used in situations where we don't necessarily want to test the logic behind our future objects, but the logic of what happens after these future objects return. Say, for instance, we are testing a web crawler and have a method that processes the results of a crawl. We could set the result of our future object to an expected value, and then build our test around this specific value.

We can call set_result like this:

```
futureObj.set_result(result)
```

## The set_exception() method

Similar to the previous set_result method, the set_exception() method sets the exception that a Future object should return.

```
futureObj.set_exception(exception)
```

# Cancelling callable

Sometimes, within your systems, you may wish to cancel jobs before they are processed by your executor objects. This would be analogous to cancelling, say, a print job in real life-- we've somehow decided that we no longer need to print out a document within our print queue, and we cancel it.

However, on a typical printer, we can't cancel the task when it's midway through execution. This also applies to tasks that we submit to either our ThreadPoolExecutors or ProcessPoolExecutors.

Cancelling tasks submitted to an executor can be done by calling the cancel() function on that specific task as follows:

```
with ThreadPoolExecutor(max_workers=2) as executor:
    myTask = executor.submit(someTask, (1))
    print(myTask.cancel())
```

The cancel function returns a boolean value which is either true if we successfully managed to cancel the future object, or false if unsuccessful. In the preceding example, you would see that it returns false unless you submit jobs prior to myTask that keeps the executor object occupied.

# Example

Let's take a look at this in more detail in a full-fledged example. Here, we define some arbitrary task to keep our ThreadPoolExecutor occupied--this is called someTask, and prints out that it's executing something before sleeping for n seconds.

In our main function, we again use the with command to instantiate our ThreadPoolExecutor as a context manager, and within the boundaries of this context manager, we then submit four distinct tasks. Immediately after submitting all four tasks, we then attempt to print the outcome of task3.cancel().

Note that we have defined max_workers=2 for our ThreadPoolExecutor, and as such, by the time we call task3.cancel(), the executor should be preoccupied running tasks 1 and 2, and shouldn't yet have started task 3:

```
import time
import random
from concurrent.futures import ThreadPoolExecutor

def someTask(n):
```

```
        print("Executing Task {}".format(n))
        time.sleep(n)
        print("Task {} Finished Executing".format(n))

def main():
    with ThreadPoolExecutor(max_workers=2) as executor:
        task1 = executor.submit(someTask, (1))
        task2 = executor.submit(someTask, (2))
        task3 = executor.submit(someTask, (3))
        task4 = executor.submit(someTask, (4))

        print(task3.cancel())

if __name__ == '__main__':
    main()
```

# Output

If we were to run the preceding program, then all four tasks would be submitted to `ThreadPoolExecutor`. Tasks 1 and 2 would then be picked up by the two available workers within the pool. While the pool is occupied with these two tasks, we then attempt to cancel task 3. Due to the fact it hasn't yet started, you should then see that it outputs true on the console. Tasks 1, 2, and 4 are then the only tasks to be executed and completed by our program:

```
$ python3.6 10_cancellingCallable.py
Executing Task 1
Executing Task 2
True
Task 1 Finished Executing
Executing Task 4
Task 2 Finished Executing
Task 4 Finished Executing
```

# Getting the result

Typically, in some scenarios, we fire and forget tasks to our executor objects, and we aren't too worried about any return values. However, there are times when we need to retrieve and store these results for further processing.

When we utilize the `executor.map` function, retrieving the results is pretty simple, below our call to `executor.map` we can utilize the following code in order to retrieve the results when they are returned:

```
for result in results:
    print(result)
```

# Example

The following code demonstrates a working example of how we can retrieve the results using the preceding method. We start with an array of values, and then call `executor.map` to map every value in this array to a task that our executor can pick up and process:

```
import time
import random
from concurrent.futures import ThreadPoolExecutor
from concurrent.futures import as_completed

values = [2,3,4,5,6,7,8]

def multiplyByTwo(n):
    time.sleep(random.randint(1,2))
    return 2 * n

def done(n):
    print("Done: {}".format(n))

def main():
    with ThreadPoolExecutor(max_workers=3) as executor:
        results = executor.map(multiplyByTwo, values)

        for result in results:
            done(result)

if __name__ == '__main__':
    main()
```

# Output

If we were to run the preceding program, we would see that this method preserves the order in which the tasks were submitted to the array:

```
$ python3.6 13_results.py
Done: 4
Done: 6
Done: 8
Done: 10
Done: 12
Done: 14
Done: 16
```

# Using as_completed

There are cases where we decide that the map function isn't fit for our needs, and as such, we would need to store all of the future objects that we submit to our ThreadPoolExecutor in an array of future objects.

By doing it this way, we can still take advantage of the as_completed method from the concurrent.futures module, and process the results of all the tasks we submit to our executor as and when they are returned.

# Example

In this example, we'll take in a small array of links that we wish to validate are working on our site. We'll utilize the urllib.request module in order to request these URLs, and then see what http status code they return:

```
import time
from urllib.request import Request, URLError, urljoin, urlopen
from concurrent.futures import ThreadPoolExecutor, as_completed

URLS = [
'http://localhost:1313',
'http://localhost:1313/about',
'http://localhost:1313/get-involved/',
'http://localhost:1313/series/blog/',
]

def checkStatus(url):
    print("Attempting to crawl URL: {}".format(url))
    req = Request(url, headers={'User-Agent': 'Mozilla/5.0'})
```

```python
        response = urlopen(req)
        return response.getcode(), url

def printStatus(statusCode):
    print("URL Crawled with status code: {}".format(statusCode))

def main():
    with ThreadPoolExecutor(max_workers=3) as executor:

        tasks = []
        for url in URLS:
            task = executor.submit(checkStatus, (url))
            tasks.append(task)

        for result in as_completed(tasks):
            printStatus(result)

if __name__ == '__main__':
    main()
```

# Output

If we were to run the last crawler, then we'll see that it prints out the URLs that it is attempting to crawl. As and when each request completes, the program then outputs the future object and its status.

You should note that the preservation of order is not guaranteed here. You cannot rely on the order of the tasks that you submit to the executor to return in the same order. Some tasks might take longer to complete. If you wish to maintain the ordering, then you will have to rely on a sorting algorithm, and return the index alongside the results returned:

```
$ python3.6 14_asCompleted.py
Attempting to crawl URL: http://localhost:1313
Attempting to crawl URL: http://localhost:1313/about
Attempting to crawl URL: http://localhost:1313/get-involved/
Attempting to crawl URL: http://localhost:1313/series/blog/
URL Crawled with status code: (200, 'http://localhost:1313')
URL Crawled with status code: (200, 'http://localhost:1313/get-involved/')
URL Crawled with status code: (200, 'http://localhost:1313/series/blog/')
URL Crawled with status code: (200, 'http://localhost:1313/about')
```

# Setting callbacks

Callbacks are something we'll be covering in a hell of a lot more detail in Chapter 9, *Event-Driven Programming*, and Chapter 10, *Reactive Programming*, when we look at both event-driven programming and reactive programming. The best way to visualize callbacks is to imagine you ask someone to do something that takes quite a bit of time. You, typically, wouldn't sit idle while that person completed the task; you would go off and do other things with your time.

Instead, you would ask them to call you back when they had completed their task. In programming, we'd appropriately call this a callback, and they are an incredibly powerful concept that we can use in conjunction with our ThreadPoolExecutors.

Upon the submission of a task to our ThreadPoolExecutor, we can specify a callback for the said function using the add_done_callback function like this:

```
with ThreadPoolExecutor(max_workers=3) as executor:
    future = executor.submit(task, (2))
    future.add_done_callback(taskDone)
```

This would then ensure that the taskDone function is called when our task is complete. With this simple function call, we saved ourselves the hassle of watching each and every task that we submit ourselves, and then, subsequently, kicking off some other function once it's done. These callbacks are incredibly powerful in the way that they handle everything for us with very little work on our end.

# Example

Let's have a look at a full-fledged sample piece of code that utilizes this callback functionality. We'll begin by by defining two functions: the task function, which will just print out that it's processing whatever we pass into it, and the taskDone function, which will be our callback function.

Within this taskDone function, we first check to see if our future object has been cancelled or whether it has been completed. We then print out the appropriate output to the console.

Below this, we define our main function, which simply creates `ThreadPoolExecutor` and submits a single task to it while also setting its callback:

```
from concurrent.futures import ThreadPoolExecutor

def task(n):
    print("Processing {}".format(n))

def taskDone(fn):
    if fn.cancelled():
        print("Our {} Future has been cancelled".format(fn.arg))
    elif fn.done():
        print("Our Task has completed")

def main():
    print("Starting ThreadPoolExecutor")
    with ThreadPoolExecutor(max_workers=3) as executor:
        future = executor.submit(task, (2))
        future.add_done_callback(taskDone)

    print("All tasks complete")

if __name__ == '__main__':
    main()
```

# Output

When we execute the preceding Python program, we should see that our `ThreadPoolExecutor` starts, our task is then submitted, and picked up by said executor, and the callback function executes as expected:

```
$ python3.6 04_settingCallbacks.py
Starting ThreadPoolExecutor
Processing 2
Our Task has completed
All tasks complete
```

## Chaining callbacks

In certain scenarios, you may find your callback functions growing with complexity, and it might make sense to split large callback functions into multiple functions. Thankfully, we can add multiple callbacks to a single future object, and chain them together to produce the desired results:

```
with ThreadPoolExecutor(max_workers=3) as executor:
  future = executor.submit(task, (2))
  future.add_done_callback(taskDone)
  future.add_done_callback(secondTaskDone)
```

It's important to note that each of these callbacks will be executed in the order in which they were added.

# Exception classes

In the previous chapter, we looked at how you could handle exceptions within normal child threads in Python by utilizing a queue primitive in order to pass the exception from the child thread to another thread. This was, however, somewhat hacky in the way that things were done, and, thankfully, with `ThreadPoolExecutors`, we no longer have to worry about this, as it's all handled for us.

In the same way that we retrieve the results from our future objects, so too can we return the exceptions.

## Example

In this example, we'll define an `isEven` function, which takes in a value. Within this function, it first does a check to see if the type of the object passed into it is an integer. If it isn't, then it raises a new exception.

After this type check, it then checks to see if the number is even or not. If it is even, then it returns true, and if not, it returns false:

```
from concurrent.futures import ThreadPoolExecutor
import concurrent.futures
import threading
import random

def isEven(n):
  print("Checking if {} is even".format(n))
  if type(n) != int:
```

```
            raise Exception("Value entered is not an integer")
        if n % 2 == 0:
            print("{} is even".format(n))
            return True
        else:
            print("{} is odd".format(n))
            return False

    def main():
        with ThreadPoolExecutor(max_workers=4) as executor:
            task1 = executor.submit(isEven, (2))
            task2 = executor.submit(isEven, (3))
            task3 = executor.submit(isEven, ('t'))

        for future in concurrent.futures.as_completed([task1, task2, task3]):
            print("Result of Task: {}".format(future.result()))
    if __name__ == '__main__':
        main()
```

# Output

When we run the preceding program, you'll see that the program attempts to check if 2, 3, and *t* are even. 2 and 3 are successfully processed, and the executor with *t* ends up throwing an exception.

You should also see the results of the tasks printing out followed by the exception thrown by the third task's invalid input:

```
$ python3.6 12_exceptionThread.py
Checking if 2 is even
2 is even
Checking if 3 is even
3 is odd
Checking if t is even
Result of Task: True
Result of Task: False
Traceback (most recent call last):
 File "12_exceptionThread.py", line 28, in <module>
 # ...
    raise Exception("Value entered is not an integer")
Exception: Value entered is not an integer
```

# ProcessPoolExecutor

`ProcessPoolExecutors` can be used and created in much the same way as your standard `ThreadPoolExecutors`. It subclasses the Executor class the same way the `ThreadPoolExecutor` class does, and thus, features many of the same methods within it.

## Creating a ProcessPoolExecutor

The process for creating a `ProcessPoolExecutor` is almost identical to that of the `ThreadPoolExecutor` except for the fact that we have to specify that we've imported that class from the `concurrent.futures` module, and that we also instantiate our executor object like this:

```
executor = ProcessPoolExecutor(max_workers=3)
```

## Example

The following example features a very simple full example of how you can instantiate your own `ProcessPoolExecutor` and submit a couple of tasks into this pool. It should be noted that our task function here isn't that computationally expensive, so we may not see the full benefit of using multiple processes, and it could, in fact, be significantly slower than your typical single-threaded process.

We'll use the `os` module to find the current PID of each of the tasks that we execute within our pool:

```python
from concurrent.futures import ProcessPoolExecutor
import os

def task():
    print("Executing our Task on Process {}".format(os.getpid()))

def main():
    executor = ProcessPoolExecutor(max_workers=3)
    task1 = executor.submit(task)
    task2 = executor.submit(task)

if __name__ == '__main__':
    main()
```

# Output

When we run this, we'll see that both our submitted tasks are executed as well as the Process IDs in which they were executed. This is a very simple example, but it's good at verifying that we are indeed running our tasks across multiple processes:

```
$ python3.6 06_processPool.py
Executing our Task on Process 40365
Executing our Task on Process 40366
```

# Context Manager

The next method we'll look at when working with `ProcessPoolExecutors` is to use them as a context manager like we've previously done with `ThreadPoolExecutor`. We can do this by using the `with` command as follows:

```
with ProcessPoolExecutor(max_workers=3) as executor:
… submit tasks etc…
```

Context managers handle the allocation and release of certain resources for you, and as such, this is the preferable way of handling your process pools. I also find that the syntax for doing it this way trumps other methods, and it can help you write cleaner and more succinct code.

# Example

In this example, we'll look at how we can employ a context manager to make our code nicer and more readable. We'll make it slightly more interesting in the sense that we'll pass arguments to our task function within our submit function call:

```
from concurrent.futures import ProcessPoolExecutor

def task(n):
    print("Processing {}".format(n))

def main():
    print("Starting ThreadPoolExecutor")
    with ProcessPoolExecutor(max_workers=3) as executor:
        future = executor.submit(task, (2))
        future = executor.submit(task, (3))
        future = executor.submit(task, (4))

    print("All tasks complete")
```

```
if __name__ == '__main__':
    main()
```

# Output

When you run the preceding program, you'll see that each of the tasks executes, and prints the value that we've passed into each task:

```
$ python3.6 02_processPoolExe.py
Starting ThreadPoolExecutor
Processing 2
Processing 3
Processing 4
All tasks complete
```

# Exercise

In order to get comfortable with `ProcessPoolExecutors`, I suggest you try to write a program that creates black and white versions of a large number of different photos. For this task, I recommend you download Pillow, which is a fork of the Python Imaging Library.

Image processing is computationally expensive, as each pixel within the image has to be processed and recalculated when converting to black and white.

The main requirements are as follows:

- The process must utilize the `ProcessPoolExecutor` class
- The project should be able to process multiple images in parallel, but ensure it does not process the same image on two different processes

# Getting started

Just to get you started, you can refer to the following sample code for how you can convert an image from a normal RGB image to a black and white version of itself:

```
from PIL import Image
image_file = Image.open("convert_image.png") # open colour image
image_file = image_file.convert('1') # convert image to black and white
image_file.save('result.png')
```

# Improving the speed of computationally bound problems

So we've seen how we can use both `ThreadPoolExecutor` and the `ProcessPoolExecutor` within our Python applications, but knowing when to use them is also important. The difference between both comes down to their underlying mechanisms.

`ThreadPoolExecutor` is named as such because it utilizes threads in order to achieve concurrent execution. `ProcessPoolExecutor` utilizes processes.

We've covered the differences between processes and threads and when to use them in a number of previous chapters, but I feel it's good to reinforce this point with a code example. In this example, we'll check to see if any of the values within an array of large values is prime or not. In order to determine if it's prime or not, we'll utilize the sieve of Eratosthenes, which, in Python, looks something like this:

```python
def is_prime(n):
    if n % 2 == 0:
        return False

    sqrt_n = int(math.floor(math.sqrt(n)))
    for i in range(3, sqrt_n + 1, 2):
        if n % i == 0:
            return False
    return True
```

## Full code sample

The following is the entire code sample which runs through our array of primes using both `ThreadPoolExecutor` and `ProcessPoolExecutor`. In this particular sample, we'll also utilize the `timeit` module that we explored in detail in the previous chapter:

```python
import timeit
from concurrent.futures import ThreadPoolExecutor
from concurrent.futures import ProcessPoolExecutor
import math

PRIMES = [
    112272535095293,
    112582705942171,
    112272535095293,
    115280095190773,
    115797848077099,
    1099726899285419
```

```
]

def is_prime(n):
    if n % 2 == 0:
        return False

    sqrt_n = int(math.floor(math.sqrt(n)))
    for i in range(3, sqrt_n + 1, 2):
        if n % i == 0:
            return False
    return True

def main():

    t1 = timeit.default_timer()
    with ProcessPoolExecutor(max_workers=4) as executor:
        for number, prime in zip(PRIMES, executor.map(is_prime, PRIMES)):
            print('%d is prime: %s' % (number, prime))

    print("{} Seconds Needed for
ProcessPoolExecutor".format(timeit.default_timer() - t1))
    t2 = timeit.default_timer()
    with ThreadPoolExecutor(max_workers=4) as executor:
        for number, prime in zip(PRIMES, executor.map(is_prime, PRIMES)):
            print('%d is prime: %s' % (number, prime))
    print("{} Seconds Needed for
ThreadPoolExecutor".format(timeit.default_timer() - t2))

if __name__ == '__main__':
    main()
```

# Output

If we were to run the last program, we'll see that both the process pools iterate through every element in the array, printing out whether or not each value is prime or not before printing out the total time for execution.

This is followed, immediately, by the thread pool executor, which follows exactly the same process of calculating the prime before printing out the total execution time. You should see an output that is similar to this on your terminal:

```
$ python3.6 08_poolImprovement.py
112272535095293 is prime: True
...
1099726899285419 is prime: False
2.8411907070549205 Seconds Needed for ProcessPoolExecutor
```

```
112272535095293 is prime: True
...
1099726899285419 is prime: False
4.426182378898375 Seconds Needed for ThreadPoolExecutor
```

`ProcessPoolExecutor` in this case, managed to work through the list in approximately 2.8 seconds, while the total time needed for `ThreadPoolExecutor` was 4.4 seconds. This represents an almost 60% increase in the total processing time for utilizing threads.

If we tried to do this in a single-threaded manner, we would see that the time taken for the program to run through our array of values would be slightly faster than the execution time for our `ThreadPoolExecutor`. If you wish to test this yourself, then you can add the following code to the bottom of the `main` function in the previous example:

```
t3 = timeit.default_timer()
for number in PRIMES:
  isPrime = is_prime(number)
  print("{} is prime: {}".format(number, isPrime))
print("{} Seconds needed for single threaded
execution".format(timeit.default_timer()-t3))
```

# Improving our crawler

Now that we've had an in-depth look at both `ThreadPoolExecutors` and `ProcessPoolExecutors`, it's time to actually put these newly learned concepts into practice. In `Chapter 5`, *Communication between Threads*, we started developing a multithreaded web crawler that was able to crawl every available link on a given website.

 The full source code for this Python web crawler can be found at this link: `https://github.com/elliotforbes/python-crawler`.

It didn't, however, output the results in the most readable format, and the code could be improved using `ThreadPoolExecutors`. So, let's have a look at implementing both more readable code and more readable results.

# The plan

Before we get started, we need to define a general plan as to how we are going to improve our crawler.

# New improvements

A few examples of the improvements we might wish to make are as follows:

- We want to refactor our code to use `ThreadPoolExecutors`
- We want to output the results of a crawl in a more readable format such as a CSV file or JSON files
- We want to capture more information on each and every page that we crawl so that we can try to improve our sites using this data

These three things will pose a good starting point as to what we can improve. There are a couple of more things we'll be looking to improve upon, such as exposing this web crawler service as a RESTful API, in `Chapter 9`, *Event-Driven Programming*.

# Refactoring our code

Okay, so the first thing we are going to do is refactor the way we implement multithreading in our application. We want to move away from us having to manage the startup and shutdown of all our threads, and, instead, leave that in the capable hands of `ThreadPoolExecutor`.

So, if we look back at our crawler code, in order to start up numerous threads, we would have to do something like this:

```
import threading
import queue
from crawler import *
from CheckableQueue import *

THREAD_COUNT = 20
linksToCrawl = CheckableQueue()

def createCrawlers():
  for i in range(THREAD_COUNT):
    t = threading.Thread(target=run)
    t.daemon = True
    t.start()

def run():
  while True:
    url = linksToCrawl.get()
    try:
      if url is None:
        break
```

```
        Crawler.crawl(threading.current_thread(), url, linksToCrawl)
    except:
      print("Exception thrown with link: {}".format(url))
    linksToCrawl.task_done()

def main():
  url = input("Website > ")
  Crawler(url)
  linksToCrawl.put(url)
  createCrawlers()
  linksToCrawl.join()
  print("Total Links Crawled: {}".format(len(Crawler.crawledLinks)))
  print("Total Errors: {}".format(len(Crawler.errorLinks)))

if __name__ == '__main__':
  main()
```

However, using `ThreadPoolExecutor`, we can condense this down to just a couple of lines now using our `with` command. Our code has become more succinct and easier to follow as a result:

```
import threading
import queue
from concurrent.futures import ThreadPoolExecutor
from crawler import *
from CheckableQueue import *

THREAD_COUNT = 20
linksToCrawl = CheckableQueue()

def run(url):
    try:
        Crawler.crawl(threading.current_thread(), url, linksToCrawl)
    except:
        print("Exception thrown with link: {}".format(url))
    linksToCrawl.task_done()

def main():
    url = input("Website > ")
    Crawler(url)
    linksToCrawl.put(url)
    while not linksToCrawl.empty():
        with ThreadPoolExecutor(max_workers=THREAD_COUNT) as executor:
            url = linksToCrawl.get()
            if url is not None:
                future = executor.submit(run, url)

print("Total Links Crawled: {}".format(len(Crawler.crawledLinks)))
```

```
print("Total Errors: {}".format(len(Crawler.errorLinks)))

if __name__ == '__main__':
    main()
```

# Storing the results in a CSV file

Like them or loathe them, CSV files represent a quick and simple way of storing the results of all our scrapping, and allow us to perform analyses on these results quickly and easily using existing software such as Microsoft Excel.

In order to append our results to a CSV file, we can use the already available `csv` module that comes with Python.

We'll define an `appendToCSV` function, which will take an input and append this input as a line to our `results.csv` file, as follows:

```
Import csv
...

def appendToCSV(result):
    print("Appending result to CSV File: {}".format(result))
    with open('results.csv', 'a') as csvfile:
        resultwriter = csv.writer(csvfile, delimiter=' ', quotechar='|',
quoting=csv.QUOTE_MINIMAL)
        resultwriter.writerow(result)
```

This `appendToCSV` function will live within our main thread, and will be called as and when a result is returned from our executor object. Having this live solely within our main thread means that we don't have to worry about race conditions and place locks to guard this resource.

Now that we've defined our `appendToCSV` file, we need to actually call this method whenever we get a result. In order to do this, we'll have to update our `main` function, and add the following code to it, where we submit the URLs in our queue to the executor:

```
for future in as_completed(futures):
    try:
        if future.result() != None:
            appendToCSV(future.result())
    except:
        print(future.exception())
```

This will leave our final `main` method looking something like this:

```
def main():
url = input("Website > ")
Crawler(url)
linksToCrawl.put(url)
while not linksToCrawl.empty():
  with ThreadPoolExecutor(max_workers=THREAD_COUNT) as executor:
    url = linksToCrawl.get()
    futures = []
    if url is not None:
      future = executor.submit(run, url)
      futures.append(future)

    for future in as_completed(futures):
      try:
        if future.result() != None:
          appendToCSV(future.result())
      except:
        print(future.exception())
```

# Exercise - capture more info from each page crawl

So, we've successfully managed to add a method for capturing the results of our site crawling to a CSV file, but right now, what we are capturing is pretty minimal. As an exercise, you should try to improve the amount of data we capture on every page crawl.

You could add things like the following:

- Total time to download
- Page size in KB
- Text to HTML ratio

These represent just a few prime characteristics that you could try to capture, but it's important to note that there are potentially hundreds of others.

 Note that the code for this crawler was used to create the following website analyzer: `https://github.com/elliotforbes/python-crawler`.

# concurrent.futures in Python 2.7

For those of you stuck in the land of Python 2.7 due to bureaucracy, having to support legacy codebase, lack of appropriate packages in Python 3.* for the tasks at hand, or whatever other reason, fear not! The `futures` module is still accessible through the use of pip.

```
pip install futures
```

The preceding command will give you, essentially, everything that the Python 3.2+ version of the `concurrent.futures` module has to offer without having to migrate your codebase.

# Summary

In this chapter, we successfully covered everything you need to get started with thread pools, process pools, and future objects. We looked at the various ways you could instantiate your own thread pools and process pools as well the advantages of using thread and process pool executors over the traditional methods.

You should now have a good appreciation of how we can improve the performance of our multi-threaded, multi-processed applications by utilizing this pooled-resource concept.

We also looked at how we could improve the existing implementation of our web crawler and refactor it so that it was easier to follow, and utilized some of the key concepts featured in this chapter. In the next chapter, we'll be looking at how we can utilize multiple processes within our applications, in depth.

# 8
# Multiprocessing

In this chapter, we will look at the wonders of multiprocessing in Python, and how it can answer the question of how to achieve truly parallel execution in Python.

We'll take a look at a number of topics such as the following:

- How multiprocessing allows us to eliminate the impact of the GIL
- The life of the processes in Python--how to spin up child processes, identify these processes, and ultimately kill them when we no longer need them
- How to utilize the multiprocessing pool API
- Communication and Synchronization between our multiple processes

By the end of this chapter, you will be quite comfortable writing your own programs that leverage the true parallel power of multiple processes.

 Thankfully, for those of you still stuck in the past, most of the concepts we are going to cover in this chapter are indeed available in Python 2.7. The multiprocessing module was introduced in version 2.6.

# Working around the GIL

The **global interpreter lock** (**GIL**) can be a truly performance-hindering mechanism at times for our CPU-bound tasks. Throughout this book, we've been looking at techniques, such as asynchronous programming, which could minimize the impact that this global interpreter lock has on our Python system's performance.

However, with the use of multiprocessing, we can effectively bypass this limitation altogether, through the utilization of multiple processes. By utilizing multiple processes, we utilize multiple instances of the GIL, and, as such, we aren't confined to only executing the bytecode of one thread within our programs at any one time.

Multiprocessing in Python allows us to express our programs in such a manner that we can fully utilize the processing power of our CPUs.

# Utilizing sub-processes

Within Python, we have the ability to spin up multiple processes that can be executed on separate cores within our CPU.

# Example

In this example, we'll create a child process which will simply execute some print statements. This represents the simplest way you can spin up child processes using the multiprocessing module, and it's probably the clunky way you could go about implementing multiprocessing in your Python applications:

```python
import multiprocessing

def myProcess():
    print("Currently Executing Child Process")
    print("This process has it's own instance of the GIL")
    print("Executing Main Process")
    print("Creating Child Process")

myProcess = multiprocessing.Process(target=myProcess)
myProcess.start()
myProcess.join()
print("Child Process has terminated, terminating main process")
```

# Output

Upon running this rather simple Python program, you should see that first the main process executes its print statement before going on to spin up and execute a child process:

```
$ python3.6 08_subprocess.py
Executing Main Process
Creating Child Process
Currently Executing Child Process
This process has it's own instance of the GIL
Child Process has terminated, terminating main process
```

# The life of a process

Within the multiprocessing module, we have three distinct methods of starting processes within our Python programs:

- Spawn
- Fork
- Forkserver

While you may never call upon this knowledge while you are crafting your multiprocess programs in Python, it's worthwhile to know how the underlying mechanisms work, and how they differ from one operating system to another.

 I'd recommend that you check out the official Python documentation which can be found here: `https://docs.python.org/3.6/library/multi processing.html#contexts-and-start-methods`.

# Starting a process using fork

Forking is the mechanism used on Unix systems in order to create child processes from the parent process. These child processes are almost identical to their parent process and similar to the real world: children inherit all of the resources available to the parent.

The fork command is a standard system command found in the Unix ecosystem.

# Spawning a process

By spawning a separate process, we spin up a second distinct Python interpreter process. This includes its own distinct global interpreter lock, and, as such, each process is able to execute things in parallel, as we are no longer constrained by the limitations of a simple global interpreter lock.

Each freshly spawned process inherits only the resources it requires in order to execute whatever is passed into its run method. This is the standard mechanism that Windows machines use when spinning up new processes, but it can also be used on Unix systems.

# Forkserver

Forkservers are a somewhat strange mechanism for creating distinct processes, and it's a mechanism that's only available on select Unix platforms that support passing file descriptors over Unix Pipes.

If a program selects this mechanism for starting processes, then what typically happens is that a server is instantiated. This server then handles all the requests for creating any processes, so when our Python program attempts to create a new process, it first sends a request to this newly instantiated server. This server then creates the process for us, and we are free to use it within our programs.

# Daemon processes

Daemon processes follow much the same pattern as the daemon threads that we encountered earlier on in this book. We are able to daemonize the running processes by setting their daemon flag to True.

These daemon processes will then continue to run as long as our main thread is executing, and will only terminate either when they have finished their execution, or when we kill our main program.

# Example

In the following example, we'll look at just how simple it is to define and start your own daemon processes in Python:

```python
import multiprocessing
import time

def daemonProcess():
    print("Starting my Daemon Process")
    print("Daemon process started:
{}".format(multiprocessing.current_process()))
    time.sleep(3)
    print("Daemon process terminating")
    print("Main process: {}".format(multiprocessing.current_process()))

myProcess = multiprocessing.Process(target=daemonProcess)
myProcess.daemon = True
myProcess.start()
print("We can carry on as per usual and our daemon will continue to
execute")
time.sleep(11)
```

# Breaking it down

In the preceding program, we first import the necessary multiprocessing and time modules. We then go on to define a function, which we'll set as the target of the daemon process that we are about to create.

Within this `daemonProcess` function, we first print out that we are starting our process, and then we go on to print out the current process. After this is done, we simply sleep for 3 seconds, and then print out that our daemon thread is terminating.

Below our `daemonProcess` function definition, we first print out the current process, and then instantiate our process and set the daemon flag of this process to true. Finally, we carry on with the work our main process has to do, and then our program terminates shortly after.

# Output

If we were to run this program, then you should see that it first outputs the main process from our `current_process()` call. We start our daemon process, and then call the same `current_process()` function from within that process.

Note the differences between our main process and our daemon process. You should notice that Process-1 states that it is started and displays that it is indeed a daemon process.

```
$ python3.6 00_daemonProcess.py
Main process: <_MainProcess(MainProcess, started)>
We can carry on as per usual and our daemon will continue to execute
starting my Daemon Process
Daemon process started: <Process(Process-1, started daemon)>
Daemon process terminating
```

It should be noted that you cannot create child processes from daemon processes; if you try this, it will fail on calling `process.start()`.

# Identifying processes using PIDs

All processes living within an operating system feature a process identifier, typically known as the PID. When working with multiple processes within our Python programs, you may expect our program to only have one process identifier, but this isn't the case.

Instead, each and every sub process that we spawn within the confines of our Python programs receive their own PID numbers to separately identify them within the operating system. Separate processes having their own assigned PIDs can be useful when it comes to performing tasks such as logging and debugging.

We can capture the process identifiers of any of our Python sub processes such as this:

```
Import multiprocessing
print(multiprocessing.current_process().pid)
```

The last code snippet will print out the current process identifier for that particular Python program when executed.

# Example

In this full-fledged example, we'll spin up a single child process, and pass in our `childTask` function as it's target for execution:

```
import multiprocessing
import time

def childTask():
```

```
   print("Child Process With PID:
{}".format(multiprocessing.current_process().pid))
   time.sleep(3)
   print("Child process terminating")

def main():
   print("Main process PID:
{}".format(multiprocessing.current_process().pid))
   myProcess = multiprocessing.Process(target=childTask)
   myProcess.start()
   myProcess.join()

if __name__ == '__main__':
   main()
```

# Output

This preceding program should output the PIDs of both the main process and the created child process, as follows:

```
$ python3.6 01_identifyProcess.py
Main process PID: 85365
Child Process With PID: 85367
Child process terminating
```

This is just to quickly bring you up to speed with getting the process identifier for the current process. However, it's important to note that you can attain things other than the PID from your current process.

Much like your `threading.Thread` class, you can do things such as name your individual processes. Say you have two processes working on a certain type of tasks, and two other working on another distinct type of task. When logging the output of these tasks, you don't want to see a string of "process-1 did $x$", "process-2 did $y$".

Instead, you can name your child processes to be more meaningful--this only helps you further down the line when it comes to the fateful day that you have to debug a production issue, and find out exactly what went wrong.

To name a process after it has been created you can do something like this:

```
import multiprocessing

def myProcess():
    print("{} Just performed
X".format(multiprocessing.current_process().name))
```

```
def main():
    childProcess = multiprocessing.Process(target=myProcess, name='My-
Awesome-Process')
    childProcess.start()
    childProcess.join()
if __name__ == '__main__':
    main()
```

This last code will output something like this:

```
$ python3.6 12_nameProcess.py
My-Awesome-Process Just performed X
```

Whenever it comes to writing production applications, do all you can to ensure traceability within your application. You will, more often than not, have to support the applications that you develop, so, ensure that you help your future self out by making logging as verbose as possible.

# Terminating a process

Being able to terminate child processes that we have spun up is important. Within smaller Python scripts that you run ad hoc on your local machine, the importance of cleaning up after yourself might not be that apparent. However, when it comes to larger enterprise Python programs that run on expensive servers indefinitely, this becomes very important.

With long running systems, we need to ensure that we aren't spinning up thousands upon thousands of idle processes, and leaving them to, essentially, hog the system resources. Therefore, being able to terminate these processes is considered quite important.

In order to terminate processes in Python, we can utilize the .terminate() function on our Process objects like this:

```
myProcess.terminate()
```

# Example

In this example, we are going to spin up a single child process, which will simulate executing something for 20 seconds. Upon startup of this process within our main function, we will immediately call the aforementioned terminate function in order to terminate this newly created process:

```
import multiprocessing
import time
```

```
def myProcess():
    current_process = multiprocessing.current_process()
    print("Child Process PID: {}".format(current_process.pid))
    time.sleep(20)
    current_process = multiprocessing.current_process()
    print("Main process PID: {}".format(current_process.pid))

myProcess = multiprocessing.Process(target=myProcess)
myProcess.start()
print("My Process has terminated, terminating main thread")
print("Terminating Child Process")
myProcess.terminate()
print("Child Process Successfully terminated")
```

Upon execution of this program, you should notice that it terminates before the child process is able to complete its full 20 seconds of blocking. This shows that we've been successful in the termination of our child thread.

# Getting the current process

Being able to identify individual processes can be important from a logging and debugging point of view, so, it's useful to know how you can retrieve the PID for all of the processes within your Python applications. We can retrieve this in much the same way we used to retrieve the current thread when we looked at multithreading.

We can use the following code in order to retrieve the current **process ID** (**PID**):

```
import multiprocessing
print(multiprocessing.current_process().pid)
```

This preceding code snippet will retrieve the current process identifier for the process that is currently executing.

# Subclassing processes

In Chapter 3, *Life of a Thread*, we looked at how we could create threads by subclassing the threading.Thread class. We can apply this same style to create processes.

# Example

In this example, we'll look at how we can implement our own classes that subclasses the `multiprocessing.Process` class. We'll define a class aptly called `MyProcess`, which will include two functions: constructor and "run".

Within the constructor, you'll notice that we make a call to super(`MyProcess`, `self`).`__init__`(). This call initializes our process for us, and turns our class from an ordinary Python object into a process.

In the run method, we'll simply print out the current process ID to show that we've successfully subclassed the `Process` class.

```python
import multiprocessing

class MyProcess(multiprocessing.Process):
    def __init__(self):
        super(MyProcess, self).__init__()
    def run(self):
        print("Child Process PID:
{}".format(multiprocessing.current_process().pid))

def main():
    print("Main Process PID:
{}".format(multiprocessing.current_process().pid))
    myProcess = MyProcess()
    myProcess.start()
    myProcess.join()

if __name__ == '__main__':
    main()
```

# Output

When we run the preceding program, we'll see that the main process first prints out its PID before it goes on to create and start a second child process. This child process should then print out its different PID.

```
$ python3.6 10_subclass.py
Main Process PID: 24484
Child Process PID: 24485
```

Once we've successfully subclassed our `multiprocessing.Process` class, we can start to do more interesting things such as spinning up multiple processes in quick succession, as follows:

```
import os
...
processes = []
for i in range(os.cpu_count()):
  process = MyProcess()
  processes.append(process)
  process.start()

for process in processes:
  process.join()
```

This would spin up *x* distinct child processes, where *x* is the number of CPU cores currently available on your machine.

# Multiprocessing pools

When working with multiple processes within our Python applications, we have the option to leverage the very versatile `Pool` class that lives within the multiprocessing module.

The Pool implementation allows us to succinctly spin up a number of child processes within our programs, and then delegate tasks for the workers in these pools to pick up.

# The difference between concurrent.futures.ProcessPoolExecutor and Pool

We covered `concurrent.futures.ProcessPoolExecutors` in Chapter 7, *Executors and Pools*, so, what is the need for another implementation of a process pool?

The `multiprocessing.Pool` implementation of process pools utilizes an almost identical implementation in order to provide parallel processing capabilities. However, the aim of the `concurrent.futures` module was to provide a simpler interface to work with when creating process pools. This simpler interface is easy for programmers to immediately start working with both Thread and process pools. However, with this abstraction from complexity, we lose out on some of the more fine-grained controls that we may need in specific scenarios.

Due to the fact that `ThreadPoolExecutor` and `ProcessPoolExecutor` are subclasses of the same abstract class, it's also far easier to work with them and memorize their inherited methods.

When it comes to availability in terms of both Python 2 and Python 3, the multiprocessing module trumps `concurrent.futures`, as it was introduced in version 2.6 of the language, and you aren't required to work with a backported version.

In general, I'd recommend the `concurrent.futures` module over the `multiprocess.Pool` module, as it will meet your requirements most, if not all, of the time. However, you do need to know the alternatives should that fateful day come around where you meet the limitations of `concurrent.futures` and require more control.

# Context manager

We can utilize multiprocessing pools using context managers in much the same way that we utilized `ThreadPoolExecutors`. We can again leverage the `with` keyword in this fashion:

```
with Pool(4) as myPool:
    # submit tasks to our pool
```

By doing it in this preceding fashion, we are able to simplify our codebase, as we no longer have to deal with actions such as releasing the resources acquired by our pool. We can then choose to do things such as map iterables to the child processes executing within this pool with relative ease.

# Example

This next example showcases a full-fledged example of us using the Pool in the context manager fashion. We define a simple task function, and within our main function, open up our context manager. Within this, we then map all the values in our `[2,3,4]` array to the task function, and print the results:

```
from multiprocessing import Pool

def task(n):
    print(n)

def main():
    with Pool(4) as p:
        print(p.map(task, [2,3,4]))
```

```
if __name__ == '__main__':
    main()
```

# Output

The previous Python program simply prints out the three values that we mapped to our process pool.

# Submitting tasks to a process pool

More often than not, what we do with Pools will be more complex than the example given in the last subsection, and we'll have to, somehow, interact with these pools in a number of distinct ways.

This is where the power of the `multiprocess.Pool` class comes to light. It features a far more fleshed-out API that we can play with.

In order to realize the full potential of your multiprocessed Python programs, you should learn these, and become as familiar as possible with the different methods for submitting tasks to your pool objects.

# Apply

Apply is to Pools as `.submit()` is to `ThreadPoolExecutors`. This is to say, they are just about the same in the sense that you use them to submit to individual tasks to our pools objects.

In this example, we are going to define a simple `myTask` function which will take in one parameter. This is the same `myTask` function that we'll use in all the subsequent examples for this section of the book.

We then go into our `main` function, which starts our `Pool` as a context manager, and simply prints out the result of each of these tasks:

```
from multiprocessing import Pool
import time

def myTask(n):
    time.sleep(n/2)
    return n*2

def main():
```

```
        with Pool(4) as p:
            print(p.apply(myTask, (4,)))
            print(p.apply(myTask, (3,)))
            print(p.apply(myTask, (2,)))
            print(p.apply(myTask, (1,)))

    if __name__ == '__main__':
        main()
```

It should be each noted that the `.apply()` function blocks until the result is ready, so, it's not exactly ideal for doing work in parallel. If you wanted to perform work in parallel, then you should really be using the `.apply()` sister function, `apply_async`.

# Apply_async

In situations where we need parallel execution of our tasks, this is the function we'll need to use in order to submit tasks to our pool.

In this example, we are going to use a for loop to submit four tasks to our processing pool as with our newly discovered `apply_async`. We keep track of these tasks by appending them to a tasks array, and then iterate over this task array to wait for the results:

```
from multiprocessing import Pool
import time
import os

def myTask(n):
    print("Task processed by Process {}".format(os.getpid()))
    return n*2

def main():
    print("apply_async")
    with Pool(4) as p:
        tasks = []

        for i in range(4):
            task = p.apply_async(func=myTask, args=(i,))
            tasks.append(task)

        for task in tasks:
            task.wait()
            print("Result: {}".format(task.get()))

if __name__ == '__main__':
    main()
```

Upon execution of this, you should see that our four tasks are picked up by our process pool, and executed by four distinct processes. Because we call `task.wait()` in the same order that they are submitted to the tasks array, we then get an ordered output of the results printing out to our console:

```
$ python3.6 21_applyAsync.py
apply_async
Task processed by Process 99323
Task processed by Process 99324
Task processed by Process 99322
Task processed by Process 99325
Result: 0
Result: 2
Result: 4
Result: 6
```

# Map

Much like its `ThreadPoolExecutor` equivalent, the `multiprocessing.Pool` map function allows us to map every element in an iterable to a task that can be picked up by a worker in our process pool.

In this small example, we look at mapping `list = [4,3,2,1]` to our process pool using the `said` map function:

```python
from multiprocessing import Pool
import time

def myTask(n):
    time.sleep(n/2)
    return n*2

def main():
    print("mapping array to pool")
    with Pool(4) as p:
        print(p.map(myTask, [4,3,2,1]))

if __name__ == '__main__':
    main()
```

This `map` function should then go on to print out the following on the console upon execution:

```
$ python3.6 17_mapPool.py
mapping array to pool
[8, 6, 4, 2]
```

However, like our `apply` function, each of these tasks blocks till the result is ready, so, in some cases, you may need to resort to `map_async` in order to achieve fully parallel asynchronous performance.

# Map_async

The `map_async` is the asynchronous offering for all your mapping needs. It works almost exactly like your standard map function with the exception that the jobs submitted through `said` function execute asynchronously:

```
from multiprocessing import Pool
import time

def myTask(n):
    time.sleep(n/2)
    return n*2

def main():
    with Pool(4) as p:
        print(p.map_async(myTask, [4,3,2,1]).get())

if __name__ == '__main__':
    main()
```

# Imap

The `imap()` function works in a somewhat similar fashion to your standard map function except for the fact that it returns an iterable. This can be very advantageous in certain situations, and I'm a big fan of using iterables, mainly, because Python features some very elegant ways to handle iterables.

In this example, we will call `iterable = p.imap()`, passing it in both `myTask` and `list` that we wish to map to our pool. Once this has finished, we then iterate over all of the results within this iterable using the `next()` method, and print this out to the console:

```
from multiprocessing import Pool
import time

def myTask(n):
 time.sleep(n+2)
 return n+2

def main():
 with Pool(4) as p:
```

```
        for iter in p.imap(myTask, [1,3,2,1]):
            print(iter)

if __name__ == '__main__':
    main()
```

Upon execution of this program, you should see every element of the array we've passed in being doubled and printed out on our console in the order that it was submitted to our pool in.

```
$ python3.6 17_mapPool.py
3
5
4
3
```

# Imap_unordered

The `imap_unordered` is aptly named as such, because when used, it returns an iterable map, and it executes the tasks submitted to it in an unordered fashion:

```
from multiprocessing import Pool
import time

def myTask(n):
  time.sleep(n+2)
  return n+2

def main():
  with Pool(4) as p:
    for iter in p.imap_unordered(myTask, [1,3,2,1]):
      print(iter)

if __name__ == '__main__':
  main()
```

Upon execution of this preceding program, you should see something like this:

```
$ python3.6 17_mapPool.py
3
3
4
5
```

We've been returned an iterable that contains transformed elements, which are not in the same order as they were inputted. `imap_unordered` has returned the elements in the order in which they completed.

## Starmap

The starmaps are awesome in the sense that they allow us to submit a list of tuples to a pool instead of your standard single variables. This, essentially, provides us slightly more flexibility, and can be very handy in certain situations.

In this example, we'll submit the list of tuples that each contain two distinct values-- `[(4,3),(2,1)]`-- to our pool, and print the returned results:

```python
from multiprocessing import Pool
import time

def myTask(x, y):
    time.sleep(x/2)
    return y*2

def main():
    with Pool(4) as p:
        print(p.starmap(myTask, [(4,3),(2,1)]))

if __name__ == '__main__':
    main()
```

Notice that we've updated the `myTask` function in order to take in the same number of arguments as we have values in each of our tuples. We then sleep for x/2 seconds, and then return y squared.

This produces the following output:

```
$ python3.6 18_starmap.py
[6, 2]
```

# Starmap_async

This is another asynchronous implementation which we can play with. It offers all of the same functionality as `starmap` except for the fact that it executes the given tasks asynchronously:

```
from multiprocessing import Pool
import time

def myTask(x, y):
    time.sleep(x)
    return y*2

def main():
    with Pool(4) as p:
        print(p.starmap_async(myTask, [(4,3),(2,1)]).get())

if __name__ == '__main__':
    main()
```

# Maxtasksperchild

Certain applications such as Apache and `mod_wdgi`, typically, have stopgaps in their code, which allow resources to be freed up for other things from time to time. This entails processes stopping after an *x* amount of work is done, and, effectively, being recycled.

For us to achieve this within our own pools, we can pass in the `maxtasksperchild` parameter, and set this to however many tasks we want our worker processes to execute before being recycled.

In the following example, we see exactly how this would work in real terms. We've taken the previous `starmap_async` example code, modified it slightly by adding the `maxtasksperchild` parameter to our pool, and submitted another task to this pool:

```
from multiprocessing import Pool
import time
import os

def myTask(x, y):
    print("{} Executed my task".format(os.getpid()))
    return y*2

def main():
    with Pool(processes=1, maxtasksperchild=2) as p:
        print(p.starmap_async(myTask, [(4,3),(2,1), (3,2), (5,1)]).get())
```

```
        print(p.starmap_async(myTask, [(4,3),(2,1), (3,2), (2,3)]).get())

if __name__ == '__main__':
    main()
```

Upon execution of the preceding program, you should see the following output:

```
$ python3.6 20_maxTasks.py
92099 Executed my task
92099 Executed my task
92100 Executed my task
92100 Executed my task
[6, 2, 4, 2]
92101 Executed my task
92101 Executed my task
92102 Executed my task
92102 Executed my task
[6, 2, 4, 6]
```

In the preceding output, you saw two things happen. The first `starmap_async` that we submitted to our Pool gets split up into four distinct tasks; these four tasks are then picked up by the one process that we currently have running in the pool.

The process then executes two of these tasks, and is then recycled. We can see this clearly as the PID of the process increments to the next available PID on the OS after the execution of every two tasks.

# Communication between processes

When it comes to synchronization between multiple sub processes, we have a number of different options that we can leverage:

- Queues: This is your standard FIFO queue, which was covered in Chapter 5, *Communication between Threads*.
- Pipes: These are a new concept, which we'll cover in more detail very shortly.
- Manager: These provide a way for us to create data, and subsequently, share this data between different processes within our Python applications.
- Ctypes: These are objects that utilize a shared memory which can subsequently be accessed by child processes.

The aforementioned four options represent quite a formidable number of different communication mechanisms that you can utilize within your multiprocess applications. It's definitely worth spending quite a bit of time engrossed within this topic in order to ensure you are making the correct choices when it comes to communication.

This book, unfortunately, does not have enough space to cover the near-infinite number of possible solutions that could be implemented using any of these options. I would suggest that if you are curious about venturing deeper into this topic, then you should pick up High Performance Python, by Ian Ozsvald; Micha Gorelick, as it has an excellent chapter that covers these concepts in greater detail.

# Pipes

Pipes represent a way we can pass information from one process to another. We have two distinct types of pipes: anonymous pipes and named pipes. Pipes are a very typical mechanism employed within operating systems in order to pass information between their own separate processes, so, it makes sense that we employ them to do the same tasks for us in our own multiprocess programs.

## Anonymous pipes

Anonymous pipes are a simplex FIFO communication method used within operating systems for inter-process communication. Simplex, if you've never heard of the term before, means that only one direction transmits at one time. The best way to imagine this is if you had two radios; in order for these radios to work, only one person can be holding down the button and talking at one time. The other person has to listen and wait for the "Over" signal before they can start sending their own messages.

In order to achieve duplex communication, in other words, two-way communication, we have to use two anonymous pipes through which our processes communicate. These anonymous pipes are supported by most major operating system implementations, and are a great way for processes to communicate while maintaining high performance.

## Named pipes

Named pipes are almost identical to anonymous pipes except that named pipes, typically, last as long as the underlying operating system is up. Anonymous pipes only last as long as the process lasts.

# Working with pipes

Now that we have some idea of what pipes are and how they operate within our operating system, it's time to look at how we can utilize them within our Python programs.

To create a pipe in our Python programs, we need to import the os module, and then call os.pipe(). This os.pipe() method creates a pipe within our operating system, and returns a tuple which is used for reading and writing respectively. In the following example, we'll use pipeout for reading and pipein for writing:

```
import os
pipeout, pipein = os.pipe()
```

# Example

In this example, we'll create a child process, which, again, subclasses the multiprocessing.Process class:

```
import os, sys
import multiprocessing

class ChildProcess(multiprocessing.Process):

def __init__(self, pipein):
  super(ChildProcess, self).__init__()
  self.pipein = pipein

def run(self):
  print("Attempting to pipein to pipe")
  self.pipein = os.fdopen(self.pipein, 'w')
  self.pipein.write("My Name is Elliot")
  self.pipein.close()

def main():
pipeout, pipein = os.pipe()

child = ChildProcess(pipein)
child.start()
child.join()

os.close(pipein)
pipeout = os.fdopen(pipeout)

pipeContent = pipeout.read()
print("Pipe: {}".format(pipeContent))
```

```
if __name__ == '__main__':
    main()
```

Upon execution of the preceding program, we get the following output:

```
$ python3.6 11_pipes.py
Attempting to pipein to pipe
Pipe: My Name is Elliot
```

# Handling Exceptions

Being able to handle exceptions thrown in your child processes is incredibly important if you want your application to succeed. Allowing exceptions to fizzle out into the ether, and bring down child processes with no means of recovery is the worst thing you application can do.

Silently handling exceptions is one of the biggest sins of developers, and while it might be tempting to quickly silence a thrown exception, it will infuriate other developers troubleshooting issues further down the line.

When it comes to handling these exceptions, we have a number of distinct options. We can use the already covered method of communicating between child processes and parent processes in order to pass raised exceptions back to our parent process to be handled in whichever way it chooses. However, there is an alternative option to this, and that is to utilize pipes to transport these exceptions between processes.

# Using pipes

When it comes to using pipes within your Python code, we have two options, the first of which is to use the os module in order to create your pipes, and the second is to leverage multiprocessing.Pipe().

The difference between the two is that the multiprocessing.Pipe implementation is, typically, far more high level than the os.pipe implementation. A key thing to note is that you can only perform bidirectional communication using the multiprocessing.Pipe implementation, as os.pipe is unidirectional.

In this example, we look at how we can pass information from thrown exceptions from child processes back up to parent processes:

```python
import multiprocessing
import os, sys
import traceback

class MyProcess(multiprocessing.Process):
  def __init__(self, pipein):
    super(MyProcess, self).__init__()
    self.pipein = pipein

  def run(self):
    try:
      raise Exception("This broke stuff")
    except:
      except_type, except_class, tb = sys.exc_info()

      self.pipein = os.fdopen(self.pipein, 'w')
      self.pipein.write(str(except_type))
      self.pipein.close()

def main():
  pipeout, pipein = os.pipe()

  childProcess = MyProcess(pipein)
  childProcess.start()
  childProcess.join()

  os.close(pipein)
  pipeout = os.fdopen(pipeout)

  pipeContent = pipeout.read()
  print("Exception: {}".format(pipeContent))

if __name__ == '__main__':
  main()
```

# Multiprocessing managers

Within the `multiprocessing` module, we have the `Manager` class; this class can be utilized as a means of controlling Python objects, and providing thread and process safety within your Python applications.

We can initialize a new Manager like this:

```
Import multiprocessing
myManager = multiprocessing.Manager()
```

With this `manager` object, we can then start to share things such as lists and dicts across multiple processes, and typically, it's the first port of call you'd go to if you needed to implement your own form of communication.

# Namespaces

Managers come with this concept of namespaces; these namespaces feature no public methods that we can call, but they are useful in the sense that they have writable attributes.

In situations where you need a quick and dirty method for sharing several attributes across multiple processes, this is the prime candidate for doing so.

# Example

In this example, we look at how to utilize namespaces in order to share some data across both a main process and a child process:

```
import multiprocessing as mp
import queue

def myProcess(ns):
    # Update values within our namespace
    print(ns.x)
    ns.x = 2

def main():
    manager = mp.Manager()
    ns = manager.Namespace()ns.x = 1

    print(ns)
    process = mp.Process(target=myProcess, args=(ns,))
    process.start()
    process.join()
    print(ns)

if __name__ == '__main__':
    main()
```

If we then go ahead, and execute the preceding program, we should see three things happen. First, we print out the Namespace object as it stands at the start of our program's execution. This should state that x=1. We then print this out from our sub process before modifying it to a new value of 2.

We then proceed to print out the namespace again from our parent process, and this time, you should see that the x value within it has been incremented to 2:

```
$ python3.6 07_manager.py
Namespace(x=1)
1
Namespace(x=2)
```

# Queues

We've explored the queue synchronization primitive in Chapter 5, *Communication between Threads*, and while we focused primarily on how they can be used in multithreaded scenarios, it's important to note that they can also be used in conjunction with multiprocess programs.

# Example

In this verbose example, we'll explore exactly how we can implement a communication mechanism between distinct child processes using the queue synchronization primitive.

We define the myTask function, which takes in our shared queue as a parameter, and simply pops a value from the queue. Within our main function, we then define both our manager object and our shared queue using this:

```
m = multiprocessing.Manager()
sharedQueue = m.Queue()
```

We then define three separate processes that take in the myTask function as their target for execution, and the sharedQueue as their one and only argument. We then start and join each of these processes in turn:

```
from multiprocessing import Pool
import multiprocessing
import queue
import time

def myTask(queue):
    value = queue.get()
```

```
        print("Process {} Popped {} from the shared
Queue".format(multiprocessing.current_process().pid, value))
        queue.task_done()

def main():
    m = multiprocessing.Manager()
    sharedQueue = m.Queue()
    sharedQueue.put(2)
    sharedQueue.put(3)
    sharedQueue.put(4)

    process1 = multiprocessing.Process(target=myTask, args=(sharedQueue,))
    process1.start()
    process1.join()

    process2 = multiprocessing.Process(target=myTask, args=(sharedQueue,))
    process2.start()
    process2.join()

    process3 = multiprocessing.Process(target=myTask, args=(sharedQueue,))
    process3.start()
    process3.join()

if __name__ == '__main__':
    main()
```

## Output

Upon execution of this program, you should see that our three distinct processes with their three distinct PIDs pop 2, 3, and 4 respectively from this shared queue object.

```
$ python3.6 06_mpQueue.py
Process 89152 Popped 2 from the shared Queue
Process 89153 Popped 3 from the shared Queue
Process 89154 Popped 4 from the shared Queue
```

## Listeners and clients

While the majority of communication between distinct processes and sub processes might be done using your standard queue primitive or using a pipe, there does, however, lie another mechanism which we can employ. The alternative is to leverage the `multiprocessing.connection` module.

The `multiprocess.connection` module is, essentially, a high-level message-oriented API for dealing with sockets or Windows named pipes.

# Example

The official documentation for the `multiprocess.connection` module has some exemplary examples of showcasing the way that both a client and listener can interact with one another, and send messages.

In this example, we'll explore this example code in greater detail to gain a basic understanding of communication using both a listener and a client.

# The Listener class

First and foremost, we'll need to define a listener, as this will need to be started first on our system. We import the `Listener` class from the `multiprocessing.connection` module, and then define an address tuple which takes in `'localhost'` and 6000, which will be our port.

We then use `Listener` as a context manager, and wait to accept a connection on this port. Note that we set `authkey=b'secret password'`--this is to ensure that we don't receive information from rogue processes, but only from separate processes that connect to this address and port with the correct `authkey`:

```
from multiprocessing.connection import Listener
 from array import array

address = ('localhost', 6000)      # family is deduced to be 'AF_INET'

with Listener(address, authkey=b'secret password') as listener:
    with listener.accept() as conn:
        print('connection accepted from', listener.last_accepted)

        conn.send([2.25, None, 'junk', float])

        conn.send_bytes(b'hello')

        conn.send_bytes(array('i', [42, 1729]))
```

# The Client class

The next thing we need to define is `Client`, which will do the job of first connecting to our listener, and then print whatever we send from our `Listener` process.

We first have to import the `Client` class from our `multiprocess.connection` module. We then again utilize the `Client` class as a context manager passing in the address we wish to connect to as well as `authkey` that we've already defined on our `Listener` class.

Upon successful connection, we then print everything we receive from our `Listener` class. We do this in a variety of ways to showcase the flexibility of the `connection` module:

```
from multiprocessing.connection import Client
 from array import array

address = ('localhost', 6000)

with Client(address, authkey=b'secret password') as conn:
    print(conn.recv())                  # => [2.25, None, 'junk', float]

    print(conn.recv_bytes())            # => 'hello'

    arr = array('i', [0, 0, 0, 0, 0])
    print(conn.recv_bytes_into(arr))    # => 8
    print(arr)                          # => array('i', [42, 1729, 0, 0,
0])
```

# Output

Upon execution of our listener script, you will see that our listener waits indefinitely until one connection has been made; at the point at which the connection has been made, it prints that it has accepted the connection, and the IP and port from which it accepted this connection:

```
$ python3.6 23_listener.py
connection accepted from ('127.0.0.1', 56197)
```

Once we've started our listener program, we can then kick off our client program. This successfully connects to our running listener, and then prints out the array of different messages that we send to it:

```
$ python3.6 22_client.py
[2.25, None, 'junk', <class 'float'>]
b'hello'
8
array('i', [42, 1729, 0, 0, 0])
```

This should, hopefully, give you some indication of the power of the `multiprocessing.communication` module, and how you can use it to efficiently pass information between multiple processes running on the same hardware.

# Logging

I believe that as we venture deeper into the world of high performance computing with Python, we need to take a step back and re-evaluate how we've implemented logging within our multithreaded/multiprocess Python applications.

For the majority of the samples in this book, a simple print, typically, suffices when it comes to logging exactly what is going on within our programs. However, as we start to face more and more complex challenges, we need to be aware of the better solutions out there when it comes to logging our applications' output.

Having a well-crafted logging system within your application can be an exceptionally good way to understand the behavior of your application over longer periods of time.

 An exceptional resource I would recommend you check out is the official Python logging-cookbook which can be found at `https://docs.python.org/3/howto/logging-cookbook.html`.

# Example

Thankfully, logging is a default module within Python, and we can easily import this into our Python programs like this:

```
Import logging
```

Once we've done this, we configure our logging system to log more meaningful log messages to a file within our programs directory, as follows:

```
logging.basicConfig(filename='myapp.log', level=logging.INFO,
    format='%(processName)-10s %(asctime)%s:%(levelname)s:%(message)s')
```

In the preceding line, we specify the filename that we want to `log`, and the logging level to `INFO`. We then specify the format that we want each and every logging message to follow when it's appended to our `log` file.

Notice that the first thing we add to our format string is `%(processName)-10s`. This ensures that we have traceability over each and every sub process within our application.

```
import logging
from multiprocessing import Pool

logging.basicConfig(filename='myapp.log', level=logging.INFO,
format='%(processName)-10s %(asctime)%s:%(levelname)s:%(message)s')

def myTask(n):
    logging.info("{} being processed".format(n))
    logging.info("Final Result: {}".format(n*2))
    return n*2

def main():
    with Pool(4) as p:
        p.map(myTask, [2,3,4,5,6,])

if __name__ == '__main__':
    main()
```

Upon execution of the preceding code, you should see the following being input into the `myapp.logs` file.

Every line features the name of the process that has taken on each task as well as the level name and the log information being given as output:

```
ForkPoolWorker-1 %s:INFO:2 being processed
ForkPoolWorker-1 %s:INFO:Final Result: 4
ForkPoolWorker-2 %s:INFO:3 being processed
ForkPoolWorker-2 %s:INFO:Final Result: 6
ForkPoolWorker-3 %s:INFO:4 being processed
ForkPoolWorker-3 %s:INFO:Final Result: 8
ForkPoolWorker-4 %s:INFO:5 being processed
ForkPoolWorker-4 %s:INFO:Final Result: 10
ForkPoolWorker-1 %s:INFO:6 being processed
ForkPoolWorker-1 %s:INFO:Final Result: 12
```

# Communicating sequential processes

Communicating Sequential Processes, or CSP for short, is used to describe how systems that feature multiple concurrent models should interact with one another. It, typically, relies heavily on using channels as a medium for passing messages between two or more concurrent processes, and is the underlying mantra of languages like clojure and golang.

It's a concept that is certainly growing in popularity, and there are a number of fantastic talks and books on CSP that you should definitely check out.

 I'd recommend checking out Communicating Sequential Processes by C.A.R. Hoare, which was published in May of 2015, the link for which is this: http://www.usingcsp.com/cspbook.pdf.

After some brief research on the topic, it's fascinating to see how certain problem sets can be abstracted out quite easily using this style of programming as opposed to your more traditional object-oriented setups.

# PyCSP

PyCSP is a Python library that implements the core primitives found in Communicating Sequential Processes. It was originally started way back in 2006, and it's stabilized to the point where releases are becoming more infrequent. The library offers a transparent distributed communication model while relying only on standard Python Modules.

Overall, it's quite an interesting concept that sheds a new light on how you can implement your own multiprocess-based Python applications using Python's in-built decorators.

In order to install PyCSP, you'll have to use `pip` as follows:

```
python3.6 -m pip install pycsp
```

# Processes in PyCSP

The following is a very simple example of just how we can construct concurrent Python applications using the PyCSP module. As you can see, we define two distinct functions, `Process1` and `Process2`. We then decorate these functions with the `@process` annotation, and this handles turning the entirety of this method into a process for us. We then tell our PyCSP-based program to run both process 1 and process 2 in parallel to each other:

```
from pycsp.parallel import *
import time

@process
def Process1():
  time.sleep(1) # Sleep 1 second
  print('process1 exiting')

@process
def Process2():
  time.sleep(2) # Sleep 2 seconds
  print('process2 exiting')

Parallel(Process1(), Process2()) # Blocks
print('program terminating')
```

# Output

Upon execution of this preceding program, you should see that both process 1 and process 2 successfully output their print statements before the program informs us that it's terminating:

```
process1 exiting
 process2 exiting
 program exiting
```

Overall, the concept of CSP is an interesting one, and I thought it was a worthy addition to the end of this chapter even if it was just food for thought.

# Summary

In this chapter, we looked comprehensively at multiprocessing, and how it can be utilized within our systems. We followed the life of a process from its creation all the way through to its timely termination.

We looked at the various intricacies such as cross-process communication and synchronization, and we also looked at how your standard multiprocessing pools differ from the standard `ProcessPoolExecutors` that we explored in `Chapter 7`, *Executors and Pools*.

We then took a brief look at how we can implement things such as communication and synchronization between our various processes without incurring major performance penalties, or becoming the proud owners of systems plagued by race conditions.

In the next chapter, Event-driven programming, we'll be diving deep into the `asyncio` module, and understand how we can leverage this module in order to develop our own event-based Python programs.

# 9
# Event-Driven Programming

In this chapter, I'm going to introduce you to the wonderful art of event-driven programming. Event-driven programming is a paradigm that focuses on events. While this may be somewhat obvious, what isn't all that obvious is the definition of an "event" in the programming sense and what entirely this encapsulates.

We'll first look at what event-driven programming is in a general sense, and then, we'll introduce the `asyncio` module, which is predominately used for all types of event-driven Python applications.

This chapter also looks to give you an introduction to the world of asyncio programming. This could, in theory, have it's own book written about it. I'll attempt to demystify some of the more critical sections and provide some small examples of how you can utilize them within your own programs.

All in all, we'll be covering the following topics in this chapter:

- Event-driven programming--what is it and how does it work?
- The `asyncio` module in depth
- Debugging asyncio-based programs
- The Twisted event-driven networking engine
- Gevent

This should be enough to get you up and running to create your own event-driven systems in Python.

# Event-driven programming

Event-driven programs are very different from the Python applications that we have got so used to writing within the confines of the previous chapters of this book. Typically, each of these prior programs follows a set flow, and while some sections of a program may be nondeterministic in terms of execue main memory, and independentram very much follows a deterministic approach:

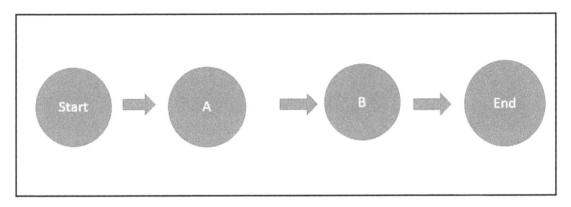

With event-driven programs, we typically have an event loop that constantly listens for incoming events. Once this event loop is started, it's entirely down to the events inputted into the system that determine what is then executed and what order they have to be executed in. An example of this would be an event-driven program that listens to keyboard input: we have no way of determining what key will be pressed next, but we will have a certain function mapped to the said key when our program receives this `key-press` event.

In the following diagram, you'll see an example of the flow that an event-driven program typically follows. We see it start up and then enter a **Wait** state. This wait state goes on indefinitely until the program is shut down through either the triggering of a specific event or a system crash.

During this **Wait** state, we are constantly listening for events and then passing them off to event handlers. Now, while this diagram only shows one particular event mapped to one handler, it should be noted that in some event-driven programs, the number of events and handlers could be theoretically infinite:

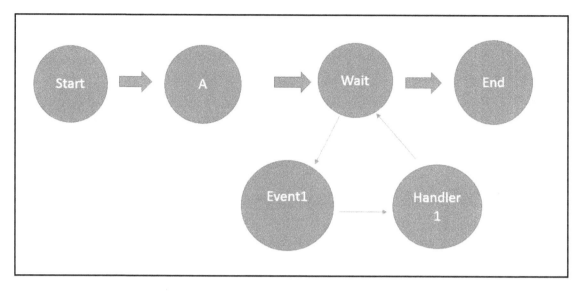

Source: https://mywebgranth.wordpress.com

This makes it somewhat ideal for systems such as OS. If we had to write an OS in a procedural manner, then you would typically see an incredibly hard to follow code base that resembles an Italian specialty in the form of spaghetti code as opposed to a well-designed system.

By leveraging an event-driven paradigm for our systems, we greatly simplify our overall program's structure and make it easier to increase its functionality or debug any issues in the future.

# The event loop

The main component of any event-driven Python program has to be the underlying event loop. Let's take the `asyncio` event loop as an example. Within this event loop, we can (from the official documentation):

- Register, execute, and cancel calls
- Launch sub-processes and the associated transports for communication with an external program
- Delegate costly function calls to a pool of threads

Essentially, all an event loop does is wait for events to happen before matching each event to a function that we have explicitly matched with the said type of event.

A good example of this would be a simple web server. Let's say we have an endpoint on our server that serves our website, which features a multitude of different pages. Our event loop essentially listens for requests to be made and then matches each of these requests to its associated webpage.

Each of the requests made to our web server in the preceding example would be considered a separate event. These events are then matched to a set function that we predefine whenever a said event is triggered.

# Asyncio

Asyncio was introduced to the Python programming language in version 3.4 and added some excellent functionality and it has been an overall hit with the Python community.

Asyncio is a module that allows us to easily write single-threaded, concurrent programs utilizing coroutines, which we'll cover later on in this chapter. It also does a lot of other clever stuff such as multiplexing I/O access over sockets as well as other resources, and provides us with an array of synchronization primitives that allow us to write thread-safe programs with relative ease.

Within the module, we have a number of distinct concepts as follows:

- The event loop
- Futures
- Coroutines
- Tasks
- Transports
- Protocols

Each of these concepts serve their own distinct purpose that can be intertwined to create readable, highly-performant Python programs. We'll look at each of these concepts in more depth throughout the rest of this chapter.

The `asyncio` module features a wealth of different tools and classes for writing programs in an event-driven manner, and I highly recommend that you check out the official documentation at `https://docs.python.org/3/library/asyncio.html`.

# Getting started

In this example, we'll utilize the `get_event_loop()` method, which returns an asyncio event loop. We'll then run this loop using the `run_until_complete()` method, which will take in a very simple coroutine.

We'll be covering coroutines in greater detail later on in this chapter, but for now, it's important to know that these coroutines are essentially functions designed for concurrent execution within asyncio:

```python
import asyncio
async def myCoroutine():
    print("Simple Event Loop Example")

def main():
    loop = asyncio.get_event_loop()
    loop.run_until_complete(myCoroutine())
    loop.close()

if __name__ == '__main__':
    main()
```

Upon execution of the preceding Python program, you should see the `Simple Event Loop Example` output on the console. This is a relatively simple program, but it features its own event loop with which we can now build up our understanding of event-driven programs.

# Event loops

Now that we've created our very own simple event loop based program, it's time to explore some of the possible methods associated with these event loops so that we understand how to effectively interact with them.

# The run_forever() method

The `run_forever()` method does exactly what it says on the tin. This method starts your event loop and blocks forever.

In this next example, we will create a never-ending event loop that constantly runs two distinct coroutines:

```python
import asyncio

@asyncio.coroutine
def hello_world():
    yield from asyncio.sleep(1)
    print('Hello World')
    asyncio.async(hello_world())

@asyncio.coroutine
def good_evening():
    yield from asyncio.sleep(1)
    print('Good Evening')
    asyncio.async(good_evening())

print('step: asyncio.get_event_loop()')
loop = asyncio.get_event_loop()
try:
    print('step: loop.run_until_complete()')
    asyncio.async(hello_world())
    asyncio.async(good_evening())
    loop.run_forever()
except KeyboardInterrupt:
    pass
finally:
    print('step: loop.close()')
    loop.close()
```

# The run_until_complete() method

The `run_until_complete` method is one that we've used previously in this chapter, and it allows us to give our event loop a specific amount of work before terminating itself:

```python
import asyncio
import time

async def myWork():
print("Starting Work")
time.sleep(5)
print("Ending Work")

def main():
loop = asyncio.get_event_loop()
loop.run_until_complete(myWork())
loop.close()
```

```
if __name__ == '__main__':
main()
```

The preceding code will start an event loop and then execute the myWork() async function before closing upon completion of the said function.

# The stop() method

The stop() method again does exactly what it says on the tin. It will cause a loop that's currently running indefinitely through the run_forever() method to stop at the next suitable opportunity:

```
import asyncio
import time

async def myWork():
print("Starting Work")
time.sleep(5)
print("Ending Work")

def main():
loop = asyncio.get_event_loop()
loop.run_until_complete(myWork())
loop.stop()
print("Loop Stopped")
loop.close()

if __name__ == '__main__':
main()
```

# The is_closed() method

The is_closed() method simply returns True if our event loop happens to have been closed by calling the close() method:

```
print(loop.is_closed()) # prints True or False
```

## The close() function

The `close()` function closes our non-running event loop and clears out any pending callbacks. It does not wait for the executor to finish and brings our event loop to quite a brutal end. I'd be careful using this in certain situations where a graceful shutdown is necessary, as this could lead to complications with non-terminated connections to resources such as databases and brokers:

```
loop.close()
```

# Tasks

Tasks within asyncio are responsible for the execution of coroutines within an event loop. These tasks can only run in one event loop at one time, and in order to achieve parallel execution, you would have to run multiple event loops over multiple threads.

I like to think of tasks within asyncio in a similar regard to how we'd think of tasks when used in conjunction with executors or pools, like we've demonstrated in the previous chapters.

In this section, we'll look at some of the key functions that we can use in order to work with tasks within our asyncio-based programs.

# Example

In this example, we'll look at how we can define a generator function that will generate five distinct coroutines for our event loop to schedule and execute. In order to schedule these coroutines, we'll use the `ensure_future()` method, which you'll learn about in more detail further on in the chapter:

```python
import asyncio
import time

@asyncio.coroutine
def myTask(n):
 time.sleep(1)
 print("Processing {}".format(n))

@asyncio.coroutine
def myGenerator():
 for i in range(5):
     asyncio.ensure_future(myTask(i))
 print("Completed Tasks")
```

```
    yield from asyncio.sleep(2)

def main():
 loop = asyncio.get_event_loop()
 loop.run_until_complete(myGenerator())
 loop.close()

if __name__ == '__main__':
 main()
```

Upon execution of the preceding program, you should see that the five tasks are successfully generated, scheduled, and executed, and each of them prints out their current status in the console:

```
$ python3.6 04_generator.py
Completed Tasks
Processing 0
Processing 1
Processing 2
Processing 3
Processing 4
```

# The all_tasks(loop=None) method

The `all_tasks` method returns a set of tasks for a given event loop. If no event loop is passed in, then it defaults to showing only all of the tasks for the current event loop:

```
import asyncio

async def myCoroutine():
print("My Coroutine")

async def main():
await asyncio.sleep(1)

loop = asyncio.get_event_loop()
try:
loop.create_task(myCoroutine())
loop.create_task(myCoroutine())
loop.create_task(myCoroutine())

pending = asyncio.Task.all_tasks()
print(pending)
 loop.run_until_complete(main())
finally:
loop.close()
```

Upon execution of the preceding program, you should see a set of three coroutines printed out to the console. These are denoted as pending as they haven't yet been scheduled to run on our current event loop:

```
$ python3.6 16_asyncioTasks.py
{<Task pending coro=<myCoroutine() running at 16_asyncioTasks.py:3>>, <Task
pending coro=<myCoroutine() running at 16_asyncioTasks.py:3>>, <Task
pending coro=<myCoroutine() running at 16_asyncioTasks.py:3>>}
My Coroutine
My Coroutine
My Coroutine
```

# The current_tasks() function

Gauging what current tasks are executing can be useful in a number of situations. If needed, you could effectively iterate through the list of current tasks executing on the event loop and attempt to cancel them if you wish.

In this example, we will schedule three distinct tasks using the `create_task` function and pass in our `myCoroutine` function as its input:

```
import asyncio
async def myCoroutine():
print("My Coroutine")

async def main():
current = asyncio.Task.current_task()
print(current)

loop = asyncio.get_event_loop()
try:
loop.create_task(myCoroutine())
loop.create_task(myCoroutine())
loop.create_task(myCoroutine())
loop.run_until_complete(main())
finally:
loop.close()
```

Upon execution, you should see that the coroutines are all successfully executed, and by the time our main coroutine is executed, the only coroutine pending is the one currently executing:

```
$ python3.6 16_asyncioTasks.py
My Coroutine
My Coroutine
My Coroutine
```

```
<Task pending coro=<main() running at 16_asyncioTasks.py:8>
cb=[_run_until_complete_cb() at
/Library/Frameworks/Python.framework/Versions/3.6/lib/python3.6/asyncio/bas
e_events.py:176]>
```

# The cancel() function

The `cancel` function allows us to request the cancellation of futures or coroutines:

```
import asyncio

async def myCoroutine():
print("My Coroutine")

async def main():
current = asyncio.Task.current_task()
print(current)

loop = asyncio.get_event_loop()
try:
task1 = loop.create_task(myCoroutine())
task2 = loop.create_task(myCoroutine())
task3 = loop.create_task(myCoroutine())
task3.cancel()
loop.run_until_complete(main())
finally:
loop.close()
```

Upon execution of the preceding program, you should see that both `task1` and `task2` are successfully executed. The third task that we scheduled, due to the cancel call we made, is never actually executed.

Now, this is just a simple example of how we can cancel a task, and we did it in such a way that we pretty much guarantee our third task is cancelled. However, out in the wild, there is no guarantee that the `cancel` function will definitely cancel your pending task:

```
$ python3.6 16_asyncioTasks.py
My Coroutine
My Coroutine
<Task pending coro=<main() running at 16_asyncioTasks.py:8>
cb=[_run_until_complete_cb() at
/Library/Frameworks/Python.framework/Versions/3.6/lib/python3.6/asyncio/bas
e_events.py:176]>
```

# Task functions

In the previous section, we looked at the functions that can be used with individual task objects, but how can we work with a collection of different tasks? Well, the asyncio module provides a series of task functions that allow us to work with and manipulate multiple tasks at the same time with relative ease.

## The as_completed(fs, *, loop=None, timeout=None) function

The `as_completed` function allows us to work with the results returned from all of our executed tasks as and when they are returned. These results could then be fed into a series of other coroutines for further processing or just simply logged somewhere depending on what your needs are.

We can use the `as_completed()` function as follows and iterate over the completed futures as and when they are returned:

```
for f in as_completed(fs):
    result = yield from f
    # Use result
```

## The ensure_future(coro_or_future, *, loop=None) function

The `ensure_future` function will schedule the execution of a `coroutine` object--wrap it in a future and then return a `task` object:

```
import asyncio
...
async def myCoro():
 print("myCoro")
...
task = asyncio.ensure_future(myCoro())
...
```

## The wrap_future(future, *, loop=None) function

This function acts as a simple adapter for converting `concurrent.futures.Future` objects into `asyncio.Future` objects.

You could then convert the created `concurrent.futures.Future` objects as follows:

```
with ThreadPoolExecutor(max_workers=4) as executor:
    future = executor.submit(task, (4))
    myWrappedFuture = asyncio.wrap_future(future)
```

# The gather(*coroes_or_futures, loop=None, return_exceptions=False) function

The `gather` function is a somewhat complicated beast. It takes in a set of coroutines or futures and then returns a `future` object that aggregates the results from the inputted set:

```
import asyncio

async def myCoroutine(i):
print("My Coroutine {}".format(i))

loop = asyncio.get_event_loop()
try:
loop.run_until_complete(asyncio.gather(myCoroutine(1), myCoroutine(2)))
finally:
loop.close()
```

Upon execution of this code, you should see that both of the coroutines that we passed into our `asyncio.gather` function were successfully completed before the termination of our program's event loop:

```
$ python3.6 16_asyncioTasks.py
My Coroutine 1
My Coroutine 2
```

# The wait() function

The `wait` function simply blocks our program until all of the futures or coroutines passed into the first parameter of this function have successfully completed:

```
import asyncio

async def myCoroutine(i):
print("My Coroutine {}".format(i))

loop = asyncio.get_event_loop()
try:
tasks = []
for i in range(4):
```

```
    tasks.append(myCoroutine(i))
loop.run_until_complete(asyncio.wait(tasks))
finally:
loop.close()
```

Upon execution of this program, you should see that we've successfully created our four coroutines, and they've all been successfully completed before our program terminated:

```
$ python3.6 16_asyncioTasks.py
My Coroutine 0
My Coroutine 1
My Coroutine 2
My Coroutine 3
```

# Futures

We've already been exposed to one kind of future object when we were looking in depth at executors and pools in Chapter 7, *Executors and Pools*. The asyncio module, however, provides a slightly different implementation with which we can play in our Python programs.

The asyncio.futures.Future object implementation of futures is almost identical to the concurrent.futures.Future object in terms of the underlying concepts. They are created with the intention that they will eventually be given a result some time in the future. They also feature all of the same methods that your standard future objects have.

There are, however, three distinct changes that have been outlined in the official documentation, which can be found at https://docs.python.org/3/library/asyncio-eventloop.html#futures. These changes are worth noting to avoid frustration in the future:

- The result () and exception() function do not take a timeout parameter and raise an exception when the future isn't done yet
- Callbacks registered with the add_done_callback() format are always called through the call_soon_threadsafe() event loops
- The future class is not compatible with the wait and as_completed functions in the concurrent.futures package

# Example

In this next example, we will look at how we can wrap a coroutine that we defined as `myCoroutine` in a `future` object and then handle it as such within a main coroutine that we'll define.

In this example, it's important to note the use of `await` before our call to `asyncio.ensure_future`. The `ensure_future()` method is the method that both schedules our coroutine for execution while also wrapping it in a future, so we have to ensure that this is completed before we try to access `result()`:

```
import asyncio

async def myCoroutine(future):
await asyncio.sleep(1)
future.set_result("My Future Has Completed")

async def main():
future = asyncio.Future()
await asyncio.ensure_future(myFuture(future))
print(future.result())

loop = asyncio.get_event_loop()
try:
loop.run_until_complete(main())
finally:
loop.close()
```

# Output

Upon execution of the preceding program, you should see that our coroutine has successfully been *converted* into a future object, and we can access it with the same `.result()` method that we'd typically expect to use:

```
$ python3.6 12_future.py
My Future Has Completed
```

# Coroutines

Coroutines in asyncio are similar to the standard `Thread` object that you'd find within the threading module. By utilizing coroutines within our asyncio-based application, we are essentially enabling ourselves to write asynchronous programs with the main exception that they run in a single-threaded context.

They are quite possibly the most important part of the asyncio module as they are typically where the magic happens within your event-based programs. If you look at any major asyncio-based program, you should notice a heavy utilization of these coroutine objects.

There are a couple of different ways we can implement our own coroutines, the first of which is to implement an *async def* function, which is a feature added to Python 3.5 and is definitely the method I recommend the most. If we were to implement a coroutine using this method, it would look something like this:

```python
import asyncio

async def myCoroutine():
    print("My Coroutine")

def main():
    loop = asyncio.get_event_loop()
    loop.run_until_complete(myCoroutine())
    loop.close()

if __name__ == '__main__':
    main()
```

The second method is to utilize generators in conjunction with the `@asyncio.coroutine` decorator:

```python
import asyncio

@asyncio.coroutine
def myCoroutine():
    print("My Coroutine")

def main():
    loop = asyncio.get_event_loop()
    loop.run_until_complete(myCoroutine())
    loop.close()

if __name__ == '__main__':
    main()
```

# Chaining coroutines

In certain situations, you may wish to chain the calling of your coroutines together in order to achieve maximum performance within your Python systems.

The official documentation again has an excellent code sample that demonstrates this concept of chaining very well. Within this code, we have two distinct coroutines denoted by *async def*. The compute coroutine returns the summation of $x + y$ after having performed a blocking sleep for 1 second.

Let's assume, however, that we want to rely on the result of a second coroutine within our first coroutine as follows:

```python
import asyncio

async def compute(x, y):
  print("Compute %s + %s ..." % (x, y))
  await asyncio.sleep(1.0)
  return x + y

async def print_sum(x, y):
  result = compute(x, y)
  print("%s + %s = %s" % (x, y, result))

loop = asyncio.get_event_loop()
loop.run_until_complete(print_sum(1, 2))
loop.close()
```

Upon execution of the preceding script, you should see that the following is outputted:

```
$ python3.6 06_chainCoroutine.py
1 + 2 = <coroutine object compute at 0x1031fc0f8>
/Library/Frameworks/Python.framework/Versions/3.6/lib/python3.6/asyncio/eve
nts.py:126: RuntimeWarning: coroutine 'compute' was never awaited
 self._callback(*self._args)
```

This essentially states that the compute function within our `print_sum()` method call was never awaited and the program tried to carry on as if it had received the result.

In order to overcome this particular issue, we need to utilize the await keyword. This await keyword blocks the event loop from proceeding any further until the called coroutine returns its result. The main drawback of this, however, is that, in this particular example, we lose the benefits of asynchronicity and we are back to standard synchronous execution. It's up to you to determine where the use of await is necessary as it does give you very quick and easy deterministic execution but you take hits on performance.

The `print_sum` coroutine instantiates a result variable that is equal to whatever the compute coroutine returns:

```python
import asyncio

async def compute(x, y):
    print("Compute %s + %s ..." % (x, y))
    await asyncio.sleep(1.0)
    return x + y

async def print_sum(x, y):
    result = await compute(x, y)
    print("%s + %s = %s" % (x, y, result))

loop = asyncio.get_event_loop()
loop.run_until_complete(print_sum(1, 2))
loop.close()
```

If we look at the sequence diagram that comes from the official documentation for this program, you should be able to see clearly how this chaining of coroutines is broken down in real terms:

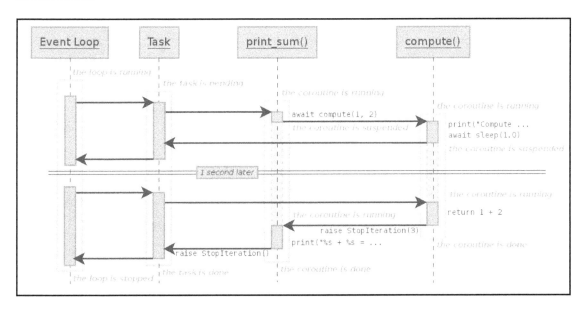

Source: https://docs.python.org/3/library/asyncio-task.html

# Output

If we then try to run the preceding program, you should see that our coroutines have been successfully chained together and that our `print_result` coroutine is now successfully awaiting the result of our `compute` function:

```
$ python3.6 06_chainCoroutine.py
Compute 1 + 2 ...
1 + 2 = 3
```

# Transports

Transports are classes that come included within the asyncio module that allow you to implement various types of communication. In total, there are four distinct types of transports that each inherit from the `BaseTransport` class:

- `ReadTransport`
- `WriteTransport`
- `DatagramTransport`
- `BaseSubprocesTransport`

This `BaseTransport` class has five methods that are subsequently transient across all four transport types listed earlier:

- `close()`: This closes the transport
- `is_closing()`: This returns true if the transport is closing or is already closed
- `get_extra_info(name, default=None)`: This returns optional transport information.
- `set_protocol(protocol)`: This does exactly what it says on the tin
- `get_protocol()`: This returns the current protocol

# Protocols

Protocols are a somewhat weird concept within the `asyncio` module. They are classes that we define that must follow a predefined interface. Interfaces, if you've never encountered them before, act as a kind of contract that ensures that a class is written in such a manner that it meets the contracts criteria.

Again, the concept of protocols lies out of the remit of this chapter, but I'd encourage research into them as they can be excellent modes of transports within your Python programs. The official documentation for both transports and protocols can be found at `https://docs.python.org/3/library/asyncio-protocol.html`.

# Synchronization between coroutines

The coroutines in asyncio run in a non-deterministic manner, and as such, there is still the possibility of our code running into race conditions regardless of the fact that it's only ever running on a single thread.

Due to the fact we can still be hit by dreaded race conditions, it's important to know how we can use the previously covered synchronization primitives in conjunction with the `asyncio` module.

In this section, we'll take a look at locks, events, conditions, and queues, as well as look at small examples of how these work within our event-driven Python programs. In the interest of brevity, I'm only going to give full code examples for both locks and queues as I feel these are going to be the two most commonly used concepts when it comes to synchronization between your asyncio coroutines.

## Locks

Locks within the `asyncio` module are almost identical in terms of practical functionality when compared with the standard lock implementation you'll find living within the `threading` module.

The `asyncio` module implementation allows us to put locks around critical sections of our asyncio-based programs in order to ensure that no other coroutines are executing that same critical section simultaneously.

In order to instantiate a lock from the `asyncio` module, we have to do something like this:

```
Import asyncio
myLock = asyncio.Lock()
```

Let's take a look at a fully fledged example of this. We'll begin by defining an async coroutine called `myWorker`, which will take in our lock as our parameter. Within this `myWorker` coroutine, we will attempt to acquire the lock using the `with` keyword. Once we've attained this lock, we then execute our critical status, which in this instance happens to be a simple `print` statement.

Within our main coroutine, we then instantiate the lock that we'll be passing to our `coroutine` function. We then await the execution of two instances of our `myWorker` coroutine before completing:

```
import asyncio
import time

async def myWorker(lock):
  with await lock:
    print(lock)
    print("myWorker has attained lock, modifying variable")
    time.sleep(2)
  print(lock)
  print("myWorker has release the lock")

async def main(loop):
  lock = asyncio.Lock()
    await asyncio.wait([myWorker(lock),
myWorker(lock)])

loop = asyncio.get_event_loop()
try:
  loop.run_until_complete(main(loop))
finally:
  loop.close()
```

If we were to execute this program, you should see that each worker, in turn, acquires the lock and performs what it has to perform before releasing the said lock and effectively allowing our second coroutine to take it up and execute its own critical section of code:

```
 $ python3.6 asyncioLock.py
<asyncio.locks.Lock object at 0x103121dd8 [locked]>
myWorker has attained lock, modifying variable
<asyncio.locks.Lock object at 0x103121dd8 [unlocked]>
myWorker has release the lock
<asyncio.locks.Lock object at 0x103121dd8 [locked]>
myWorker has attained lock, modifying variable
<asyncio.locks.Lock object at 0x103121dd8 [unlocked]>
myWorker has release the lock
```

# Queues

The `asyncio.Queue` implementation gives us another near identical implementation to that given to us in the standard queue module already present in Python.

In this example, we'll create both a producer and a consumer. The producer will produce `articleIds` between 1 and 5, while the consumer will try to read all of these articles. For both the producer and consumer, we'll define an appropriately named coroutine. Within our `newsProducer` coroutine, we'll perform the `put` command once every second that will put an ID onto our passed-in `asyncio.Queue`.

Within our `newsConsumer` function, we'll constantly try to perform a get request in order to retrieve an article ID from our shared queue. We'll then print out that we've consumed the said article ID and proceed to try and consume the next article:

```
import asyncio
import random
import time

@asyncio.coroutine
def newsProducer(myQueue):
  while True:
    yield from myQueue.put(random.randint(1,5))
    yield from asyncio.sleep(1)

@asyncio.coroutine
def newsConsumer(myQueue):
  while True:
    articleId = yield from myQueue.get()
    print("News Reader Consumed News Article {}", articleId)

myQueue = asyncio.Queue()

loop = asyncio.get_event_loop()

loop.create_task(newsProducer(myQueue))
loop.create_task(newsConsumer(myQueue))
try:
loop.run_forever()
finally:
loop.close()
```

When we execute the preceding program, you should see a constant stream of print statements coming from our `newsConsumer` coroutine. This demonstrates that we've successfully utilized our `asyncio.Queue` object for both our producer and consumer and have now achieved the communication that we desired:

```
$ python3.6 13_asyncioQueue.py
News Reader Consumed News Article {} 4
News Reader Consumed News Article {} 1
News Reader Consumed News Article {} 4
News Reader Consumed News Article {} 2
...
```

# Events and conditions

Events, as we have covered in `Chapter 4`, *Synchronization between Threads*, allow us to block multiple consumers from progressing from a set point until a flag has been set. We can instantiate them as follows:

```
myEvent = asyncio.Event()
```

Conditions again allow us to block tasks until a point where they are notified that they can continue by another coroutine. We can instantiate this as follows:

```
myCondition = asyncio.Condition()
```

# Semaphores and BoundedSemaphores

The `asyncio` module provides us with its own implementation of both the semaphore primitive as well as the `BoundedSemaphore` primitive that you would also find within the `threading` module.

This gives us the exact same functionality to the implementation we saw in `Chapter 4`, *Synchronization between Threads*. It is a counter that will decrement with each call to acquire and increment with each call to release. Again, this allows us to do things such as controlling the number of coroutines by accessing a given resource and can help ensure that issues such as resource starvation don't become an issue within our programs.

These can be instantiated as follows:

```
import asyncio
...
mySemaphore = asyncio.Semaphore(value=4, *, loop=None)
...
boundedSemaphore = asyncio.BoundedSemaphore(value=4, *, loop=None)
```

# Sub-processes

We've seen in the past that single process programs sometimes cannot meet the demands required of them in order for our software to function properly. We looked at various mechanisms in the previous chapters on how we can improve performance using multiple processes, and thankfully, asyncio comes with the ability for us to still leverage the power of sub-processes within our event-driven based programs.

I am not a fan of using this mechanism for improving performance as it can drastically heighten the complexity of your programs. However, this isn't to say that there aren't situations where this would be useful, and as such, I should make you aware of the official documentation, which can be found at `https://docs.python.org/3/library/asyncio-subprocess.html`

# Debugging asyncio programs

Thankfully, when it comes to debugging asyncio-based applications, we have a couple of options to consider. The writers of the asyncio module have very kindly provided a debug mode, which is quite powerful and can really aid us in our debugging adventures without the overhead of modifying the system's code base too dramatically.

# Debug mode

Turning on this debug mode within your asyncio-based programs is relatively simply and requires just a call to this function:

```
loop.set_debug(True)
```

Let's take a look at a fully fledged example of this and how it differs from your standard logging. In this example, we'll create a very simple event loop and submit some simple tasks to the event loop:

```
import asyncio
import logging
import time

logging.basicConfig(level=logging.DEBUG)

async def myWorker():
    logging.info("My Worker Coroutine Hit")
    time.sleep(1)

async def main():
    logging.debug("My Main Function Hit")
    await asyncio.wait([myWorker()])

loop = asyncio.get_event_loop()
loop.set_debug(True)
try:
    loop.run_until_complete(main())
finally:
    loop.close()
```

Upon execution of this, you should see the following chunk of code being outputted:

```
$ python3.6 11_debugAsyncio.py -Wdefault
DEBUG:asyncio:Using selector: KqueueSelector
DEBUG:root:My Main Function Hit
INFO:root:My Worker Coroutine Hit
WARNING:asyncio:Executing <Task finished coro=<myWorker() done, defined at
11_debugAsyncio.py:7> result=None created at
/Library/Frameworks/Python.framework/Versions/3.6/lib/python3.6/asyncio/tas
ks.py:305> took 1.004 seconds
DEBUG:asyncio:Close <_UnixSelectorEventLoop running=False closed=False
debug=True>
```

You should notice the extra log statements that wouldn't otherwise have been included within your logs. These extra log statements provide us with a far more granular idea of what's going on with regards to our event loop.

In this simple example, the debug mode was able to catch the fact that one of our coroutines took longer than 100 MS to execute as well as when our event loop finally closed.

You should note that this debug mode of asyncio is very useful for doing things such as determining what coroutines are never yielded from and thus, killing your program's performance. Other checks that it can be performed are as follows:

- The `call_soon()` and `call_at()` methods raise an exception if they are called from the wrong thread
- Logging the execution time of the selector
- The `ResourceWarning` warnings are emitted when transports and event loops are not closed explicitly

This is just for starters. Overall, this is a rather powerful tool to have and gives you an option other than your typical Pdb as a means of looking deeper into your programs. I implore you to check out the official documentation of asyncio's debug mode at `https://docs.python.org/3/library/asyncio-dev.html#asyncio-debug-mode`, as it provides a few far more in-depth examples that you can peruse at your own leisure.

# Twisted

Twisted in Python is a very popular and very powerful event-driven networking engine that can be used for a huge range of different projects such as web servers, mail clients, subsystems, and more.

Twisted is an amalgamation of both high- and low-level APIs that can be effectively utilized to create very powerful, elegant programs without masses of boilerplate code. It is both asynchronous and event-based by design and could be compared to the asyncio module as a more fully fleshed out older sibling.

If you are interested in learning far more on the Twisted framework then I fully recommend Twisted Network Programming Essentials, 2nd Edition, by Abe Fettig and Jessica McKellar

# A simple web server example

Twisted is absolutely ideal for doing things such as serving websites. We can set up a simple TCP server that listens on a particular endpoint that can serve files from a relative file location to someone requesting it in a browser.

In this example, we'll set up a very simple web server that serves local content from a `tmp` directory within the same directory as your program.

We will first import the necessary parts of the `twisted.web` and `twisted.internet` modules. We will then define an instance of the file resource that maps to the directory we wish to serve. Below this, we will create an instance of the site factory using our newly defined resource.

Finally, we will map our `Site` factory to a TCP port and start listening before calling `reactor.run()`, which drives our entire program by handling things such as accepting any incoming TCP connections and passing bytes in and out of the said connections:

```
from twisted.web.server import Site
from twisted.web.static import File
from twisted.internet import reactor, endpoints

resource = File('tmp')
factory = Site(resource)
endpoint = endpoints.TCP4ServerEndpoint(reactor,
8888)
endpoint.listen(factory)
reactor.run()
```

We'll serve this very simple `.html` file, which features a `<h1>` tag within its body. Nothing special, but it represents a good starting point for any website:

```
<!DOCTYPE html>
<html lang="en">
<head>
 <meta charset="UTF-8">
 <meta name="viewport" content="width=device
width, initial-scale=1.0">
 <meta http-equiv="X-UA-Compatible"
content="ie=edge">
 <title>Twisted Home Page</title>
</head>
<body>
 <h1>Twisted Homepage</h1>
</body>
</html>
```

Upon running the preceding code, navigate to `http://localhost:8888` in your local browser, and you should see our newly created website in all it's glory being served up.

This represents just a very small fraction of what the Twisted framework is capable of, and unfortunately, due to concerns for the brevity of this book, I cannot possibly divulge all of its inner workings. The overall power of this framework is incredible, and it has been a joy working with it in the past.

# Gevent

The `gevent` networking library is based purely on top of coroutines. It's very similar in nature when compared to Twisted and provides us with a similar range of functionality that we can leverage to build our own network-based event-driven Python applications.

Its features include the following:

- A fast event loop
- Lightweight execution units based on greenlets
- An API that reuses concepts from the Python standard library
- Cooperative sockets and SSL modules
- TCP/UDP/HTTP servers
- Thread pools
- Sub-process support

It also includes a number of other features. It features a healthy collection of internal methods and classes that enable us, as developers, to develop some pretty powerful and flexible systems. If you are interested in reading up on everything that it provides, then I suggest you check out the official documentation, which can be found at `http://www.geven t.org/contents.html`.

# Event loops

Much like the `asyncio` module, `gevent` utilizes the concept of an event loop. This event loop is incredibly efficient in design as it handles events as and when they are registered within the event loop. It lets the OS handle the delivery of event notifications and focuses on making real progress on the events as opposed to wasting valuable resources polling for events.

# Greenlets

The core of the `gevent` framework is the greenlet. Greenlets, if you haven't worked with them before, are a very lightweight coroutine written in C that are cooperatively scheduled. They provide us with a very lightweight *thread-like* object that allows us to achieve concurrent execution within our Python programs without incurring the cost of spinning up multiple threads.

These lightweight pseudo threads are spawned by the creation of a greenlet instance and subsequently call its start method. These lightweight pseudo threads then execute a certain amount of code before cooperatively giving up control and allowing another pseudo thread to then take over. This cycle of repeated work and then giving up is repeated over and over again until the program has accomplished it's target and terminated.

We can define greenlets through the use of functions such as spawn as follows:

```python
import gevent

def myGreenlet():
 print("My Greenlet is executing")

gevent.spawn(myGreenlet)
gevent.sleep(1)
```

Alternatively, we can also define them through the use of sub-classing as follows:

```python
import gevent
from gevent import Greenlet

class MyNoopGreenlet(Greenlet):
  def __init__(self, seconds):
    Greenlet.__init__(self)
    self.seconds = seconds

  def _run(self):
    print("My Greenlet executing")
    gevent.sleep(self.seconds)

  def __str__(self):
    return 'MyNoopGreenlet(%s)' % self.seconds

g = MyNoopGreenlet(4)
g.start()
g.join()
print(g.dead)
```

# Simple example-hostnames

In this simple example, we'll introduce the use of gevent within your Python applications. We'll write something that takes in an array of three distinct URLs, and then, we'll spawn an array of gevents in order to retrieve the IP addresses of these URLs using the `socket.gethostbyname()` function.

We'll then use `joinall()` for these gevents, giving them a timeout of 2 seconds, and finally, we'll print the array of IP addresses this returns:

```
import gevent
from gevent import socket

def main():
    urls = ['www.google.com', 'www.example.com',
'www.python.org']
    jobs = [gevent.spawn(socket.gethostbyname, url)
for url in urls]
    gevent.joinall(jobs, timeout=2)
    print([job.value for job in jobs])

if __name__ == '__main__':
    main()
```

## Output

When you run the preceding program, you should see output that looks similar to this one:

```
$ python3.6 19_geventSimple.py
['216.58.211.100', '93.184.216.34', '151.101.60.223']
```

# Monkey patching

One concept that was new to me when I was researching the gevent library was the concept of monkey patching. It has absolutely nothing to do with monkeys unfortunately and is, instead, focused on the dynamic modification of a class or module at runtime.

A great example of how this works is if you imagine you have a Python program that contains a method that retrieves a value from an external dependency such as a database, a REST API, or something else. We can utilize monkey patching as a means of stubbing out this method so that it does not hit our external dependency when we are running our unit tests.

Why does this necessarily fall under a gevent though? Well, in gevent, we can utilize monkey patching in order to carefully replace functions and classes with cooperative counterparts. An example of how powerful this can be is if you consider the standard socket module. DNS requests are by default serialized and, thus, are incredibly slow when done in bulk.

In order to perform these DNS requests concurrently, we can utilize monkey patching! Using `gevent.monkey`, we can monkey patch the functions and classes in the socket module with cooperative counterparts, thus solving all our performance issues:

```
from gevent import monkey; monkey.patch_socket()
import urllib2 # it's usable from multiple greenlets now
```

If you want to learn more about this magical performance improving technique, then I recommend you check out the official documentation at `http://www.gevent.org/intro.html#monkey-patching`.

# Summary

In this chapter, we covered the paradigm of event-driven programming before covering how asyncio works and how we can use it for our own event-driven Python systems.

We went in depth into the asyncio module and the various ways you can do things such as construct your event loops, chain coroutines within this loop, and set up event handlers, to name but a few things.

In the next chapter, we'll look at how you can create reactive programs using the powerful `RxPy` module and cover how the reactive programming paradigm differs from your typical event-based programs.

# 10
# Reactive Programming

While event-driven programming might revolve around events, in reactive programming, we deal purely with data. In other words, every time we receive a new piece of data, we consider this to be an event. Due to this definition, you could technically call it a branch of event-driven programming. However, due to its popularity and the differences in the way it does things, I couldn't help but put reactive programming in a chapter of its own.

In this chapter, we will dive deeper into one of the most popular libraries available in Python when it comes to reactive programming, RxPY. We'll cover in depth some of the features of this library and how we can utilize this to create our own asynchronous programs.

We'll come to terms with some of the basics necessary of RxPY to get us started:

- Dealing with observers and observables
- Lambda functions and how we can use them
- The multitude of operators and how we can chain these to achieve a desired state
- The differences between both hot and cold observables
- Multicasting

We'll also take a brief look at the PyFunctional library, and how this differs from RxPY and how we can leverage that in certain scenarios. You should note that some of these examples from the official documentation have also been covered in a video course called *Reactive Python for Data Science* by *Thomas Nield*. I highly recommend this course as Thomas covers a lot of material that I've not had a chance to in this chapter. You can find this course at http://shop.oreilly.com/product/0636920064237.do.

# Basic reactive programming

Reactive programming is a paradigm that is totally unlike that of your more traditional imperative style of programming. Being aware of the strengths and weaknesses of reactive programming could help you turn software disasters into potential successes.

With reactive programming, we can totally destroy the imperative style and instead focus on representing our data as a stream of events. We can subscribe to these subsequent streams and take action upon receiving these events. This helps us simplify our system's flow that could quickly become very unwieldy and unmaintainable if we were to follow a more traditional architecture and style.

Reactive libraries take away the complexity of us having to push our events to various functions within our systems, and enable us to effectively work with data as queryable, real-time streams. We can essentially fashion programs that will run infinitely against an infinite stream of events such as constant stock quotes or social media interactions.

This reactive programming paradigm has been taken up by the likes of data scientists who may have streams of statistical data or sensory data coming in, which they have to analyze and make decisions.

## Maintaining purity

In a reactive paradigm, it's important that we try to make all our transactions stateless. By enforcing stateless transactions, we essentially reduce the number of potential side-effects that could impact our program's execution.

This pure style of programming is one that functional programmers tend to live by, and it's proving to be an incredibly powerful paradigm when it comes to designing highly resilient distributed systems. Overall, it's something that I would try and follow right from the start as you develop these new systems.

## ReactiveX, or RX

Reactive Extensions, or RX, first hit the scenes in around 2010 and has been heavily adopted by large tech companies such as Netflix using `RxJava`. It has since grown into something far bigger and more prevalent within the industry.

It comes in many different flavors for each of the different programming languages currently out there. The most popular of these are as follows:

- `RxJava` for Java
- `RxJS` for JavaScript
- `RxPy` for Python
- `RxSwift` for Swift

> The full list of Rx flavors can be found at `https://github.com/ReactiveX`.

Reactive Extensions for Python, or `RxPY` as it has been condensed to, is a library for composing asynchronous and event-based programs using observable collections and LINQ-style query operators in Python. I first came across a similar version of ReactiveX when I was working with the new Angular framework, and my experience with it was great. It let me turn a web socket stream into an observable, which could subsequently be watched from within my Angular application and displayed, in real-time, in the browser.

`RxPY` is equally useful, and it paves the way for you to write some incredibly interesting applications while handling the underlying complexity of dealing with observers and observables.

One of the best examples I could envisage this library being used is in, say, a stock trading application. You could in theory have an API that constantly checks the price of certain stocks and in turn stream it back to your `RxPY`-based stock trading application if certain conditions were met. Say, for instance, a stock that you own falls in value by 20 percent, you could subscribe to this type of event and then react to this situation in whatever way you wish, be it to sell off the stock or to buy more of it.

# Installing RxPY

Installing `RxPY` can be done with ease using pip as follows:

```
pip install rx
```

You should note that `RxPY` runs on both Python 2.7+ and 3.4+ as well as `PyPy` and `IronPython`.

# Observables

Observables are the most important part of our RxPy applications. We define these observables that can emit events to any observer that is currently registered to receive events from the said observable. The key thing to note is that these observers utilize a push mechanism in order to notify subscribers of new events as opposed to a pull mechanism.

# Creating observers

In RxPY, nearly anything can be turned into an observable, which makes it immensely powerful as a library, and when it comes to consuming from these observables, we have a many options. If we need to, we could utilize a quick and easy lambda function or we could define a fully fledged class that handles it all for us.

# Example

In this example, we'll implement `PrintObserver`, which will subclass the `rx.Observer` class. This will implement the three necessary functions required: `on_next()`, `on_completed()`, and `on_error()`. Each of these three functions has an important role to play within our observers:

- `on_next(self, value)`: This is called whenever the observer receives a new event.

- `on_completed(self)`: This is called whenever our observable notifies it that it has completed its task.

- `on_error(self, error)`: This is called whenever we wish to handle error cases. Thankfully, in our simple example, we shouldn't have to worry about this.

This will be a relatively simple example that will just print out the values received when the `on_next()` function is called, but it should give you the basic idea of how to define your own observers.

 Note: The following code snippet was taken from the official RxPY documentation.

Let's examine this code snippet that features a very simple RxPY observer and observable:

```python
from rx import Observable, Observer


def push_five_strings(observer):
        observer.on_next("Alpha")
        observer.on_next("Beta")
        observer.on_next("Gamma")
        observer.on_next("Delta")
        observer.on_next("Epsilon")
        observer.on_completed()


class PrintObserver(Observer):

    def on_next(self, value):
        print("Received {0}".format(value))

    def on_completed(self):
        print("Done!")

    def on_error(self, error):
        print("Error Occurred: {0}".format(error))

source = Observable.create(push_five_strings)

source.subscribe(PrintObserver())
```

When we execute the preceding Python program, you should see that the five distinct strings are all printed out one after the other before the `on_completed()` function is called. This signals to our observer that there will be no further events, and the program then terminates:

```
$ python3.6 07_createObservable.py
Received Alpha
Received Beta
Received Gamma
Received Delta
Received Epsilon
Done!
```

# Example 2

In the following example, we will take a look at how to build a very simple stock trading system that decides whether or not to buy a stock. If the stock matches the criteria, then we will emit a buy order to our observer, which then processes it. I should probably point out that while this might not make you a millionaire, I do expect something in the way of royalties in the off chance that it does:

```python
from rx import Observable, Observer

stocks = [
{ 'TCKR' : 'APPL', 'PRICE': 200},
{ 'TCKR' : 'GOOG', 'PRICE': 90},
{ 'TCKR' : 'TSLA', 'PRICE': 120},
{ 'TCKR' : 'MSFT', 'PRICE': 150},
{ 'TCKR' : 'INTL', 'PRICE': 70},
]

def buy_stock_events(observer):
  for stock in stocks:
    if(stock['PRICE'] > 100):
      observer.on_next(stock['TCKR'])

  observer.on_completed()

class StockObserver(Observer):

def on_next(self, value):
  print("Received Instruction to buy
{0}".format(value))

def on_completed(self):
  print("All Buy Instructions have been received")

def on_error(self, error):
  print("Error Occurred: {0}".format(error))

source = Observable.create(buy_stock_events)
source.subscribe(StockObserver())
```

# Breaking it down

In our code sample, we defined a dictionary array that stores our ticker symbols marked by TCKR and the stock prices of each of these stocks, represented by PRICE. It should be noted that these are entirely fictitious and that their stock prices don't mean anything.

We then went on to define our `buy_stock_events` observable, which iterates through this array of stocks and prices, and, using a very complex algorithm, checks to see if we should buy this stock. If the stock meets our criteria, then we emit an event with the stock's TCKR as the key for the event. Once we've finished iterating through all of our stocks, we then call `on_completed()`, which informs our observers that we have finished working our way through the stocks and no more buy orders should be expected.

Finally, below our `StockObserver` class definition, we created our Observable object, which takes in our `buy_stock_events` function as its main argument. We then subscribed to this observable with a new instance of our `StockObserver` class.

# Output

If we were to now run this program on our machine, it would iterate through our five stocks and compare their prices and see if they were greater than 100. It sees that APPL, TSLA, and MSFT, all meet this criteria, and it emits these buy instructions. Our `StockObserver` object receives these emissions, and then acts accordingly and prints out that it received the orders.

Once all five stocks have been looped through, the observable emits that it's finished and our `StockObserver` object then shuts up shop:

```
$ python3.6 00_observables.py
Received Instruction to buy APPL
Received Instruction to buy TSLA
Received Instruction to buy MSFT
All Buy Instructions have been received
```

# Lambda functions

The preceding way can sometimes be rather verbose for some scenarios where an entire class is unnecessary. In scenarios like this, we can engage the help of something called lambda functions.

Lambda functions, if you haven't encountered them yet, are constructs that allow us to create anonymous functions. In certain situations such as this one, it can be quite powerful. Using lambda functions, we could effectively rewrite the preceding program as shown in the next example.

# Example

In this example, we'll examine how you can utilize a simple lambda function in order to "execute" a trade on a given stock ticker:

```
from rx import Observable

stocks = [
{ 'TCKR' : 'APPL', 'PRICE': 200},
{ 'TCKR' : 'GOOG', 'PRICE': 90},
{ 'TCKR' : 'TSLA', 'PRICE': 120},
{ 'TCKR' : 'MSFT', 'PRICE': 150},
{ 'TCKR' : 'INTL', 'PRICE': 70},
]

def buy_stock_events(observer):
for stock in stocks:
  if(stock['PRICE'] > 100):
    observer.on_next(stock['TCKR'])
observer.on_completed()


source = Observable.create(buy_stock_events)

source.subscribe(lambda value: print("Received Instruction to buy
{0}".format(value)))
```

# Breaking it down

In the preceding code, we kept the same observable that we implemented in the previous example, but you'll notice one key difference. We no longer have this rather verbose `StockObserver` class definition and have replaced it with a far more terse one liner, which features all of the same functionality:

```
source.subscribe(lambda value: print("Received Instruction to buy
{0}".format(value)))
```

In this particular example, we minimized our code base and made our code more maintainable as we don't have to pour over an entire class definition to see what's happening. However, it should be noted that while this was advantageous here, trying to cram all of your code into a single lambda expression could actually hamper your code's readability and make maintenance work and bug fixes a nightmare.

# On_next, on_completed, and on_error in lambda form

So, one key thing you should notice from the preceding example is that while it is more terse, we seem to have lost the ability to define the on_next, on_completed, and on_error functions as we had done in the previous example. Fear not though, we can still implement these three functions as lambda functions as follows:

```
from rx import Observable

stocks = [
{ 'TCKR' : 'APPL', 'PRICE': 200},
{ 'TCKR' : 'GOOG', 'PRICE': 90},
{ 'TCKR' : 'TSLA', 'PRICE': 120},
{ 'TCKR' : 'MSFT', 'PRICE': 150},
{ 'TCKR' : 'INTL', 'PRICE': 70},
]

def buy_stock_events(observer):
for stock in stocks:
  if(stock['PRICE'] > 100):
    observer.on_next(stock['TCKR'])
observer.on_completed()

source = Observable.create(buy_stock_events)

source.subscribe(on_next=lambda value:
print("Received Instruction to buy
{0}".format(value)),
              on_completed=lambda:
print("Completed trades"),
              on_error=lambda e: print(e))
```

# Output

In the preceding code, within our source.subscribe call, we've defined the three distinct lambda functions necessary for our subscriber, and we've mapped them to their appropriate calls. You should see an almost identical output to the previous program as well as our newly added *Completed trades* message, which lets us know that our `on_completed` function has successfully mapped:

```
$ python3.6 10_allLambda.py
Received Instruction to buy APPL
Received Instruction to buy TSLA
Received Instruction to buy MSFT
Completed trades
```

# Operators and chaining

Operators work as an intermediary between the emission and the subscriber. They can effectively transform raw data being outputted into a format that is more pleasantly digested by your subscribers.

In total, RxPY features over 130 distinct operators from which you can derive new observables, and the fact that we can chain these operators together make them very powerful indeed. It's important to note that most operators that operate on an Observable also return an Observable that can be subscribed to. It is due to this fact that we can do cool things such as chain multiple operators together to achieve our desired end state.

## Filter example

Let's first take a look at how we can chain some very simple operators together in order to only print out the lengths of a string only when it is above five characters in length.

We'll take an array of five strings, map them to their lengths using the `.map()` operator, and then filter these for all strings less than five using the `.filter()` operator. We'll then have a subscriber subscribe to the mapped and filtered emissions using a simple lambda function that prints the length:

```
from rx import Observable

source = Observable.from_(["Alpha", "Beta", "Gamma", "Delta", "Epsilon"])

lengths = source.map(lambda s: len(s))
```

```
filtered = lengths.filter(lambda i: i >= 5)

filtered.subscribe(lambda value: print("Received {0}".format(value)))
```

# Breaking it down

In the preceding code example, we first defined our source using the `Observable.from_` function, passing in an array of five letters of the Greek alphabet into it.

We then went on to map the lengths of these strings into a lengths variable using `source.map` and provided a `lambda` function that transforms our string into it's length.

Then, we went on to filter these lengths using a `lambda` function that returns only those values that match the greater than or equal to five criteria.

Finally, we subscribed to this filtered stream of events using a final `lambda` function that merely prints out the received lengths of each string.

# Chained operators

If we were to represent the preceding example using the chaining mechanism that we talked about earlier, then it would look something like this:

```
from rx import Observable

Observable.from_(["Alpha", "Beta", "Gamma", "Delta", "Epsilon"]) \
    .map(lambda s: len(s)) \
    .filter(lambda i: i >= 5) \
    .subscribe(lambda value: print("Received {0}".format(value)))
```

This code features absolutely no difference in functionality to the previous code example and is in fact, in my opinion, easier to read as we don't have to follow where the output of each operator is being stored.

# The different operators

In this section, we'll take a very brief look at a handful of different operators available within the RxPY. Unfortunately, for the sake of brevity, I will have to omit some from the list as I can't possibly cover the 130+ different operators available within this section of the book. If you do, however, want to see a more complete list, then I implore you to check out the official list of operators at http://reactivex.io/documentation/operators.html. This list is language agnostic and just gives you an overview of what is available, and it's a fantastic resource to have bookmarked when working with ReactiveX.

## Creating observables

When it comes to creating observables in RxPY, we have quite a large number of options. So far, we've leveraged operators such as *Create* and *From* as well as *Interval* in order to create, but there are more out there.

You have a standard *Create* operator, which creates an Observable from scratch by calling the observer methods programmatically. *Defer*, on the other hand, only creates an Observable at the point at which an observer subscribes and will actually create a completely unique Observable object for each call to subscribe.

## Transforming observables

When it comes to transforming observables, we have slightly fewer options than when it comes to creating observables. We have the following operators that we can utilize to transform any of the observables within our Python programs.

The few most notable operators could be defined as follows:

- Buffer: This buffer periodically gathers items from an already created Observable and bundles it into a single emission. We can effectively use this to somewhat stem the flow of systems that output millions upon millions of emissions.

- FlatMap: We've already had a look at combining observables using the merge_all operator, but the FlatMap operator gives us an alternative solution when it comes to merging these observables into one Observable.

- Map: This transforms all emissions from a given Observable and then applies a function to each of the said items.

There are other operators such as scan and window operators that lie within this remit, but these should be adequate to get you started.

## Filtering observables

RxPY provides quite a deep API for filtering observables as well. We've already used the de facto `Filter` operator in one of our previous examples, but there are others such as `Distinct`, `ElementAt`, `Sample`, and `Take`, which I recommend you get familiar with.

Again, the following list contains only a subset of the available operators when it comes to filtering:

- `Distinct`: This stops an Observable from emitting duplicate items. This is the very operator that takes care of the complexities for filtering lists of duplicates for you.

- `Take`: This takes a subset of the first *n* items emitted by an Observable.

- `ElementAt`: This returns the element at position *n* emitted by an Observable.

## Error-handling observables

Error handling is something that every programmer must consider for essentially every piece of software on or off the planet. `RxPY`-based programs are no exception, and thankfully, `RxPY` provides us with two very helpful error-handling operators:

- `Catch`

- `Retry`

# Hot and cold observables

Within ReactiveX, we have this underlying concept of hot and cold observables that you should be aware of when creating observables with multiple subscribers.

Within an RxPY program, we can have any one of the following observables:

- hot observables: These actively publish notifications regardless of whether or not they have subscribers
- cold observables: These only emit when they have subscribers listening in on them

Say, for instance, you have an observable that watches for news on particular stocks and shares. You currently have one subscriber listening into this observable and acting upon the emissions. Now, imagine a scenario where we need to add a second or even a third subscriber to this Observable.

In this particular scenario, our Observable would not replay the already played out events to our second and third subscribers. It would instead just ensure that they receive its subsequent emissions. This would be an example of a hot observable.

If our Observable was indeed able to replay the already played emissions, then it would be an example of a cold Observable.

# Emitting events

In RxPY, we are able to create composite observables that work with both data and normal events that you'd find in event-driven programming the same way.

# Example

In the next example, we will look at how we can combine data emissions events with keyboard input so that we can kill our stream of events should we wish to:

```
from rx import Observable

Observable.interval(1000) \
    .map(lambda i: "{0} Mississippi".format(i)) \
    .subscribe(lambda s: print(s))

input("Press any key to quit\n")
```

# Breaking it down

What we've essentially done in the preceding code is create an observable that emits the result of *i* concatenated with *Mississippi* every 1,000 milliseconds. We then subscribed to these events with a very simple lambda function that simply prints out whatever has been emitted.

We included the call to `input()` in order to block until we wish to end the program. This is due to the fact that `Observable.interval()` operates on a separate thread, and without this call, our program would end somewhat prematurely.

# Output

This then leaves us with an output that looks something like this until the point at which we quit the program:

```
0 Mississippi
1 Mississippi
2 Mississippi
3 Mississippi
4 Mississippi
5 Mississippi
6 Mississippi
. . .
```

# Multicasting

So far, in the examples that I've presented earlier, we've only dealt with cases where there has only been one Observable and one Observer. However, one of the most powerful aspects of the RxPY library is the fact that our observables can multicast emissions out to numerous subscribers.

The need for multicasting comes from the fact that having multiple subscribers subscribe to the one observable would result in discrepancies with regards to the events that both of these subscribers receive. However, using multicasting, we can effectively eliminate these discrepancies and ensure that all of our subscribers, regardless of how many we have, will receive identical events.

Take, for instance, the following lines of code:

```
from rx import Observable
from random import randint

three_emissions = Observable.range(1, 3)

three_random_ints = three_emissions.map(lambda i: randint(1, 100000))

three_random_ints.subscribe(lambda i: print("Subscriber 1 Received: {0}".format(i)))
three_random_ints.subscribe(lambda i: print("Subscriber 2 Received: {0}".format(i)))
```

This code features a simple observable that emits three random events, each containing a generated random number that ranges anywhere from 1 to 100,000. If we were then to execute the preceding code, you may have expected to see both subscriber 1 and subscriber 2 receive the same events. However, if we have a look at the output of the said program, you'll see this isn't the case:

```
$ python3.6 03_multicast.py
Subscriber 1 Received: 21097
Subscriber 1 Received: 19863
Subscriber 1 Received: 68053
Subscriber 2 Received: 69670
Subscriber 2 Received: 11348
Subscriber 2 Received: 8860
```

# Example

In this example, we'll extend the previous example and flesh it out a bit. We'll define a `Subscriber` class, which will subclass the `Observer` class. This class will implement the `on_next()`, `on_completed()`, and `on_error()` functions and simply print out any value passed to them.

We'll then use the same `three_random_ints` Observable that we defined in the previous example and publish these emissions using the `.publish()` function.

Below this, we'll subscribe three distinct subscribers to our Observable before calling the `.connect()` function, which defines that all our subscribers are ready so that they receive the same stream of emissions:

```
from rx import Observable, Observer
from random import randint
```

```
class Subscriber(Observer):

    def __init__(self, ident):
        self.id = ident

    def on_next(self, value):
        print("Subscriber: {} Received:
{}".format(self.id, value))

    def on_completed(self):
        print("Subscriber: {} Received
Events".format(self.id))

    def on_error(self, error):
        print("Error Occurred: {}".format(error))

three_emissions = Observable.range(1,3)
three_random_ints = three_emissions.map(lambda i:
randint(1, 10000)).publish()

three_random_ints.subscribe(Subscriber("Grant"))
three_random_ints.subscribe(Subscriber("Barry"))
three_random_ints.subscribe(Subscriber("Sophie"))
three_random_ints.connect()
```

# Output

You'll see in the output of our program that all three subscribers receive all three of our news events before finally receiving the completed emission:

```
$ python3.6 14_multicasting.py
Subscriber: Grant Received: 211
Subscriber: Barry Received: 211
Subscriber: Sophie Received: 211
Subscriber: Grant Received: 7120
Subscriber: Barry Received: 7120
Subscriber: Sophie Received: 7120
Subscriber: Grant Received: 2802
Subscriber: Barry Received: 2802
Subscriber: Sophie Received: 2802
Subscriber: Grant Received Events
Subscriber: Barry Received Events
Subscriber: Sophie Received Events
```

# Combining observables

There might be times where we have two distinct observables that emit data at different times. We may, in this scenario, wish to combine both of these observables so that we still effectively have one Observable that our subscribers can subsequently subscribe to.

If we imagine a stock trading program that places stock trades based off breaking news, then you would probably have multiple observables both watching for new news posts and then emitting these events to other components within our system. In this scenario, we could effectively aggregate all these observables into one golden news source that could effectively feed the rest of our stock trading program.

When it comes to actually implementing the component that combines our observables, we could leverage a number of different operators available to us within RxPY. These are as follows:

- And()/Then()/When()

- CombineLatest()

- Join()

- Merge()

- StartWith()

- Switch()

- Zip()

It's worth playing around with these and trying to fully understand them as each of them can be leveraged differently within your programs.

# Zip() example

In this example, we'll use the .zip() operator in order to combine both the letters Observable as well as the intervals Observable into one Observable. Then, we will use the .subscribe() operator in order to subscribe a very simple Observer to this newly combined Observable object:

```
from rx import Observable
```

```
list1 = [23, 38, 43, 23]

letters = Observable.from_(list1).to_blocking()
intervals = Observable.interval(1000)

def main():
Observable \
    .zip(letters, intervals, lambda x, y: (x*y, y))
\
    .subscribe(lambda t: print(t))

if __name__ == '__main__':
main()
input("Press any key to quit\n")
```

## Output

Upon running the preceding program, you should see the following output in the console. First, you should see the input blocking the program from prematurely ending and then a stream of four tuples, the first value of which represents the relative value in list1 times the current interval value, and the second of which is just the interval value:

```
$ python3.6 06_combining.py
Press any key to quit
(0, 0)
(38, 1)
(86, 2)
(69, 3)
```

## The merge_all() operator

Another option to combine your observables is to use the merge_all() operator in order to merge two or more distinct observables into one observable that we can subscribe to.

In this example, we'll define two very simple observables from two arrays of numbers. We will then create an array of observables that we'll call "sources" and subsequently use the merge_all() operator on this newly created array in order to combine them all into an amalgamation of all of our two original observables:

```
from rx import Observable

list1 = [23, 38, 43, 23]
list2 = [1,2,3,4]
```

```
source1 = Observable.from_(list1)
source2 = Observable.from_(list2)
sources = [source1, source2]

def main():
Observable.from_(sources) \
  .merge_all() \
  .subscribe(lambda x: print(x))
if __name__ == '__main__':
main()
input("Press any key to quit\n")
```

## Output

When you output this, you should see a very eclectic output that accounts to a combination of both of our original observables:

```
$ python3.6 11_mergeAll.py
23
38
1
43
2
23
3
4
Press any key to quit
```

## Concurrency

While the majority of code covered within this chapter up to this point has been of a single process nature, it is definitely worth noting that concurrency is still achievable and RxPY provides two distinct operators that allow for concurrent execution:

- subscribe_on()

- observe_on()

Both of the preceding operators require a scheduler, which can be provided using something like ThreadPoolScheduler in order to create a pool of reusable worker threads.

# Example

We'll again leverage the code that the official library provides in its documentation as it is a fantastic example of just how you can achieve concurrency within your own RxPY programs.

In this example, we'll use the rx.concurrency ThreadPoolScheduler class as our necessary cross-thread scheduler. We will then create three distinct observables that emit events at various intervals:

```
import multiprocessing
import random
import time
from threading import current_thread

from rx import Observable
from rx.concurrency import ThreadPoolScheduler

def processHeavyCalc(value):
time.sleep(random.randint(5,20) * .1)
return value

# calculate number of CPU's, then create a
ThreadPoolScheduler with that number of threads
optimal_thread_count = multiprocessing.cpu_count()
pool_scheduler =
ThreadPoolScheduler(optimal_thread_count)

# Create Process 1
Observable.from_(["Alpha", "Beta", "Gamma",
"Delta", "Epsilon"]) \
  .map(lambda s: processHeavyCalc(s)) \
  .subscribe_on(pool_scheduler) \
  .subscribe(on_next=lambda s: print("PROCESS 1:
{0} {1}".format(current_thread().name, s)),
            on_error=lambda e: print(e),
            on_completed=lambda: print("PROCESS 1
done!"))

# Create Process 2
Observable.range(1, 10) \
  .map(lambda s: processHeavyCalc(s)) \
```

```
    .subscribe_on(pool_scheduler) \
    .subscribe(on_next=lambda i: print("PROCESS 2:
{0} {1}".format(current_thread().name, i)),
            on_error=lambda e: print(e),
on_completed=lambda: print("PROCESS 2 done!"))

# Create Process 3, which is infinite
Observable.interval(1000) \
    .map(lambda i: i * 100) \
    .observe_on(pool_scheduler) \
    .map(lambda s: processHeavyCalc(s)) \
    .subscribe(on_next=lambda i: print("PROCESS 3: {0}
{1}".format(current_thread().name, i)),
            on_error=lambda e: print(e))

input("Press any key to exit\n")
```

# Output

When we run this program, you should see that we've successfully achieved concurrent thread execution within our program. You should see the initial "Press any key to exit" print out, which blocks until it is satisfied.

We will then see each of our three processes execute concurrently, and their constant stream of print statements is thoroughly intertwined and not executed synchronously:

```
$ python3.6 09_concurrency.py
Press any key to exit
PROCESS 1:<concurrent.futures.thread.ThreadPoolExecutor object at
0x102abda20>_0 Alpha
PROCESS 2: <concurrent.futures.thread.ThreadPoolExecutor object at
0x102abda20>_1 1
PROCESS 1: <concurrent.futures.thread.ThreadPoolExecutor object at
0x102abda20>_0 Beta
PROCESS 3: <concurrent.futures.thread.ThreadPoolExecutor object at
0x102abda20>_2 0
PROCESS 2: <concurrent.futures.thread.ThreadPoolExecutor object at
0x102abda20>_1 2
PROCESS 3: <concurrent.futures.thread.ThreadPoolExecutor object at
0x102abda20>_3 100
PROCESS 1: <concurrent.futures.thread.ThreadPoolExecutor object at
0x102abda20>_0 Gamma
```

```
PROCESS 2: <concurrent.futures.thread.ThreadPoolExecutor object at
0x102abda20>_1 3
PROCESS 3: <concurrent.futures.thread.ThreadPoolExecutor object at
0x102abda20>_3 200
PROCESS 2: <concurrent.futures.thread.ThreadPoolExecutor object at
0x102abda20>_1 4
PROCESS 1: <concurrent.futures.thread.ThreadPoolExecutor object at
0x102abda20>_0 Delta
. . .
```

# PyFunctional

`PyFunctional` is a library that's worth noting at this point as it follows a similar paradigm to that of reactive programming. It essentially enables us to create functional programs using the Python programming language.

Both functional and reactive programming tend to utilize pure functions that feature no side effects and store no additional state. We define functions that will always return the same results regardless of what else is happening within our programs. The key difference between both `PyFunctional` and `RxPY` is the fact that while we handle streams in a very similar fashion in both libraries, the way that this data is handled is somewhat different. `RxPY` is far more focused on the way that data and subsequently events are handled within systems. `PyFunctional` is more focused on the transformation of data using functional programming paradigms.

`PyFunctional` is specifically useful as it allows us to easily create data pipelines using chained functional operators. The library was originally conceived by a PhD student in AI called Pedro Rodriguez and draws inspiration from both Spark and Scala and tries to enable us to write very elegant code using `LINQ` style chained operators in order to easily manipulate our data streams.

## Installation and official docs

You can install PyFunctional using the pip installer as follows:

```
pip install pyfunctional
```

This allows us to import from the functional module, which you will see an example of in the next example section.

For more comprehensive documentation on the `PyFunctional` module, I recommend you check out the official GitHub repository for the module, which can be found at `https://git hub.com/EntilZha/PyFunctional`, or the official site, which can be found at `http://www.p yfunctional.org/`.

# Simple example

Let's take a look at a very simple example to show you how you can write functional programs using the `PyFunctional` module. This will act as a toe-dipping example that should hopefully give you the gist of some of the basic things you can accomplish with the `PyFunctional` module.

In this example, we'll leverage `seq`, which acts as the stream object with which we can iterate and manipulate. We'll first map this sequence using a lambda function that doubles every value. After this, we'll filter for values where `x` is greater than 4, and finally, we'll reduce the sequence into a summation of all the remaining values:

```
from functional import seq

result = seq(1, 2, 3, 4)\
    .map(lambda x: x * 2)\
    .filter(lambda x: x > 4)\
    .reduce(lambda x, y: x + y)
print("Results: {}".format(result))
```

# Output

You should see that 14 is printed out as the sum of our map; filter and reduce chaining:

```
$ python3.6 12_pyFunctional.py
Results: 14
```

# Streams, transformations, and actions

Within PyFunctional, there are three distinct types of functions that we can segregate its API into:

- Streams

- Transformations

- Actions

Each of these have their own distinct roles to play within the library. With streams, we can read in the data that we wish to manipulate or utilize. Transformations are the functions that can transform the data from these streams, and actions cause a series of these transformations to evaluate to a concrete value.

When we call `seq()` and pass data into it as an argument, we are essentially converting the data into a stream, which we can transform and manipulate to our will.

# Filtering lists

When it comes to tasks such as filtering, `PyFunctional` provides an incredibly diverse range of operators that we can leverage to transform our streams into our desired results.

In this example, we'll show just how simple it is to do something such as filter an array of stock transactions before mapping the results to an array and then summing this array to find the total costs of a given transaction.

We'll leverage the `namedtuple` module from collections in order to define a `Stock` tuple. With this `namedtuple` structure, we'll then define an array of stock transactions that consists of the stock ticker and the cost of, the said transaction:

```
from functional import seq
from collections import namedtuple

Stock = namedtuple('Stock', 'tckr price')
stocks = [
  Stock('AMZN', 100),
  Stock('FACE', 200),
  Stock('JPM', 80),
  Stock('TSLA', 500),
  Stock('TSLA', 450)
]

costs = seq(stocks)\
  .filter(lambda x: x.tckr == 'TSLA')\
  .map(lambda x: x.price)\
  .sum()

print("Total cost of TSLA transactions: {}".format(costs))
```

# Output

Upon execution of the preceding program, you should see that we are able to successfully filter our array of stocks for all *TSLA* stock transactions. We will then map and sum our filtered list and output the total cost of these transactions to the console. The output should look something like this:

```
$ python3.6 13_pyfilter.py
Total cost of TSLA transactions: 950
```

# Reading/writing SQLite3

The `PyFunctional` library is surprisingly good at working with SQLite3 and features a multitude of different operators, which turn a traditionally more complex task of querying DBS and writing to them somewhat more palatable.

For instance, when querying a `sqlite3` database, we can leverage `seq.sqlite3(db, query).to_list()` in order to query a number of rows from a database and transform them into a list. This is just pure syntactic sugar and makes your code bases more succinct and ultimately more readable.

The official example they give in their documentation is when querying all the users from a database. They pass in the relative database path to their `sqlite3` database and then call `select * from user` in order to return all users. The `to_list()` operator then transforms the rows returned by the SQL query back into your standard list in Python that you can manipulate and bend to your will:

```
db_path = 'examples/users.db'
users = seq.sqlite3(db_path, 'select * from user').to_list()
# [(1, 'Tom'), (2, 'Jack'), (3, 'Jane'), (4, 'Stephan')]]

sorted_users = seq.sqlite3(db_path, 'select * from user order by
name').to_list()
# [(2, 'Jack'), (3, 'Jane'), (4, 'Stephan'), (1, 'Tom')]
```

When it comes to the all important task of writing things back to a database in `sqlite3`, we can have a range of different options:

```
import sqlite3
from collections import namedtuple

with sqlite3.connect(':memory:') as conn:
    conn.execute('CREATE TABLE user (id INT, name TEXT)')
```

```
    conn.commit()
    User = namedtuple('User', 'id name')

    # Write using a specific query
    seq([(1, 'pedro'), (2, 'fritz')]).to_sqlite3(conn, 'INSERT INTO user
(id, name) VALUES (?, ?)')

    # Write by inserting values positionally from a tuple/list into named
table
    seq([(3, 'sam'), (4, 'stan')]).to_sqlite3(conn, 'user')

    # Write by inferring schema from namedtuple
    seq([User(name='tom', id=5), User(name='keiga',
id=6)]).to_sqlite3(conn, 'user')

    # Write by inferring schema from dict
    seq([dict(name='david', id=7), dict(name='jordan',
id=8)]).to_sqlite3(conn, 'user')

    # Read everything back to make sure it wrote correctly
    print(list(conn.execute('SELECT * FROM user')))

    # [(1, 'pedro'), (2, 'fritz'), (3, 'sam'), (4, 'stan'), (5, 'tom'), (6,
'keiga'), (7, 'david'), (8, 'jordan')]
```

These all represent distinct ways of writing a list back to our metaphorical user table for this section.

# Compressed files

PyFunctional handles compressed files that have been compressed with gzip, lzma/xz, and bz2 with ease. It automatically handles the detection of whether or not a file is compressed, so you can essentially work with compressed files as if they were no different from normal files.

This may impact the speed at which you are able to manipulate these files though, as there is the overhead of working with compressed data. However, in my experience this hasn't been an extreme overhead.

When it comes to writing back to these files, you simply have to set the compression parameter to the following functions:

- `gzip` or `gz` for `gzip` compression
- `lzma` or `xz` for `lzma` compression
- `bz2` for `bz2` compression

This parameter exists on every `to_` function that exists within `PyFunctional`, and the combination of this and the automatic detection makes working with compressed files an absolute delight.

# Parallel execution

In order to enable parallel execution in your `PyFunctional` based Python program, there is only one real change you need to make to your code base. This change is replacing your usage of seq with `pseq`.

However, it should be noted that there are only three operations that currently support parallel execution:

- `map/select`

- `filter/filter_not/where`

- `flat_map`

By making this small change to your program, you change your uni-process code into code that utilizes the multiprocessing module, and thus, you should see a considerable speed improvement on some of the computationally expensive operations within your code base.

# Summary

In this chapter, we covered some of the key principles of reactive programming. We looked at the key differences between both reactive programming and typical event-driven programming, and we dived deeper into the specifics of the very popular RxPY Python library. We covered observers and observables, emitting events, and multicasting to numerous subscribers.

Hopefully, by now, you have an appreciation of some of the nuances of reactive programming, and you'll now be able to piece together your own reactive systems. You should also have some insight into how you can construct functional programs using Python, using this newly covered topic of operators in conjunction with PyFunctional.

In the next chapter, we'll discuss how you can improve the performance by leveraging the true power of your graphics card to perform tasks such as data analysis and research into big data. We'll see how to utilize the hundreds to thousands of cores that are all working in parallel and reach new performance heights using libraries such as Numba and PyOpenCL.

# 11
# Using the GPU

In this penultimate chapter, you'll learn about the various ways we can leverage the power of the GPU in order to greatly improve the performance of our Python programs. We'll take a general look at what GPUs are and what sort of advantages they can give us should we leverage them in certain scenarios within our Python programs.

We'll then look at the various Python wrappers that will enable us to use these GPUs for our more general purpose based programs without having to dive too deeply into the finer details.

Libraries such as `PyCUDA` are incredible in the sense that they enable programmers to create these high-performance applications without having to learn far more complex and low-level languages such as C and C++.

In this chapter, we'll explore a number of different libraries that are quite widely used in the GPU programming ecosystem. We'll cover the basics of how to get up and running with these libraries before showing how these concepts can be translated to run on top of both GPU and APU hardware. The libraries that we'll cover are as follows:

- `PyCUDA`
- `PyOpenCL`
- `Numba`
- `Theano`

However, first, let's look more closely at the advantages that GPUs provide over your more traditional CPUs.

# Introduction to GPUs

Graphics Processing Units, or GPUs as they are more typically shortened to, are typically marketed to and focused on the hardcore gaming market. It's typically gaming enthusiasts that expect an incredibly high-level of performance from these graphics cards in order to ensure that they have the smoothest possible experience while playing computationally expensive 3D video games.

Video games require millions upon millions of calculations per minute to be done in order for the computer to know exactly where to render 3D objects in a game. A typical scene within a game could contain anywhere from a handful of simple 3D objects to thousands of incredibly complex models. So, with each frame, we need to decide their exact relative positions, scales, rotations, and a whole multitude of other factors in order for them to be successfully rendered.

Even models that we deem to be relatively simple could be made up of hundreds or even thousands of different vertices. Look at the following car model; this would be a relatively low-polygon car by most modern games standards. However, if you look at the likes of the wheels, each of those wheels probably has 200-300+ distinct vertices:

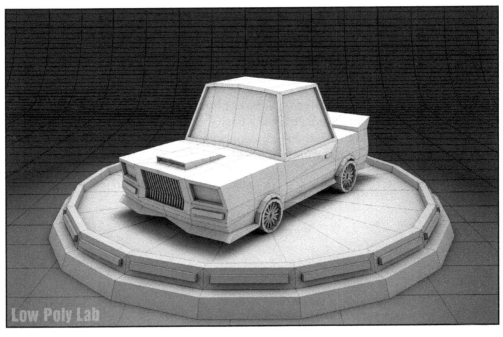

Source: https://www.lowpolylab.net/

When it comes to animating objects such as the preceding one, we have to multiply each of these individual vertices by translation and rotation matrices in order for us to obtain their updated position. Consider the fact that there might be hundreds of other objects within our scene such as buildings, characters, and so on, and the number of vertices we have to translate becomes daunting. Multiply this by the minimum 24-30 frames per second we have to do this for, and you should see that this isn't exactly an easy exercise for any machine.

# Why use the GPU?

The challenge of calculating such a high number of matrix translations per second is typically too much for an average CPU. Unfortunately, it hasn't been designed to handle such a huge number of requests per second in a highly efficient and parallel manner. This is why we require some dedicated hardware that features thousands of individual cores that are able to handle the thousands of millions of requests that are thrown at it.

In `Chapter 2`, *Parallelize It*, we touched briefly on the SIMD architecture style that these graphics cards follow. We looked at how it's excellent for doing this style of work, but we never looked at how it could be used for alternative means such as data science and machine learning.

These GPUs are absolutely phenomenal at handling the high-intensity graphics calculations that get thrown at it, but it's important to note that these can be repurposed very easily to other tasks such as statistical analysis, data mining, cryptography, and more. In this chapter, we'll look at some of the different libraries that wrap around our graphics cards, and I'll introduce you to some of the different ways that we can utilize these libraries.

# Data science

In the coming years, we will see a huge increase in the demand for data scientists. The vast majority of these jobs will be in industries such as finance where you'll be tasked with analyzing patterns and determining key characteristics of potentially billions of stock transactions.

It's a blend of art and science that requires an incredible amount of computational power in order to apply models and processes to vast quantities of data that have been captured over time by some of the largest companies in the world.

Python happens to be one of the most prevalent languages used within this field primarily due to the fact that expressing models in Python is relatively simple.

# Branches of data science

When it comes to data science, there are a number of different sub-branches, each which garners a lot of interest and is a fully qualified area of study in its own right. These main areas of study are as follows:

- Machine learning

- Classification

- Cluster analysis

- Data mining

We will talk more about them in the upcoming sections.

## Machine learning

Typically categorized into either supervised or unsupervised learning, machine learning algorithms focus on iterating over a training dataset as many times as possible while tweaking configuration to achieve optimal results. Once the algorithm has been run against a subset of the data, it is typically released on the remaining data in order to try and predict how that data will then behave.

## Classification

Classification is a subset of machine learning, which aims to classify distinct items into a set of categories. It follows the same process as machine learning in which it will train itself on a set of sample data that has already been classified. It will then attempt to classify new items into their correct categories based on what it has learned from this sample data.

## Cluster analysis

Cluster analysis is the act of grouping sets of data into a set of clusters where each of the elements within these clusters follow similar characteristics. This is typically used heavily in information retrieval where search engines will try to use algorithms such as agglomerative clustering in order to group web pages together so that they can be returned when specific search terms are entered.

The following image shows an example of a number of points of data. Using techniques such as agglomerative clustering, we can attempt to group these data points into three distinct categories. Imagine these data points were individual web pages that we had crawled. Then, let's imagine that the yellow pages are about cats, the blue pages are about dogs, and the red pages are about turtles. Agglomerative clustering allows us to effectively cluster these together:

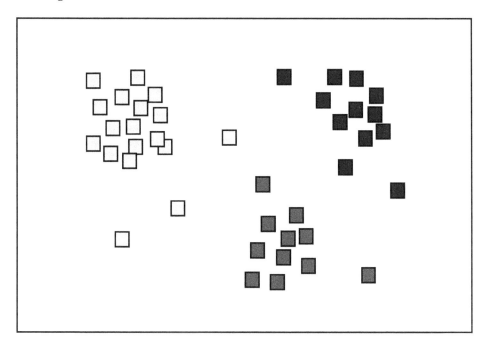

Source: https://en.wikipedia.org/wiki/Cluster_analysis#agglomerative_clustering

## Data mining

Data mining is the process of trying to extract useful information from massive sets of data. It typically follows a five-step process:

1. Identifying the data you wish to examine.

2. Preprocessing this information.

3. Transforming this data.

4. Mining the data.

5. Interpreting and reporting the results.

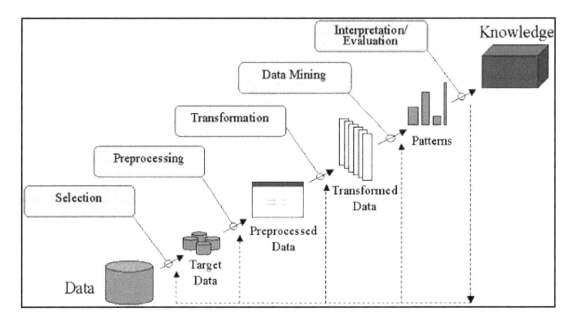

Source: http://www2.cs.uregina.ca/~dbd/cs831/notes/kdd/1_kdd.html

For a good book on this subject, I would recommend *Big Data: Using Smart Big Data, Analytics and Metrics to Make better Decisions and Improve Performance* by Bernard Marr. This focuses purely on the preceding process, which you can then action upon using any of the following Python libraries.

# CUDA

In the upcoming sections of this chapter, we'll cover libraries that rely heavily on the use of CUDA. Therefore, it's very important that you are familiar with what CUDA is precisely in the grand scheme of things and how this relates to the libraries that we'll ultimately use.

CUDA is a parallel computing platform and an API that was conceived by the NVIDIA Corporation. It's designed to make our lives as programmers simpler and help us fully leverage the power of the incredibly powerful parallelism that our GPUs have to offer for general purpose programming.

With CUDA, we are able to craft our Python programs in a way that is familiar to us while sprinkling in some of the keywords that CUDA has to offer in order to fully utilize the GPU. These keywords allow us to map appropriate sections of our code base that deal with the particularly computationally expensive calculations to massively parallel hardware and thus drastically improve performance.

# Working with CUDA without a NVIDIA graphics card

Ultimately, one of the biggest blockers to working with CUDA directly and the likes of libraries such as PyCUDA is the lack of the appropriate hardware. Fortunately, there are workarounds to this seemingly glaring issue that will enable you to utilize these libraries. However, they are unfortunately not free.

The most immediate workaround to this issue is to potentially utilize some of the cloud offerings that are currently available on the market. AWS, for instance, allows you to work with servers that feature NVIDIA hardware and pay only for the time that you are actively using it. This is a relatively more affordable method of getting started, but it requires more investment in the form of time required to learn to set up and manage the AWS infrastructure.

The second and the most straightforward option is to go out and purchase a NVIDIA-based graphics card for your work machine. This presents a fixed upfront cost, and I can fully appreciate how unaffordable this can be, especially for the latest generation of graphics cards with the highest specifications.

You should note that while the first option may be more affordable in the short term, I have seen instances where people have left GPU instances running for extended periods of time without their knowledge and have racked up a bill that is substantially higher than the total cost of a new graphics card.

# PyCUDA

PyCUDA is a Python library that exposes the power of NVIDIA's CUDA parallel computation API to us as Python developers.

The official documentation for PyCUDA can be found at https://mathema.tician.dc/software/pycuda/. This includes the official source code and a mailing list for those interested.

In this section, we'll cover some basic examples as to how you can utilize PyCUDA for your computationally heavy programs that require the full power of your NVIDIA GPU.

# Features

PyCUDA has a number of interesting features, which I feel should be mentioned at this point:

- Object cleanup is tied to the lifetime of objects, and as such, it's easier to write code that isn't plagued by leaks and won't crash on you after extended periods of execution.

- As previously mentioned, the main benefit of PyCUDA is that it abstracts away the complexities with things such as pycude.compiler.SourceModule and pycuda.gpuarray.GPUArray.

- Automatic error checking--PyCUDA automatically converts any of the errors that we encounter on our travels into Python exceptions, so no nasty error checking code has to be written.

- Performance--The library is written in C++ which is deviously performant.

Due to length limitations, I will unfortunately not be able to provide full examples of all the concepts I cover for this library. I will leave this as an exercise for you to piece together full samples.

# Simple example

Let's take a look at the official example that is given on the homepage of PyCUDA. It presents a very simple introduction to the PyCUDA ecosystem and gives us a base upon which we can build the foundations of our PyCUDA knowledge.

At the top of our program, we will import both the necessary parts of the PyCUDA module and the NumPy module:

```
import pycuda.autoinit
import pycuda.driver as drv
import numpy

from pycuda.compiler import SourceModule
mod = SourceModule("""
__global__ void multiply_them(float *dest, float *a, float *b)
{
  const int i = threadIdx.x;
```

```
    dest[i] = a[i] * b[i];
}
""")

multiply_them = mod.get_function("multiply_them")

a = numpy.random.randn(400).astype(numpy.float32)
b = numpy.random.randn(400).astype(numpy.float32)

dest = numpy.zeros_like(a)
multiply_them(
        drv.Out(dest), drv.In(a), drv.In(b),
        block=(400,1,1), grid=(1,1))

print dest-a*b
```

# Kernels

Kernels are a concept that is transient among all graphics programming and languages. Kernel functions are a specific kind of GPU function that are meant to be called from CPU code. So, in theory, our standard Python program runs on top of the CPU and delegates work to the GPU in the form of these kernel functions.

These kernels tend to look something like this within our Python programs:

```
mod = SourceModule("""
  __global__ void doublify(float *a)
  {
    int idx = threadIdx.x + threadIdx.y*4;
    a[idx] *= 2;
  }
  """)
```

There is an excellent online book, *The OpenCL Programming Book,* which covers in detail the basics of OpenCL kernel programming. You can find that book at `https://www.fixstars.com/en/opencl/book/OpenCLProgrammingBook/first-opencl-program/`.

I highly recommend that if you are going to go down the route of working with `PyCUDA` and `Kernels`, you actively learn the ins and outs of kernel programming as it will undoubtedly help you in the long run.

# GPU arrays

GPU arrays are a very important part of the `PyCUDA` library. They do the vital job of abstracting away the complexities of working with the GPU and, instead, allow us to focus on working with something not too dissimilar from `numpy.ndarray`. The class definition looks something like this:

```
class pycuda.gpuarray.GPUArray(shape, dtype, *, allocator=None, order="C")
```

let's take a look at a quick example as to how you can initiate your own gpuarray instance. We'll instantiate an instance of our gpuarray by calling gpuarray.to_gpu(). We'll then define a.tripled which will equate to all of the contents of our randomly filled gpuarray tripled. Finally we'll print out the results to the console.

```
import numpy
import pycuda.autoinit
import pycuda.gpuarray as gpuarray

a.gpu = gpuarray.to_gpu(numpy.random.randn(2,2).astype(numpy.float64))
a.tripled = (3*a gpu).get()
print(a.tripled)
```

 Note: Due to brevity concerns, I'm not able to go into the same level of depth that the official documentation does. I highly recommend you check it out at `https://documen.tician.de/pycuda/array.html#`.

# Numba

The `Numba` Python compiler from continuum analytics helps make highly parallelizable, incredibly powerful performance from an interpreted language a reality.

 Note: The documentation on the official pydata website provides a comprehensive overview of what Numba is and how you can leverage it in your own Python programs. You can find it at `http://numba.pydata.org/#`.

In this section, we'll have a look at the ecosystem surrounding `Numba`, which takes its form in the shape of Anaconda. We'll also look at how you can then leverage `Numba` alongside numerous other packages in order to effectively and efficiently perform analysis of big data. We'll cover some of the basics of `Numba` and then work our way into the more complex aspects such as utilizing GPUs and APUs within our program.

# Overview

Numba is very cool in the sense that it generates optimized machine code from pure Python code using the LLVM compiler infrastructure. By making slight modifications to our existing code, we can see incredible differences in the way our programs performs.

# Features of Numba

Numba has three key main features, which make it incredibly attractive to us as developers. These are as follows:

- On-the-fly code generation
- Native code generation for both CPUs (by default) and GPUs
- Integration with the Python scientific software stack

It's also available across the three main operating systems for both Python 2 and Python 3, so thankfully, you don't have to jump back in time and rely on the older version of Python if you are wanting to use Numba.

# LLVM

LLVM for the uninitiated, or even just the interested, is the full moniker for a project that is made up of a collection of modular and reusable compiler and toolchain technologies. It began as a research project and has since outgrown its original shell into something that is widely respected by nearly everybody who takes an interest in compiler technologies.

It focuses on creating optimal low-level code, be that either intermediate code or binary. It's written primarily in C++ and is the underlying base for a wide number of languages and projects, such as the following:

- Ada
- Fortran
- Python
- Ruby

For those of you interested in building your own compiler, I highly recommend this article at http://gnuu.org/2009/09/18/writing-your-own-toy-compiler/.

# Cross-hardware compatibility

While this chapter may be on general programming on a GPU, you should note that Numba is incredibly versatile, in the sense that it can support the compilation of Python to run on either CPU or GPU hardware. Also, the example in this section can be run on top of a wide range of different GPUs that are not necessarily of the NVIDIA variety.

## Python compilation space

Before going deeper into the Numba library, I feel it's important to understand the key differences between how your standard CPython program is compiled and executed, and how your Numba Python program is compiled and executed. This is shown in the following comparison:

CONTINUUM ANALYTICS

### Space of Python Compilation

| | Ahead Of Time | Just In Time |
|---|---|---|
| **Relies on CPython / libpython** | Cython Shedskin Nuitka (today) Pythran **Numba** | **Numba** HOPE Theano Pyjion |
| **Replaces CPython / libpython** | Nuitka (someday) | Pyston PyPy |

# Just-in-Time (JiT) versus Ahead-of-Time (Aot) compilation

This concept of two different types of compilation may be somewhat alien to a lot of people, so I feel it's important to highlight the differences between these two different types and when and where each type is used.

Just-in-Time (JiT) compilation is something that can remove the interpreter overhead of the Python code that you've written, which can result in a drastic speed up of your program. By removing the overhead of interpretation, we come closer in terms of performance to that of a compiled language such as your standard C or C++. While Numba does employ JiT compilation, it's important to note that though it may help remove the overhead of interpretation, you will likely never see a speed up that brings your code in line in terms of performance to that of C; it merely helps bring us closer.

Ahead-of-time, or AoT compilation, is where a function is compiled into an on-disk binary object that can then be distributed and executed independently. This is the technique that languages such as C, C++, or Fortran typically employ. The benefits of this are that no interpretation of code is necessary, and your machine is focused on just running the pre-built binary file as opposed to compiling the binary code and executing it at the same time.

# The Numba process

From the first glance at the `Numba` documentation, you may think that the easiest way to improve the total performance of Python code is to just append the `@jit` decorator to every function within your code and expect huge gains. In reality, however, this is very rarely the case, and you may find yourself not realizing the full benefits of the `Numba` library.

There is an excellent talk by Stanley Seibert, who happens to be one of the scientific software developers working at Continuum Analytics, in which he outlines five distinct steps you should follow in order to effectively use `Numba`. They are as follows:

1. Start off by creating a realistic benchmark test case. This should ideally give you realistic metrics as to how your systems function under load and should not just be your standard unit test library.
2. Utilize profilers and run this on your benchmark. An ideal candidate for this is the cProfile tool that we covered in detail in `Chapter 6`, *Debug and Benchmark*.

3. Identify hotspots within your code that require more time to execute.
4. Utilize the `@numba.jit` and `@number.vectorize` decorators as needed for your critical functions.
5. Rerun benchmarks and analyze the results to determine if what you've done has actually improved the performance of your programs.

You can find his original talk on YouTube at `https://www.youtube.com/watch?v=eYIPEDnp5C4`. I highly recommend you check it out.

# Anaconda

Before you can get started with Numba, you will have to install the Anaconda package from the Continuum Analytics website. The link to it is `https://www.continuum.io/downloads`.

Anaconda is an incredibly powerful and respected part of the Python data science ecosystem. It is open source and features a high-performance distribution of both Python and the R programming language. If you've never seen or heard about R, then I suggest you have a look at it. R is the de facto choice for data scientists and quants when it comes to performing analysis and trying to work with incredibly huge datasets.

Anaconda also comes with its own package and dependency manager, Conda. This comes flush with over 1,000 data science specific packages, at the time of writing this chapter.

# Writing basic Numba Python programs

Now that we have covered the essential underlying concepts of how `Numba` works in terms of compilation strategies, it's time to start applying these new practices to our own Python programs.

Let's begin by writing a fairly straightforward Python program. It will contain a function that will just return the summation of the two values passed into it:

```
def f(x, y):
    return x + y


f(2,3)
```

We can add lazy compilation to this by importing the `jit` decorator from `numba` and subsequently decorating our newly defined summation function, shown earlier, with this decorator as follows:

```
from numba import jit

@jit
def f(x, y):
    return x + y

f(2,3)
```

This addition of a decorator now means that our function will be compiled.

# Compilation options

The `@jit` decorator takes in a number of keywords that we can use to explicitly tell the compiler how we want our functions compiler. With these options, we can do things such as escape from the global interpreter lock (the GIL) or force the use of a specific compilation mode.

## nopython

`Numba` has two distinct compilation modes, nopython and object mode. Within our `Numba` programs, we can explicitly select what mode we'd like to compile our code against and raise an error should this compilation mode be unattainable.

The nopython mode generates code that does not directly access the Python C API. This essentially means that the code generated from this will be incredibly quick.

The object mode typically generates code that, in performance terms, isn't far off of that of a normal interpreted program:

```
@jit(nopython=True)
def func(x, y):
    return x + y
```

## nogil

If Numba is able to compile a function down to native code a la the nopython mode we mentioned earlier, we can then specify this `nogil` flag. Every time we enter one of these functions, we can release the GIL.

We've seen first hand the impact of the GIL in certain scenarios in numerous chapters within this book so having this control on such a granular level. When this happens, this function can run concurrently with other threads that are executing Python, and you should see some very decent performance gains using this:

```
@jit(nogil=True)
def func(x, y):
    return x + y
```

## The cache option

By setting the cache option, we effectively tell Numba to store the compiled code for this particular function in an on-disk cache file. This means that once the function has been compiled, it should not be recompiled on every execution of your program:

```
@jit(cache=True)
def func(x, y):
    return x + y
```

## The parallel option

The parallel option is an experimental function that aims to automatically parallelize the operations within your specified function that are known to have parallel semantics:

```
@jit(nopython=True, parallel=True)
def func(x, y):
    return x + y
```

 Note: This particular feature must be used in conjunction with the nopython option as shown earlier.

# Issues with Numba

One of the most important things you should be aware of when building software systems using Numba is that it does have its limitations. Type inference is not always possible in certain scenarios, and when this issue rears its ugly head, you'll be left scratching your own head wondering where the issue is.

Let's take a look at the example they give in their Troubleshooting and tips section. Imagine we had a function that featured the @jit(nopython=True) decorator. This takes in arguments x and y and returns the summation of the two arguments.

```
@jit(nopython=True)
def f(x, y):
    return x + y
```

If we pass in values 2 and 3 into our function; f(2,3); then we should see numba working as expected and returning 5. This means that type inference was successful, but what happens when we pass in something like f(1, (2,))? These two values are of differing types and as such numba fails to infer what they should be and throws an error that looks like:

```
>>> f(1, (2,))
Traceback (most recent call last):
  File "<stdin>", line 1, in <module>
    [...]
  File "/home/antoine/numba/numba/typeinfer.py", line 242, in resolve
    raise TypingError(msg, loc=self.loc)
numba.typeinfer.TypingError: Failed at nopython frontend
Undeclared +(int64, (int32 x 1))
File "<stdin>", line 2
```

# Numba on the CUDA-based GPUs

Now that we've come to terms with the basics of Numba, it's time to see how this translates to using it with GPUs.

# Numba on AMD APUs

As of version 0.21 of Numba, we've seen the support for programming on top of Heterogeneous System Architecture (HSA). HSA, for those who have never heard of it before, is a standard that essentially aims to combine the performances of both CPUs and GPUs and give them a shared memory space.

If you want to read up more on the release of this feature, then you can check out `https ://www.continuum.io/blog/developer/programming-amd-apus-numba`. To give you a brief idea of the power of what APUs can achieve in terms of performance, you should have a look at the following graph. This displays the speedup ratio of programs running on top of these APUs versus their performance on NumPy, relative to the number of elements they would have to each process:

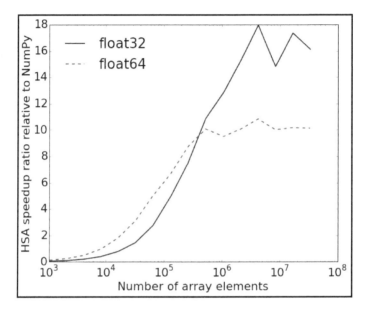

Source: https://www.continuum.io/blog/developer/programming-amd-apus-numba

You should see that as the number of elements in an array grows linearly, the performance that you are able to achieve using HSA grows almost exponentially until it hits around the 11x speedup mark, at which point it starts to take a more linear progression before capping off at around 15-18x speedup.

# Accelerate

Anaconda's Accelerate package is a package that enables us to leverage the exceptional performance of Intel CPUs as well as Nvidia's GPUs. It's an add-on to the anaconda package that from the documentation features:

- Binding to several CUDA libraries such as `cuBLAS`, `cuFFT`, `cuSPARSE`, `cuRAND`, and `CUDA Sorting`

- Speed-boosted linear algebra operations in `NumPy`, `SciPy`, `scikit-learn`, and `NumExpr` libraries using Intel's Math Kernel Library
- Accelerated variants of NumPy's built-in UFuncs
- Increased-speed Fast Fourier Transformations (FFT) in NumPy

Much like the other libraries in this chapter, it's designed specifically to cope with huge datasets.

The official documentation of Anaconda's Accelerate can be found at `https://docs.contin uum.io/accelerate/#` It's unfortunately quite a sparse documentation at the time of writing this book.

# Theano

If you are interested in niche topics such as deep learning and machine learning, then it's very probable that you may have considered using Theano. Theano is a Python library that is ideal for working with multi-dimensional arrays such as NumPy's ndarrays, and it's exceptionally performant when it comes to doing so. Theano relies on the GPU in order to provide performance that can surpass C on a typical CPU many times over.

# Requirements

Theano is available for those of us on either Python 2.7 or on a version of Python greater than 3.3 but less than version 3.6. You'll also need to install NumPy and SciPy. For a fuller list of requirements, I recommend you check out the official requirements documentation, which can be found at `http://deeplearning.net/software/theano/requirements.html`.

# Getting started

Theano is incredibly easy to get started with, and it was a pleasure learning it for the purpose of this chapter. The official documentation for the library is surprisingly good and features some excellent examples for getting up to speed and crafting your own performant Python applications.

# Very simple example

In this very simple example, we'll start by defining a simple function that will just take in two numbers and add them together. Now, I'll grant you that this may not be the most interesting way to showcase the theano library, but bear with me:

```
from theano import *
import numpy
import theano.tensor as T

x = T.dscalar('x')
y = T.dscalar('y')
z = x + y
f = function([x,y],z)
print(f(2,3))
```

If we were to run that, you should see that there are no real surprises and it outputs 5.0 to the console:

```
$ python3.6 02_theano.py
5.0
```

# Adding two matrices

Now, let's build on top of this and define a function that will sum two matrices. Again, we'll follow the exact same format of our previous example, except for the fact we'll use dmatrix instead of dscalar:

```
from theano import *
import numpy
import theano.tensor as T

x = T.dmatrix('x')
y = T.dmatrix('y')
z = x + y
f = function([x,y],z)

print(f(\
[[2,3],[4,5]],\
[[2,3],[4,5]]\
))
```

If we then run this program, you should see that `theano` has successfully summed the two matrices before. We will then print out the results to the console:

```
$ python3.6 03_matrices.py
[[  4.   6.]
 [  8.  10.]]
```

## Fully-typed constructors

The `theano` library has a pretty comprehensive array of `TensorType`. We've already touched upon the dmatrix type and the dscalar type, but it's important to note that there are a large number of other options available to you. These effectively allow us to leverage some of the strengths of a strongly typed system. You can see the complete list of all fully typed constructors at http://deeplearning.net/software/theano/library/tensor/basic.html#all-fully-typed-constructors.

These range from scalars that represent the most basic unit to things such as vectors, matrices, rows and cols, and tensor objects. If you are going to deal with a lot of computational modeling of problems, then this list should hopefully help you in your modeling efforts.

## Using Theano on the GPU

`Theano` has been designed to abstract away from developers the intricacies of modeling their computational models. It allows us to write simple code that relies upon incredibly powerful hardware without too much modification on our part.

Currently, it offers two distinct methods of enabling the utilization of GPUs for the programs that we write using it. One enables the utilization of any OpenCL device as well as any NVIDIA cards, and another that will only support NVIDIA cards.

In order to use the GPU, you'll have to set the "device" configuration flag to equal CUDA for the first, more open method as follows:

```
$ THEANO_FLAGS='device=cuda' python3.6 04_gpu.py
```

Alternatively, you can set `device=gpu` for the older, less inclusive method:

```
$ THEANO_FLAGS='device=gpu' python3.6 04_gpu.py
```

# Example

We'll leverage the very convenient example that is provided by the `theano` documentation to test whether or not we have successfully been able to leverage the GPU:

```
from theano import function, config, shared, tensor
import numpy
import time

vlen = 10 * 30 * 768  # 10 x #cores x # threads per core
iters = 1000

rng = numpy.random.RandomState(22)

x = shared(numpy.asarray(rng.rand(vlen),
config.floatX))

f = function([], tensor.exp(x))
print(f.maker.fgraph.toposort())
t0 = time.time()
for i in range(iters):
   r = f()
t1 = time.time()
print("Looping %d times took %f seconds" % (iters,
t1 - t0))
print("Result is %s" % (r,))

if numpy.any([isinstance(x.op, tensor.Elemwise)
and
            ('Gpu' not in type(x.op).__name__)
            for x in f.maker.fgraph.toposort()]):
  print('Used the cpu')
else:
  print('Used the gpu')
```

When you run the preceding program by itself, you should see something similar to this output in the console:

```
$ python3.6 04_gpu.py
[Elemwise{exp,no_inplace}(<TensorType(float64, vector)>)]
Looping 1000 times took 2.136130 seconds
Result is [ 1.23178032  1.61879341  1.52278065 ...,  2.20771815  2.29967753
  1.62323285]
Used the cpu
```

Note the fact that it prints out that it used the CPU and not the intended GPU. We can enforce the utilization of the GPU by setting THEANO_FLAGS=device=cuda0 and then running our Python program after this as follows:

```
THEANO_FLAGS=device=cuda0 python3.6 04_gpu.py
Mapped name None to device cuda0: GeForce GTX 680 (cuDNN version 5004)
[GpuElemwise{exp,no_inplace}(<GpuArrayType<None>(float64, (False,))>),
HostFromGpu(gpuarray)(GpuElemwise{exp,no_inplace}.0)]
Looping 1000 times took 1.202734 seconds
Result is [ 1.23178032  1.61879341  1.52278065 ...,  2.20771815  2.29967753
  1.62323285]
Used the gpu
```

This should then print out that we have successfully used the GPU as opposed to the CPU.

# Leveraging multiple GPUs

If you are lucky enough to be able to afford a system that features two high-performance graphics cards, you'll be happy to know that theano provides you with the capability of using both of these GPUs in parallel. I should warn you now that this is an experimental part of the library and, as such, there is the potential that it could still lead to anomalies in the results of your programs.

The official documentation for this can be found at
http://deeplearning.net/software/theano/tutorial/using_multi_gpu
.html.

# Defining the context map

When it comes to leveraging multiple GPUs, we need to first map each of these devices so that we can then delegate them work. These mappings can be formed of any number of devices and are made up of a context name plus -> plus the name of the device that typically looks like cuda0 or something to that effect:

```
$ THEANO_FLAGS="contexts=dev0->cuda0;dev1->cuda1" python -c 'import theano'
Mapped name dev0 to device cuda0: GeForce GTX TITAN X
Mapped name dev1 to device cuda1: GeForce GTX TITAN X
```

# Simple graph example

In this example from their documentation, we'll look at how we can achieve the full utilization of two graphics cards in parallel:

```
import numpy
import theano

v01 = theano.shared(numpy.random.random((1024, 1024)).astype('float32'),
                    target='dev0')
v02 = theano.shared(numpy.random.random((1024, 1024)).astype('float32'),
                    target='dev0')
v11 = theano.shared(numpy.random.random((1024, 1024)).astype('float32'),
                    target='dev1')
v12 = theano.shared(numpy.random.random((1024, 1024)).astype('float32'),
                    target='dev1')

f = theano.function([], [theano.tensor.dot(v01, v02),
                         theano.tensor.dot(v11, v12)])

f()
```

When you run this with two distinct devices, you should see a linear improvement in the speed that it takes to execute. You should note that at this point, if you don't have multiple graphics cards, there is still the option to run this on one device by mapping multiple contexts to that device.

You can achieve this by using the following line of code:

```
THEANO_FLAGS="contexts=dev0->cuda0;dev1->cuda0" python myApp.py
```

# PyOpenCL

OpenCL, or Open Computing Language in its full form, is a low-level API for heterogeneous computing that runs on CUDA-powered GPUs. PyOpenCL represents the Python implementation of this API that enables us to write Python applications that leverage the power of a whole range of different platforms from CPUs, GPUs, DSPs and FPGAs.

 The official documentation for the PyOpenCL library can be found at https://documen.tician.de/pyopencl/.

# Example

Let's dissect the example that comes in the official documentation. This will act as a perfect starting point, which we can expand upon later.

We will first import all the necessary modules at the top and alias NumPy and PyOpenCL as np and cl, respectively. We will then generate two random numbers of type numpy.float32. We will then create some context within our PyOpenCL program, by calling this with no parameters. This function will interactively allow you to choose what platforms and devices that your program should run on top of, which is pretty helpful to get you up and running quickly.

After we've created our context, we will then create both our command queues, which take in our newly created context.

We will then proceed to define our Program object, which takes in our context, an empty string for the devices, and finally our binary that takes shape in the form of an OpenCL kernel:

```
from __future__ import absolute_import, print_function
import numpy as np
import pyopencl as cl

a_np = np.random.rand(50000).astype(np.float32)
b_np = np.random.rand(50000).astype(np.float32)

ctx = cl.create_some_context()
queue = cl.CommandQueue(ctx)
```

```
mf = cl.mem_flags
a_g = cl.Buffer(ctx, mf.READ_ONLY | mf.COPY_HOST_PTR, hostbuf=a_np)
b_g = cl.Buffer(ctx, mf.READ_ONLY | mf.COPY_HOST_PTR, hostbuf=b_np)

prg = cl.Program(ctx, """
__kernel void sum(
    __global const float *a_g, __global const float *b_g, __global float
*res_g)
{
  int gid = get_global_id(0);
  res_g[gid] = a_g[gid] + b_g[gid];
}
""").build()

res_g = cl.Buffer(ctx, mf.WRITE_ONLY, a_np.nbytes)
prg.sum(queue, a_np.shape, None, a_g, b_g, res_g)

res_np = np.empty_like(a_np)
cl.enqueue_copy(queue, res_np, res_g)

# Check on CPU with Numpy:
print(res_np - (a_np + b_np))
print(np.linalg.norm(res_np - (a_np + b_np)))
```

# Output

I'm running this on my Macbook Pro, which features integrated graphics. You can see that it first asks me to choose what platform I should run the code on and then which device on that platform I should run it against:

```
$ python3.6 06_example.py
Choose platform:
[0] <pyopencl.Platform 'Apple' at 0x7fff0000>
Choice [0]:0
Choose device(s):
[0] <pyopencl.Device 'Intel(R) Core(TM) i5-4288U CPU @ 2.60GHz' on 'Apple'
at 0xffffffff>
[1] <pyopencl.Device 'Iris' on 'Apple' at 0x1024500>
Choice, comma-separated [0]:1
Set the environment variable PYOPENCL_CTX='0:1' to avoid being asked again.
[ 0.  0.  0. ...,  0.  0.  0.]
0.0
```

# Summary

So, let's recap over what we have covered. We looked at what GPUs are in depth as well as how we could utilize them for more general purpose tasks. We covered some of the more realistic scenarios that data scientists would typically encounter and why these are ideal scenarios for us to leverage these GPU wrapper libraries.

We then looked at some of the major libraries that exist today that allow us to leverage the full power of our graphics processing hardware. You should now have some idea as to how to get started writing your own GPU- as well as APU-based applications, whether this be for data science purposes or otherwise.

In the final chapter of this book, we'll take a look back at the different techniques we covered within this book and summarize some of the key places to use them.

# 12
# Choosing a Solution

In this final chapter, we'll look very briefly at some of the libraries that I have unfortunately been unable to cover in this book. These will be cursory glances to merely let you know that there are alternatives on the market. I'm leaving the onus on you to research on these libraries and get up and running with them if you desire.

We'll also look briefly at the process you should follow in order to effectively choose what libraries and what programming paradigms you leverage for your Python software projects. We'll also cover some of the books and learning resources out there that can aid you in your learning.

## Libraries not covered in this book

As a disclaimer, there have been a number of different libraries that I researched while writing this book. However, due to concerns of brevity, I've had to cap the number of libraries that I could cover within each chapter.

It would be remiss of me to not present to you some of the excellent resources currently available that present far more in-depth coverage of some of the topics I've unfortunately not been able to expand upon. I also feel that it's worthwhile knowing what further material is available that will continue to expand your knowledge of software engineering with Python.

# GPU

The GPU presents one of the topics that I feel I could not cover in detail within this book. There lies an incredible amount of potential in the utilization of the GPU to improve the performance of your applications, and as such, it's one for which I highly encourage further study.

## PyGPU

PyGPU is one such library that I would encourage further research into. PyGPU is designed specifically for your image-processing needs, and much like the other GPU based libraries, it abstracts away the complexities of dealing with low-level GPU APIs in order to achieve monumental speeds.

It's an embedded language within Python that features most of Python's core features such as higher order functions, iterators, and list comprehensions, and it's specifically designed for ease of use when constructing GPU algorithms.

 The official documentation for PyGPU can be found at `http://fileadmin .cs.lth.se/cs/Personal/Calle_Lejdfors/pygpu/`.

# Event-driven and reactive libraries

The event-driven and reactive programming paradigm is one that I find very interesting. It provides a very intuitive way of solving a somewhat challenging problem, and I've had a lot of fun crafting some sample projects for this book using both `asyncio` and `RxPY`. It's important to note that there are other libraries available that fill different needs though.

## Tornado

Tornado is a Python web framework and asynchronous networking library. It utilizes non-blocking network I/O and can subsequently scale to tens of thousands of connections.

 The official documentation for Tornado can be found at `http://www.torn adoweb.org/en/stable/`.

It's also very easy to get up and running with a simple Hello World application, which is the basis of a very simple RESTful API. It looks like this:

```
import tornado.ioloop
import tornado.web

class MainHandler(tornado.web.RequestHandler):
    def get(self):
        self.write("Hello, world")

def make_app():
    return tornado.web.Application([
        (r"/", MainHandler),
    ])

if __name__ == "__main__":
    app = make_app()
    app.listen(8888)
    tornado.ioloop.IOLoop.current().start()
```

# Flask

Flask is in the same vein as Tornado. It, however, considers itself a micro framework. It features an API that is actually far simpler to get up and running with, and you can achieve the same results as the preceding Tornado example in a total of five lines of code.

An example of a very simple flask application can be found below:

```
from flask import Flask
app = Flask(__name__)

@app.route("/")
def hello():
    return "Hello World!"
```

The official documentation for Flask can be found at `http://flask.pocoo.org/`.

# Celery

Celery is an asynchronous task, queue/job queue based on distributed message passing, and it goes hand in hand with some of the aforementioned web frameworks such as Tornado and Flask. However, it requires some form of broker technology setup, which adds an extra layer of complexity to your software systems, but is sometimes essential.

These message brokers, if you haven't used them before, are intermediary stops that enable us to do things such as communication between micro services. They are very heavily used in enterprise systems, and as such, I would recommend that you read up on them if that's the environment you are going to be working in.

Celery is currently compatible with four distinct brokers:

- RabbitMQ
- Redis
- Amazon SQS
- Zookeeper (experimental compatibility)

 Official documentation for the Celery project can be found at `http://www.celeryproject.org/`.

# Data science

Since university, I've always had an interest in data science, more specifically the art of data retrieval and how large systems such as Google work in order to deliver you the best possible search results. If you haven't had a chance to look into it yourself, then I highly encourage it!

# Pandas

Pandas is an open-source library that provides you with very high performance and is used heavily in data analysis projects. It's more focused on the preparation of data as opposed to analysis and modeling. It's supposed to perform the work that you'd typically expect something like the R programming language to solve.

For data scientists, Pandas is a fantastic supplementary tool that is designed to aid you in your data science work. The official documentation for Pandas can be found at `http://pandas.pydata.org/`.

## Matplotlib

Matplotlib offers high-quality 2D visualization of all of the data that you would typically be performing analysis upon. It's designed specifically to abstract away the difficulties of working with graphs and lets you focus on what really matters.

The official documentation for matplotlib can be found at `https://matplotlib.org/`.

## TensorFlow

TensorFlow is a rather exciting open source library that is typically used for numerical computation using a thing known as data flow graphs. Data-Flow Graphs or DFGs for short are *graphs that represent data dependencies between a number of operations (Prof Brewer, University of California).*

Overall TensorFlow is an incredible framework that allows you to build complex AI leveraging concepts such as deep learning neural networks. It was originally opensourced by Google back in November of 2015 and since then has gone on to become majorly successful, garnering it's own TensorFlow conference hosted in Mountain View, CA.

*If you wish to learn more about TensorFlow and how you would use it then I highly recommend you check out their 'Getting Started' guide which can be found here: https://www.tensorflow.org/get_started/get_started*

# Designing your systems

Throughout the course of this book, we looked at a multitude of different concepts that each suit different problem sets. In this section of the chapter, we will look at when and where each of these distinct concepts are best used.

You should note that this is mostly advisory; as with everything, there is no silver bullet. What works for one individual may not work for others. If you are designing enterprise systems, then I implore you to perform as much research as is heavenly possible before diving into writing any code.

Some problems will require an eclectic mix of different solutions. Software architecture is an art that requires a great deal of time and effort to become proficient at but it's incredibly rewarding once you have become proficient.

# Requirements

Before any design work can be done, a considerable amount of time should be spent on gathering the requirements of your key stakeholders for your project. The amount of time and effort spent on this portion should be proportionate to the number of stakeholders. If the project is just for personal use, then it's entirely OK to hack away and play around; but for serious projects, serious requirements gathering must be done.

When it comes to requirements gathering, there are two distinct types of requirements that must be determined. These are functional and nonfunctional requirements, both of which you should have a good understanding of and spend considerable time gathering.

## Functional requirements

The first category of these requirements, your functional requirements, defines what the system must do.

Let's take, for instance, a project that will try to trade on the stock market and earn us a bit of money. This system should feature the following Functional requirements:

- The system must be able to poll the price of a stock every 5 seconds and then act, if necessary, upon that stock change
- The system must be able to make buy and sell trades against "X" stockbroker
- The system must be able to keep track of every trade that it executes for compliance reasons

## Non-functional requirements

Non-functional requirements are requirements that determine how a system does something.

Let's now look at the nonfunctional requirements for the system we described in the functional requirements section:

- Performance: The system must be performant enough to keep up with the heavy number of calculations that will need to be done
- The system must be able to handle faults well. We don't want a repeat of a company going broke in 45 minutes due to errors. Refer to `https://dougseven.c om/2014/04/17/knightmare-a-devops-cautionary-tale/`.
- Scalability: The program should be able to scale when we eventually start to make millions from our successful trading algorithms
- Documentation: Most, if not all, software should be documented to some degree, especially if you are designing enterprise systems.

# Design

Once you have a definitive set of requirements, both functional and nonfunctional, then and only then can you begin to start designing how your software is going to look with regards to structure.

When it comes to designing your final solution, I can't emphasize enough on spending as much time as possible researching what is out there and available. Before I start a project, I can spend days, if not weeks, PoC-ing small concepts with various libraries before I settle on one.

One thing to watch is what licenses come with each of the particular libraries in question. You need to ensure that you are using a library that will allow you to sell your finished product should that be the goal. If you go down the route of using a library that has a restrictive license, then you could find yourself chained into giving them royalties. For the majority of libraries featured in this book, however, there are no real issues when it comes to licensing.

# Computationally expensive

We've somewhat covered what the difference is between the use of threads versus processes when your system is either I/O bound or CPU bound. However, I feel it's important to highlight what libraries you should be employing for these different scenarios.

For these computationally heavy applications, you'll typically have to rely on libraries and modules such as the following ones:

- The multiprocessing module: This is for apps that require a fast computation of relatively small datasets. Ensure that the computation warrants the use of multiple processes before going down this route.
- Libraries such as PyCUDA and Theano: This is for apps that require fast computation of huge datasets. It is typically used for big data projects.

## Event-heavy applications

If your application processes events, be they user-inputted events or programmatically generated events, then you would typically use libraries such as the following ones:

- `Asyncio`: This is ideal for your standard event-based programs.
- `Twisted`: This is ideal for networking event-driven system. Think web servers.
- `RxPy`: This is ideal for systems that deal with data-based events.

## I/O-heavy applications

If your application will spend a lot of time performing I/O-based tasks, then it's a good idea to leverage the modules such as the standard threading module or, more favorably, the `concurrent.futures` module:

- The `threading` module, which we have covered in a number of the earlier chapters within this book
- The `concurrent.futures` module, specifically concepts such as `ThreadPoolExecutor`, which we covered in `Chapter 7`, *Executors and Pools*

I'd specifically lean towards using the `concurrent.futures` module as its API abstracts away some of the complexities of using multiple threads and is therefore, ideal for these types of projects.

## Recommended design books

While this book may have covered a multitude of different Python libraries, it doesn't cover that much detail about when and where you should use these particular libraries. There are a number of excellent books currently available that go into a great depth on the art of software design. Here, you'll find the two books that I believe are the most worthwhile.

## Software Architecture with Python

Software Architecture with Python by Anand Balachandran is an excellent book that covers a number of important topics in an almost encyclopedic fashion. Within the covers lie a vast wealth of information on quite a number topics, such as the following ones:

- Writing modifiable and readable code
- Testability
- Writing applications that scale
- Python design patterns

It covers quite a number of other, very important topics to consider when practicing the art of software architecture.

## Python: Master the Art of Design Patterns

Python: Master the Art of Design Patterns covers topics such as object-oriented Python programming and a multitude of different design patterns that you can employ within your software systems.

This is an excellent read for those of you wanting a more rounded education in the art of software design, and it complements the previous book well by covering in more detail the various well-known design patterns.

# Research

If you take one thing from this chapter, it should be that design is important, and by spending as much time as possible with design, you will be saving yourself much pain and suffering.

When it comes to researching and designing large software projects, you should attempt to bear in mind the famous quote by the original Renaissance polymath, Leonardo Da Vinci:

*"Simplicity is the ultimate sophistication."*

Aim to create software systems that solve your particular problem but also represent the simplest way you could have solved the said problem. This will make the job of other developers coming into your team's life much easier once you move on to other projects.

# Summary

Unfortunately, we've reached the end of our journey learning about the ins and outs of working with concurrency in Python.

Throughout this book, we looked at the fundamental concepts of threads and processes, which has enabled us to work with more advanced concepts such as event-driven programming, reactive programming, and so on.

You should now be adept at the art of designing and building asynchronous systems that handle their workloads in a performant manner. You should also be comfortable with the different ways you can approach problems and why some ways are better than others.

If you have any questions, feel free to reach out to me either on my Twitter handle `@elliot_f` or through email at `elliot@elliotforbes.co.uk`. I'm always happy to try and lend a hand, or if you have any comments or feedback on the book, then I'm always happy to hear them!

# Index

www.ingramcontent.com/pod-product-compliance
Lightning Source LLC
Chambersburg PA
CBHW060923060326
40690CB00041B/3074